The Common-Sense Mortgage

Books by Peter G. Miller

The Common-Sense Mortgage

*The Common-Sense Guide to
Successful Real Estate Negotiation*
(with Douglas M. Bregman)

The Common-Sense Mortgage

How to Cut the Cost of Home Ownership by $100,000 or More

Third Edition

Peter G. Miller

Harper & Row, Publishers, New York
Cambridge, Philadelphia, San Francisco, Washington
London, Mexico City, São Paulo, Singapore, Sydney

Portions of this work originally appeared in slightly different form in *FACT Magazine*, *Goodlife Magazine*, *The Washington Post*, and *The Washington Weekly*.

BOMC offers recordings and compact discs, cassettes and records. For information and catalog write to BOMR, Camp Hill, PA 17012.

Designer: C. Linda Dingler

Copy editor: Viera Morse

Indexer: Auralie Logan

Library of Congress Cataloging-in-Publication Data

Miller, Peter G.
    The common-sense mortgage.

    Includes index.
    1. Mortgages. 2. Mortgage loans. 3. Housing—Finance. I. Title.
HG2040.M54   1987   332.7'22   86-46265
ISBN 0-06-055081-3
ISBN 0-06-091392-4 (pbk.)

To Caroline

Contents

Acknowledgments

Major portions of this book were first printed in *The Washington Post* as part of a weekly column on real estate finance. The sections on timesharing, reverse loans, equity-sharing, and GEM mortgages first appeared in *Goodlife* magazine (Suite B-212, 1401 West Paces Ferry Road, Atlanta, Ga. 30327). The sections on Computers and the Searching Process and the material on hidden refinancing costs were originally published by *Fact, The Money Management Magazine* (711 Third Avenue, New York, N.Y. 10017). Portions of the material concerning computer services have been rewritten and updated for this edition.

This book would not have been possible without the cooperation and assistance of many individuals and organizations. The author wishes to thank Albert B. Crenshaw, real estate editor of *The Washington Post;* Bill Winn, publisher, and Gene-Gabriel Moore, editor, *Goodlife* magazine; and Daniel M. Kehrer, editor, and Joseph Lisanti, associate editor, *Fact, The Money Management Magazine*.

Also, Katherine B. Ulmann and the United States League of Savings Institutions; Beth Van Houten and Eugene R. Eisman and the Federal National Mortgage Association; John J. Coonts, director, FHA Single Family Development Division, HUD; Victor S. Parra of the National Timesharing Council; Phyllis R.

Pleasants of the Mortgage Insurance Companies of America; Hilda Pena and the Washington Regional Office of the Veterans Administration.

And James Sherman, Talman Home Federal Savings & Loan (Chicago); James J. Hall, James J. Hall, Inc., Realtors (Silver Spring, Maryland); Douglas M. Bregman, Esq. (Bethesda, Maryland); Leon Pomerance, Esq. (Rockville, Maryland); Steven A. Skalet, Esq. (Washington, D.C.); and Charles R. Wolfe (Gaithersburg, Maryland).

The author would also like to thank Warren Dunn and the Mortgage Bankers Association of America and Martin Keithline and the Montgomery County (Maryland) Board of Realtors, who graciously provided amortization statements and other valued information that was used in the first and second editions of this guide. In this edition, all amortization statements have been recalculated by the author with the use of a business calculator, commonly available spreadsheet software and a personal computer.

Timothy Schwartz, an attorney based in Bethesda, Maryland, reviewed certain material in the text relating to tax reform and deductions for points and interest. His advice and comments have been greatly valued.

Introduction

In 1986, the United States government made a fundamental decision to change its tax policies. Lower rates for individuals coupled with higher rates for business and fewer deductions for all taxpayers will now be the order of the day.

What does this mean in terms of real estate and especially home mortgages? Basically the federal government has said the old tax rules favored forms of economic behavior which often made little economic sense. Before tax reform, for instance, many large cities had huge office towers downtown even though vacancy rates were often 18 to 21 percent. Such deals worked only because of favorable tax benefits. But now such arrangements will be decidedly less attractive. The new tax rules favor economic sanity, putting money where you can find cash benefits and the potential for appreciation.

In terms of home mortgages there has never been a case for paying excess interest; yet, because federal tax rates were as high as 50 percent, excess costs were often rationalized—since, after all, good old Uncle Sam was underwriting a large part of the bill. But as of 1988, the apparent top tax rate will be a meager 28 percent and the value of home mortgage deductions will be greatly diminished.

The new tax code outlines a very clear financial path favored by the federal government: it pays to buy and own real estate and it pays most when property is correctly financed. In this era, correctly financing real estate means finding the best loan at the lowest possible cost—the very definition of the common-sense mortgage.

The Common-Sense Mortgage is now in its third edition, and the principles which have guided this book continue in the face of tax reform. The best way to finance real estate is to examine the myriad choices available in today's marketplace and select the financing alternative which leaves the most money in your pocket.

But to examine alternative mortgage formats you have to know how each loan works, what it really costs, and how to evaluate financing options. It's not always easy to wade through conflicting claims, but this guide should make the process easier.

The public, for its part, has already responded to the issues raised by tax reform. The fastest-growing loan format in the past few years has been the simple 15-year mortgage, a financing option that cuts interest costs by more than 55 percent when compared with 30-year loans.

This is a book about money, real estate and choices. The choices you make when financing a home can save tens of thousands of dollars, and often a lot more. Designed to serve as a basic reference, consumer aid and classroom text, this guide stresses the idea that with so many loan choices now available, borrowers can customize home financing options to meet individual needs and save substantial sums of money in the process.

PETER G. MILLER

January 1987

The Common-Sense Mortgage

1
The Case for the Common-Sense Mortgage

Few of us are so rich that we can needlessly give away tens of thousands of dollars and yet it happens every day. We pay too much for home mortgages and the money we waste could easily send our kids to college, underwrite retirements or simply make home ownership more affordable to millions of people.

While much attention, debate and haggling surround real estate selling prices, financing is rarely given equal time or study and the result is that enormous sums of money—often amounts as great or greater than the original purchase price of a property—are lost to borrowers.

But why lose the money-making and money-saving advantages that sound mortgage planning can create? Reducing home interest costs is not an activity reserved for the rich or real estate pros. There is nothing illegal, immoral, unfair or abusive about cutting mortgage expenses. You don't have to be a financial whiz to succeed; there are no miracles involved, nothing difficult to understand and no tax rules to violate. Getting a good mortgage deal does not presume that you find a foolish lender or an impractical seller.

What you need is time to study your financial position, honesty to realistically evaluate where you are economically and where you're going, probing questions to find the best possible deals and professional assistance from brokers, lawyers and tax advisors. You'll have to work with lenders to arrange deals that are mutually attractive and you'll have to forget the idea that mortgage financing is a once-in-a-lifetime event: it isn't. You can finance and refinance at any time and the choices you make can put thousands of dollars in your pocket.

Whether you earn $20,000 or $200,000 a year you may think that you couldn't possibly spend an extra $50,000 on home financing without noticing. Yet if you've managed to waste "only" $50,000 you're probably doing better than most friends or neighbors. Here's where the money goes.

Suppose Mr. Matthews buys a home for $106,250. He puts down $21,250 in cash and gets a 30-year, fixed-rate mortgage for $85,000 at 10 percent interest—in other words, a "conventional" loan at market rates and terms. Monthly payments for principal and interest total $745.94.

At the end of 30 years Matthews has made 360 mortgage payments and spent a total of $268,537. Of the money paid to the lender, $85,000 was principal and $183,537 was interest—an amount substantially greater than the apparent acquisition price of the property.

But a 30-year loan is not the only way to organize a mortgage. Within the bounds of a 10 percent interest rate, Matthews—or you or I—could easily cut the interest bill for an $85,000 loan by $100,000—or more. Suppose, for example, that Matthews decides to increase his mortgage payment by $5.09 a day—not an unreasonable expense in the context of a $100,000 home or an era when a good hamburger costs five dollars anyway. Let's look at what happens:

- Monthly payments rise to $898.73.
- The debt to the lender is reduced at a far faster rate than would have been possible with payments of $745.94 per month.

- Because principal payments have been increased, the length of the loan is shortened from 360 months to 187 months. In other words, the loan term is now 15.58 years rather than 30 years.
- Interest costs are slashed by just over $100,000. (See Table 1.)

TABLE 1
How Mr. Matthews Could Save $100,000 with an $85,000 Mortgage

Loan size	$85,000	$85,000
Interest rate	10 percent	10 percent
Monthly payment	$745.94	$898.73
Extra monthly cost	None	$152.79
Number of payments	360	187
Potential interest cost	$183,536.90	$83,062.37
Potential cash saving	None	$100,474.53

Ask yourself: If you were Matthews, would you set aside $38.20 a week—hardly the cost of a meal for two at many restaurants—to cut your mortgage bill by $100,000? Is it worth spending $152.79 a month to knock out almost 15 years of mortgage payments?

Raising monthly mortgage payments is only one path to lower financing costs. In every community you can find loan plans that slash home ownership expenses. Growing Equity Mortgages (so-called "GEM" financing), wraparound loans, bond-backed mortgages and buy-downs are just some of the approaches savvy borrowers use to cut interest costs. Just as importantly, you don't need a new loan to drop interest expenses. Borrowers refinance and restructure old mortgages daily and save thousands of dollars when they do.

In many cases, lenders will help you develop money-saving strategies—while you pay less interest overall they have less risk, get their money back quicker and preserve or enlarge their buying power in the face of inflation. The interest you're not paying is more than made up by the lender's ability to issue additional loans that generate not only interest but high-profit fees and charges as well.

THE COMMON-SENSE MORTGAGE DEFINED

There is nothing sacred about being in debt for 30 years, especially since conventional mortgages—30-year, fixed-rate loans with 20 percent down—are no longer the best deals for most borrowers. What borrowers must look for today is the common-sense mortgage.

What is the common-sense mortgage? Since everyone's income and needs differ it follows that no single mortgage format works well for all borrowers. Not only are needs different; needs change. The conditions that made one loan ideal several years ago may no longer exist. A new job, more or less income, the repayment of other debts, an inheritance, retirement or a killing on the stock market may each influence mortgage thinking.

Rather than being a particular type of loan with so much down or a certain interest rate, the common-sense mortgage is a viewpoint, an idea, a way of looking at real estate debt. In very basic terms the common-sense mortgage can be defined as the best available financing for each borrower at any given time. Going further, the search for the common-sense mortgage is guided by nine basic principles.

First, borrowed money represents actual debt that must be repaid, preferably at discount or with cheaper dollars over time. Interest is a potential cost that can be controlled, reduced or eliminated through sound financial planning.

Second, mortgage rates and terms are not set in stone. Selecting a mortgage should not be viewed as a static, one-time event which ends once property is bought. Borrowers must instead search continually for profitable opportunities to acquire, refinance, curtail or restructure loans. New mortgage opportunities that lower interest costs, cut tax bills, preserve buying power and raise additional capital can be available at any time, opportunities about which borrowers will want to be aware in light of changing needs, resources and goals.

Third, when buying or refinancing property, look for loans that offer the lowest possible interest cost. Note that "the lowest possible interest cost" does not necessarily mean the lowest interest rate, say 10 percent as opposed to 12 percent. Structure counts. For instance, both a 30-year conventional mortgage and a GEM loan may each have a 10 percent interest rate, but the absolute interest cost of the conventional loan is likely to be tens of thousands of dollars higher than a GEM mortgage. How a loan is paid off can be more important than interest rates alone and the money you save can be spent or invested elsewhere.

Fourth, a mortgage must be seen as an alternative investment choice. Does it make sense to rapidly pay down your mortgage or is your money better spent on retirement plans, stock, mutual funds or other investments? What about after-tax results and the effect of inflation?

Fifth, reducing mortgage costs should not be seen as an exclusive financial option. There is no reason why an individual cannot have investments, a savings account, insurance and the best possible mortgage financing.

Sixth, saving interest and making interest are really two sides of the same coin. One thousand dollars invested today at 10 percent interest will be worth $6,727 in 20 years because of compounding. Conversely, small mortgage reductions today produce big savings over time because there is less principal on which to pay interest and less interest to compound. Note, however, that "savings" and "interest" are treated differently for tax purposes. Earned interest is generally taxable while savings are tax-free.

Seventh, leverage is an important financial tool that can be made even more valuable by cutting potential interest costs.

Eighth, personal decisions are not always economically rational. If it makes you feel good to pay off the mortgage, at least consider that feeling even if higher returns are available elsewhere.

Ninth, you and I can make financial choices that are both different yet equally valid. Our economic decisions will be based on individual needs, incomes, assets, ages and perceptions and so there is no single strategy that is always "correct." The important point is to have a strategy, to consider alternatives and to actively take those steps which produce the best financial results.

INFLATION AND THE COMMON-SENSE MORTGAGE

Over time most people who have held real estate have seen values rise, at least in cash terms. Whether such increases in value are "real" is sometimes difficult to demonstrate.

Suppose Mr. Sullivan bought a home for $125,300 in 1972 and sold it for $289,100 ten years later. Surely there is the appearance of a profit, at least in cash terms, but what could Sullivan buy with his extra dollars?

If Sullivan moves into a house of equal size in an equivalent neighborhood the probability is that it will cost him $289,100 to buy the new property. Why? Because the cost-of-living index between 1972 and 1982 rose from 125.3 to 289.1, according to the Bureau of Labor Statistics. Only if Sullivan's house sold for more than $289,100 will he gain additional buying power.

(In fact, home prices did appreciate faster than the rate of inflation in the decade between 1972 and 1982 so most property owners earned additional buying power relative to the cost of living.)

What really happened here is not so much that the value of Sullivan's home rose but rather the buying power of cash declined as a result of inflation. Thus while Sullivan had more dollars, each dollar bought less than it did ten years earlier.

While Sullivan came out even in terms of inflation not everyone was so lucky. Sullivan financed his house with a fixed-rate mortgage at 7 percent interest.

Since the rate of inflation averaged 8.7 percent between 1972 and 1982, Sullivan repaid his loan in dollars that bought less and less. The result is that Sullivan's lender, not Sullivan, lost buying power. Multiply Mr. Sullivan's experience and that of his lender by millions of real-life examples and you can quickly see how lenders lost buying power worth billions and billions of dollars in this one, ten-year period.

Today fixed-rate property loans such as Sullivan's are only one financing alternative. In addition, we have the widespread use of adjustable rate mortgages (ARMs), loans with interest rates that float up or down according to an index, and a variety of other innovative loan plans that feature graduated payments, accelerated pay-offs and even one without interest, so-called Zero Interest Plan (ZIP) financing.

The bottom line:

- The burden of inflation is being shifted from lenders to borrowers, particularly with ARM financing. While real estate ownership will remain a hedge against inflation, many real estate loans will not.
- Faster loan pay-offs with some mortgage formats mean lenders will have less exposure to inflation and thus less risk. Less risk, in turn, will permit bigger loans and lower interest rates to borrowers at every income level.
- Inflation has forced lenders to look beyond interest for profits. A growing proportion of lender revenues are now derived from the fees and charges which result from generating new loans. Lenders are also becoming more active in the "servicing" business, collecting payments and

performing other chores for mortgage investors. With these new profit centers lenders often have an incentive to favor mortgages that feature quicker loan pay-offs.

- Fixed-rate, conventional financing will command premium interest rates and steep up-front charges. Alternative forms of financing, in contrast, will be packaged with incentives for borrowers such as low initial interest rates, fewer fees up front, lower total interest costs and better payment schedules than conventional, 30-year mortgages.

- New loan formats, many created as a response to the inflation of the late 1970s and early 1980s, will allow borrowers to fine-tune their lending needs. Opportunities to cut home ownership costs will abound but to be successful borrowers will have to shop carefully in a marketplace deluged with choices.

TAXES, ECONOMICS AND THE COMMON-SENSE MORTGAGE

It is clear that widespread real estate ownership would be virtually impossible without the present tax advantages property owners enjoy. Tax deductions are crucial to homeowners because they reduce effective interest rates. If, for instance, you pay 10 percent interest but are in the 28 percent tax bracket, your true financing cost is 7.2 percent. As tax brackets rise, effective financing costs drop, so the true expense of being in debt falls less heavily on the rich. (See Table 2.)

Combining tax and inflation factors produces an interesting view of true mortgage costs. If Mr. Green's mortgage interest rate is 10 percent and he's in the 28 percent tax bracket, his out-of-pocket mortgage cost is 7.2 percent. That is, if Green spent $6,000 on mortgage interest last year his real cost was only $4,320. The other $1,680 would not otherwise have been available to Green because it would have been spent on taxes.

But if the inflation rate was 10 percent there was no "real"

TABLE 2
Tax Effects on Interest

Interest Rate (%)	Tax Bracket (%)	Effective Rate of Interest* (%)
8	15	6.80
8	28	5.76
9	15	7.65
9	28	6.48
10	15	8.50
10	28	7.20
11	15	9.35
11	28	7.92
12	15	10.20
12	28	8.64
13	15	11.05
13	28	9.36
14	15	11.90
14	28	10.08
15	15	12.75
15	28	10.80

*Not corrected for inflation.

economic cost for Green's loan because the rate of inflation (10 percent) was greater than his effective, after-tax interest rate (7.2 percent). In this case, Green's buying power actually increased because the after-tax cost of borrowing money was less than the rate of inflation. (See Table 3.)

TABLE 3
The True Cost of Mr. Green's Mortgage

Interest rate	10	percent
Tax bracket	28	percent
Effective interest rate	7.2	percent
Inflation rate	10	percent
Interest rate corrected for inflation	−3.8	percent

Does not this illustration suggest that it's always best to have the largest possible mortgage, particularly if you're in a high tax bracket? How can someone maximize his or her financial position with a mortgage that is quickly paid off or with one that features reduced interest expenses?

THE COMMON-SENSE MORTGAGE AND FINANCIAL PLANNING

To answer the questions above a mortgage must be viewed as only one of several financial necessities which should be part of a sound personal financial program. A good personal finance strategy would include not only home ownership but also

- life and health insurance, particularly to protect against catastrophic medical costs;
- the equivalent of three to six months' income in a savings account or money market fund; and
- a retirement plan.

Once your basic financial foundations are in place—home-ownership, adequate insurance, cash on hand and a good retirement program—you can begin to devise an investment strategy. Just where should you put extra dollars? Does it ever make sense to pay down your mortgage early? If you are now paying 10 percent interest or whatever figure on real estate financing, where else could you get an equal or better rate of return with as little risk?

Suppose you have an extra $1,000, a 10 percent mortgage, and your income places you in the 28 percent federal tax bracket in 1988. Where could you put your money?

By investing $1,000 in a home loan, the size of your mortgage would be reduced and thus interest costs would be cut. The interest you don't pay—$100 per year in this case—is not "income," however. It's considered a "saving" and is therefore untaxed. In effect, by investing in a mortgage you would earn something more than 10 percent, about 12.8 percent in this example.

If you're in the 28 percent bracket, excluding social security, state and local income taxes, $1,000 placed in a savings account that paid 10 percent interest would yield only $72 after taxes. To earn $100 after federal income taxes from such an account you would have to deposit $1,390.

You could also take your $1,000 and deposit that money in an IRA or Keogh Plan producing a 10 percent annual return. These retirement programs are structured so that *if you qualify* the amount you deposit each year is deductible and the income or appreciation is untaxed until withdrawn. Putting $1,000 in an approved retirement program would lower current income taxes by $280 and produce interest worth $100 before deferred taxes. To earn as much after federal taxes from a 10 percent savings account you would have to deposit $5,280.

(Note that under tax reform many past IRA contributors will no longer be able to deduct IRA contributions. IRA contributions on which regular taxes are paid will still be permitted, however. The income and appreciation from such investments will be untaxed until withdrawal. Be sure to see a qualified tax advisor for complete details and latest information.)

There is a difference between the savings account and mortgage payments. With the savings account, the $1,000 deposit produces immediate cash returns. The mortgage reduction, however, creates an economic benefit that is only realized when the property is sold, refinanced or paid off. Monthly mortgage payments remain unchanged. Borrowers who need an immediate cash benefit from the placement of their $1,000 may not be able to make the long-term commitment represented by a reduced mortgage balance even when it is economically attractive.

IRA and Keogh plans are blessed with extensive tax preferences and so they are likely to produce better after-tax returns than most investments. But these programs are of no value to older homeowners and contributions to such plans are limited.

Another "investment" choice might be to pay off credit card debt. Since the cost of consumer credit generally ranges from 18 to 21 percent, reducing credit card bills by $1,000 would produce returns of $180 to $210—money which is again a "saving" and not taxable income.

In the past, some borrowers have used real estate tax shelters to reduce taxes by ratios of one to two, one to three and sometimes more; that is, for each dollar invested tax bills dropped by two dollars, three dollars or whatever. In addition, the best tax shelters produced cash profits plus appreciation. Investing $1,000 in a shelter would produce far higher returns than a simple mortgage reduction.

The difficulty today with tax shelters is that many of the attractive deals of yesteryear have been phased out or eliminated under tax reform. However, since the rules for many forms of investment have been changed, the view here is that *relative to alternative choices under tax reform,* real estate in general continues to offer excellent investment opportunities—especially for investors with gross adjusted incomes of $100,000 or less. Rather than limited partnership tax shelters that featured little if any income, under tax reform the best deals will be required to make economic sense—properties that produce income and offer the possibility of future appreciation above the rate of inflation.

In terms of residential real estate, interest deductions on both prime residences and second homes remain intact. However, the value of mortgage interest deductions has been significantly lowered because maximum tax rates have been reduced. Here's what it means:

- If you're poor, your tax liabilities are limited or non-existent under tax reform. In essence, the mortgage interest rate you pay is likely to be your real cost of financing before inflation. In most instances you'll do better paying off credit card bills and auto loans before putting additional dollars into a mortgage.

- If you're in the middle income brackets, you appear to have a larger number of financial options than the poor. But these options are limited by the fact that home mortgage payments are likely to represent your largest monthly expense, a huge cost that influences job flexibility (Can you pay the mortgage if you quit?), family roles (Must both husband and wife work?) and life-style choices (Are you able to save money for the kids, retirement or a better vacation?). At best, tax benefits make mortgage payments more bearable.

- If you're at the upper end of the middle class, however, a portion of your income, or perhaps much of your income, won't be in the 28 percent bracket. Buried in tax reform is a five percent surcharge for couples with taxable incomes between $71,900 and $149,250, and individuals with taxable incomes between $43,150 and $89,560. These income levels —which will be adjusted for inflation in future years—have an effective federal tax rate of 33 percent.

Thus people in the middle class may find themselves paying the highest possible rates under tax reform and therefore receiving the greatest interest subsidy. The problem, however, is to earn that subsidy you must spend three dollars in interest to receive a one-dollar deduction. That's not a good deal; a better choice is to find mortgage financing with the lowest-possible interest cost, have a smaller deduction and pay the taxes.

- If you're wealthy, you'll have fewer deductions under tax reform but your maximum tax bill will drop from 50 percent of gross adjusted income to just 28 percent. This means that if you had a $10,000 mortgage interest bill in 1986, $5,000 would have been deductible. By 1988, however, a $10,000 interest cost would yield only $2,800 in tax deductions. In effect, your cost of home ownership will rise greatly under tax reform.

For the wealthy—the folks who have the greatest number of economic choices—the issue of rapidly repaying a mortgage must be seen in the light of alternative investments. Should you accelerate mortgage payments or place your money elsewhere? Where can you get the highest rate of return after taxes and inflation? Should you pay off a home mortgage merely as a matter of personal preference? Since effective mortgage costs will be higher under tax reform, and since many tax shelters have been eliminated or devalued, paying off a mortgage may be a sound choice for those who are truly rich.

The bottom line for all borrowers:

First, both taxes and interest are expenses.

Second, tax policies reward certain types of behavior. In the case of tax reform, the government might as well erect a huge neon sign from the highest building in Washington saying: "BORROW ON REAL ESTATE, BUT BORROW WISELY. FROM NOW ON, UNCLE SAM IS PAYING LESS OF THE BILL AND YOU'LL PAY MORE." The government is reducing mortgage interest subsidies by cutting tax rates. Simply put, smaller subsidies mean higher effective interest costs. If you have excess interest costs—dollars you don't really need to pay—you'll get penalized twice: once because the lender will realize more money than you need to pay, and once again because interest costs will generate smaller write-offs than in the past.

One result of tax reform will be a widespread change in borrowing habits. Rather than automatically opting for 30-year financing with high overall interest costs, many borrowers will consider shorter loans and loans with accelerated payment schedules. These financing choices will reduce interest costs by tens of thousands of dollars for individual borrowers and—multiplied by hundreds of thousands and ultimately millions of cases—the overall interest bill paid by U.S. homeowners will drop by billions of dollars each year.

Third, it's *always* cheaper to pay taxes rather than excess interest. If you're in the 28 percent tax bracket, it's far better to pay $28 in taxes than $100 in excess interest. Spending $100 on unnecessary interest creates, in this case, a $28 tax deduction. Not spending $100 in additional interest creates a $28 tax debt—but leaves $72 in your pocket.

If excess interest costs made sense, then we would have borrowers demanding 12 percent interest in a 10 percent market for loans of equal size. Yet, while borrowers constantly seek low interest *rates,* many wind up with high financing *costs.* How? Because excess interest can be created by loan *structure*—the way money is repaid—as well as high interest rates.

In example after example you can plainly see that two loans of equal size create different interest costs. If given a choice between such financing alternatives, why pick the mortgage with the higher cost? In some cases borrowers with limited finances have no option—the only loan they can afford is a stretched-out mortgage with high overall interest expenses. But many of us *do* have choices, particularly those who know that alternatives exist and that by selecting the best possible mortgage option we can save substantial amounts of money, *our* money if we don't needlessly give it away.

The point about real estate financing is that it is one of several valid investment choices, so why not buy property with a mortgage that represents the best possible arrangement in terms of interest, monthly payments, debt reduction, inflation, taxes and the value of money over time? Why not refinance or restructure when it is to your advantage?

Why not hold your mortgage to the same criteria that you would use to evaluate stocks, bonds or any other investment?

Surely you would check the stock tables every day, wait for dividends and splits, look for opportunities to buy, sell or trade, compare your stock with other issues and generally take an active interest in "your" company. Why be less concerned about your own mortgage?

LEVERAGE AND THE COMMON-SENSE MORTGAGE

It is commonly argued that borrowers should put down as little cash as possible when buying real estate. Use "other people's money" (OPM) and you'll have leverage and a better chance at big returns. If you can buy property with 10 percent down that's fine. If you can buy with 5 percent down that's better. Some argue that no money down is best of all.

There is no conflict between the idea of a common-sense mortgage and maximizing leverage. Whether you put down 5 percent, 10 percent or 20 percent you are still financing the bulk of the property so why not borrow money under the best possible terms and conditions?

A problem arises, however, when the idea of maximum debt is thought to be synonymous with maximum interest. There is no benefit in terms of leverage with steep interest costs. Putting down 5 percent to buy property and having a $100,000 interest bill is likely to be a much better deal than putting down 5 percent and paying interest costs of $200,000. Although the leverage factor is the same, the ultimate cost of the property is not.

INVESTMENT REAL ESTATE
AND THE COMMON-SENSE MORTGAGE

There are significant distinctions between real estate which is purchased for personal purposes and property that is bought for investment. Two identical townhouses in a single subdivision may be physically alike but if one is residential property and the other investment real estate, the financing of each will be influenced by different factors.

First, owners of pure residential property—real estate which is used for no purpose other than personal housing—may not claim deductions for depreciation, maintenance, utilities, repairs, improvements or condo and co-op fees. Investors can claim deductions for such expenses.

Second, residential owners may move from one personal property to another of equal or greater value and defer all taxes from the sale of the first house. Investors face taxes whenever they sell at a profit.

Third, personal property owners over the age of 55 may claim a one-time profit exclusion of up to $125,000 (at this writing) when they sell their homes. There is no similar exemption for investors.

Home ownership and investment choices are guided by different philosophies, motivations, economics, tax policies and goals. These factors mean that strategies which work well for personal real estate deals may be inappropriate or even harmful when making investment decisions and borrowers must adjust their planning to suit the type of real estate being financed.

HOW TO PROFIT FROM THIS BOOK

This book has been written to help you both make money and save money. It is designed to serve as a basic reference guide and as a tool to help you choose the best loan at any given time.

To use this book effectively you must first know how the lending system works, information which is covered in Chapter 2. Chapter 3 looks at the influence of ownership on financing and explains why condos, PUDS (Planned Unit Developments) and co-ops raise special mortgage concerns.

Picking the right mortgage is the subject of Chapter 4. To

choose the best mortgage you must be able to compare one loan format with another and to measure like loans offered by different lenders. You'll need to recognize a variety of specific loan plans and to understand how they operate, their pros and cons and what they really cost. Chapters 5 through 12 examine individual loan programs and at the end of each section you'll find a checklist, questions that will help you evaluate and compare current loan choices.

If you now have a mortgage you'll want to read Chapter 13. It describes several strategies that current borrowers can use to cut loan costs by thousands of dollars, how to get big discounts through loan curtailments and where to find hidden loan refinancing charges—costs that can sour an otherwise good deal.

Chapter 14 discusses the rapidly emerging 15-year mortgage and how it can be used both to save interest and to generate capital. Also in this chapter you'll find a section that explains how bi-weekly mortgages really work and why they're not for everyone despite big potential interest savings.

Chapter 15 is an extensive question-and-answer section based on the most frequent and interesting questions I have received while speaking around the country. This chapter responds to many of the issues and ideas raised by borrowers and probably contains a few questions you would like directly answered.

To get the best deal you must ask questions, speak to mortgage loan officers, talk with real estate brokers, consult with attorneys and tax advisors and always consider alternative approaches. You'll need paper and pencil, a calculator that can figure interest rates and monthly loan payments and a willingness to study, listen and explore.

If it seems as though finding the best financing is a lot of work, you're right. But it is also true that a properly structured mortgage can easily save the equivalent of several years' income, a fact few of us can ignore.

2
How the Lending System Works

Real estate financing is more than a matter of interest rates and loan terms. To prosper in the mortgage-lending system borrowers must first understand its language, how it works, who the players are, why they act the way they do and what they expect from you. Let's get started by looking at basic words and concepts.

THE LANGUAGE OF REAL ESTATE FINANCE

Every trade has its tools, each discipline its special words and so it is not surprising that real estate financing has a unique vocabulary.

The most frequent words you will encounter are *mortgage* and *trust* or *deed of trust*. Simply stated, mortgages and trusts are both promises to repay a loan secured by real estate. The actual terms of the loan—its length, interest rate, size, etc.—are found in a separate document, the *note*. For the general purposes of this book, the terms *mortgage* and *trust* are used interchangeably.

On a more technical basis, however, mortgages and trusts are different. A mortgage represents a direct arrangement between lender and borrower. A deed of trust is a triangular affair in which there is a borrower, a lender and trustees selected by the lender. If a borrower fails to make adequate or timely payment, the trustees have the right to foreclose on the property. In many jurisdictions, foreclosure is faster with a deed of trust than with a mortgage.

From the borrower's viewpoint, real estate loans have a potential problem. What happens at the end of the loan term if the lender is on a two-year trip to Nepal or was hit by a bus and is now comatose in a hospital? You cannot sell or refinance the property as long as your debt to the lender is outstanding. Who can sign all the papers needed to show your debt has been paid? With a deed of trust the trustees must promptly sign all requisite documents upon payment of the debt and therefore a borrower is not dependent on the availability of the lender.

There are many words and phrases commonly used in real estate finance, expressions with which borrowers should be familiar. Here is a selected list of important terms that can help you better understand how the mortgage system works.

Amortization. As payments are made to a lender each month, the size of the mortgage debt, or *principal,* declines in most cases. This process is called *amortization.* Also, see SELF-AMORTIZATION, and NEGATIVE AMORTIZATION.

Amortization Schedule. A table that shows how each monthly payment is divided into principal and interest during the term of the loan and the remaining principal balance after every mortgage payment. For a level-payment, 30-year, $85,000 loan at 10 percent interest, monthly payments would be $745.94 and an amortization schedule would look like this:

Payment	Interest	Principal	Balance
1	$708.33	$37.60	$84,962.40
2	$708.02	$37.91	$84,924.49
3	$707.70	$38.23	$84,886.26
4	$707.39	$38.55	$84,847.71
Etc.			

Annual Percentage Rate (APR). The true rate of interest for a loan over its projected life, say 30 years. May be different than the initial interest rate or the nominal interest rate before compounding.

Balloon Payment. It sometimes happens that loan payments are not sufficient to pay off a debt and the result is that at the end of the loan a large, or *balloon,* payment remains. This can be the case when monthly payments are not large enough to cover the combined value of principal and interest or when monthly payments do cover principal and interest but there are not enough of them to repay the debt in full. For instance, if the loan above terminated after three payments there would be a balloon payment of $84,886.26.

In the case of an interest-only loan, the balloon payment at the end of the loan term would be equal to the original amount borrowed. Second trusts often feature balloon payments because they tend to be short-term obligations, usually two to ten years in length.

Blanket Mortgage. A single mortgage secured by several properties.

Closing. See SETTLEMENT.

Curtailment. A payment that shortens or ends a mortgage. For example, if you have a $15,000 balance on your mortgage and pay off the entire debt the loan has been curtailed.

Deferred Interest. See NEGATIVE AMORTIZATION.

Entitlement. A right due to an individual. Used with VA mortgages. For instance, a $15,000 *entitlement* would mean that a vet could borrow that sum from a lender and the VA would guarantee its repayment. Since lenders usually want a 1:4 ratio between the value of an entitlement and the loan amount, having a $15,000 guarantee would allow a borrower to get a $75,000 loan—$15,000 backed by the VA and $60,000 secured by the borrower and the worth of the property.

Equity.   The cash value of property, less marketing expenses, after all liens have been paid off.

Escrow.   When money is held by one party for another it is usually placed in an *escrow,* or trust, account. For example, if you give a real estate broker a $10,000 deposit to purchase a house and those funds are placed in an escrow account, the broker does not have the right to use that money *(commingle)* for his own purposes.

Installment Sale.   A transaction in which the buyer pays the seller in whole or in part after title has been transferred. For example, Wilson buys a house from Davis and pays $100,000 for the property. Davis receives $20,000 at settlement and $20,000 a year plus interest for the next four years. The advantage to Davis is that his profit is spread over several years and thus he may enjoy a reduced tax rate.

Junior Lien.   Much like shoppers in a supermarket line, lenders line up to be paid when a property is foreclosed. The order of repayment is established by the loan documents recorded in local government offices. The lender with the first claim has the first mortgage or first trust, the lender with the second claim holds the second mortgage or second trust, etc. If a loan is not a first trust or mortgage it is a *junior lien.*

Leverage.   A general investment concept meaning that you have been able to borrow funds and thereby use other people's money (OPM). If you buy a home for $100,000, put down $20,000 at settlement and get an $80,000 mortgage for the balance, your *leverage* is 1 to 4. If you put down only $10,000 your leverage is 1 to 9, a better deal as long as the $10,000 you didn't put into the property can earn an equal or better return elsewhere.

Liens.   A *lien* is a claim against property. Not only are mortgages and trusts liens, but overdue property taxes, unpaid repair bills, condo fees and even water and sewage charges can all be liens. A major purpose of a title search is to be certain that all liens are known as of the day of settlement.

Locking In.   Mortgage rates are often widely advertised but the rate you see may not be the rate you get. Borrowers must ask when a rate is "locked in"; that is, guaranteed by the lender. Rates may be locked in at the time a loan application is made, several weeks later when the loan is approved or at the time of settlement. If a loan is not locked in at the time of application, then a borrower may pay higher rates if interest levels rise. Some lenders not only lock in rates at the time of application, they also guarantee that the quoted rate is the highest a borrower will pay. If interest rates fall between the time of application and settlement, borrowers pay the lowest rate.

Negative Amortization.   A loan in which monthly payments are too small to pay for either principal or interest reductions. The result is that the size of the principal balance grows by both the amount of unpaid interest and the interest on the unpaid interest. *Negative amortization* will produce a balloon payment at the end of the loan in most cases. However, with some formats, such as graduated payment mortgages, there can be negative amortization in the first years of the loan, but higher payments later in the loan term eliminate the possibility of a balloon payment. For example: With a 30-year, $85,000 loan at 10 percent interest a self-amortizing loan would require monthly payments of $745.94. If the payments were only $700, negative amortization would develop.

Payment	Interest	Principal	Balance
1	$700	0	$ 85,008.33
2	$700	0	$ 85,016.73
3	$700	0	$ 85,025.20
Etc.			

Other People's Money (OPM). Money that you borrow from other people or lenders. To get the maximum amount of leverage you want to borrow the largest possible amount of money and have it work for you.

Package Mortgage. A single mortgage used to acquire not only a house but personal goods as well, such as a microwave oven.

Points. A *point,* or a *loan discount fee,* is an amount equal to 1 percent of the value of a mortgage. This sum is paid or credited to a lender at settlement. The purpose of points is to raise the lender's yield. (For more information about points, *see* YIELD AND POINTS.)

Principal, Interest, Taxes and Insurance (PITI). The four basic costs of home ownership that most concern lenders. For example, a lender might say that only 28 percent of your gross income can be devoted to PITI if you are to qualify for financing.

Refinance. A situation in which new financing is placed on a property. The addition of a second trust would be a "partial" refinancing. Replacing one loan with another would be a "total" refinancing.

Restructure. A loan that remains in place but with new terms. If you increase your monthly payments by $25 you have *restructured* your loan. By making the additional payments you will reduce the principal debt at a faster rate than originally planned, so you will pay less interest and have fewer payments.

For example, if you have an $85,000 loan at 10 percent interest it will take 30 years to repay the loan with monthly payments of $745.94. If the monthly payment is raised $25 to $770.94, the loan could be repaid in a little more than 25 years.

Self-Amortization. When monthly payments for principal and interest allow a loan to be repaid over its term without any balloon payment, *self-amortization* has occurred. See AMORTIZATION SCHEDULE for illustration.

Settlement. *Settlement,* or *closing,* is nothing more than an accounting of who owes what to whom as a result of a real estate sale. Not only must the buyer pay the seller but the seller may have to pay off old loans, brokerage fees, etc. It is at settlement that transfer taxes, points, adjustments between buyer and seller (for such items as oil in the furnace or prepaid taxes), title insurance, and other costs are first collected from buyer and seller and then paid out or credited as required.

Take Back. An expression used in real estate to mean that a loan has been made directly to a purchaser by the seller as in, "seller Conklin will *take back* a $30,000 second trust from buyer Hastings."

Usury. In many jurisdictions there is a maximum rate of interest permitted for certain types of loans. If the interest rate is above the limit, there is *usury.* The usury limit varies not only between jurisdictions but according to loan types. There may, for instance, be one usury limit for first trusts and another rate for seconds.

YIELD AND POINTS

For most borrowers, the cost of mortgage financing—and the lender's income—can be measured in terms of interest. But interest is only one mortgage expense; there are others and they greatly influence the cost of financing.

Mortgage rates are described by both a nominal rate, say 10 percent, and the APR, or *annual percentage rate*, a figure that is generally higher than the nominal interest cost, perhaps 10.75 percent in this case. The difference between the nominal and APR figures is the result of interest compounding and possibly other factors. When comparing loans the APR figure should always be used.

In a growing number of situations, however, it is difficult to cite a specific interest cost. With adjustable rate mortgages (ARMs), for example, there may be an attractive interest rate initially but that figure is subject to change. Rate fluctuations over the life of a variable-rate loan are not predictable, so determining a set APR is not possible.

There are many situations in which borrowers select one lender over another on the basis of interest rates. While it certainly pays to shop for interest rates, other expenses should not be ignored. Consider these costs:

Fees.   Many lenders charge to process loan applications and these costs vary. Ask if all or part of the fee will be refunded in the event an application is rejected.

Charges.   Most lenders require borrowers to pay for a credit report and appraisal. Some lenders, however, have additional requirements such as surveys and photos and these items are also an expense of financing.

Reserves.   Different lenders have different reserve requirements, money held by the lender to assure the payment of property taxes, condo fees or mortgage insurance premiums. Reserves can be a major cash drain at settlement, so be certain to compare lender practices in this area.

Perhaps the single lender charge that causes the most confusion is a *loan discount fee*, or *point*. A point is equal to 1 percent of the value of a mortgage and is paid or credited to a lender at settlement.

The purpose of points is to raise the lender's yield. Suppose you get an $85,000 loan at 10 percent interest. The lender charges one point, or $850, and so at settlement you receive $84,150. The lender has loaned only $84,150 but expects you to repay the full face value of the loan, $85,000—plus interest.

In terms of interest rates, a point is usually valued at one-eighth of 1 percent over the 30-year term of a conventional mortgage. Using this figure, one might expect that if a lender is making one loan at 10 percent and another mortgage at 9 percent interest, the lower rate note would require the payment of eight points.

As a practical matter, however, loans do not last 30 years. Most loans are repaid within 12 years, not so much a result of borrowers making additional payments as the fact that people move and refinance with some frequency. For the loan above, lenders would surely ask for less than eight points, perhaps three to three and a half points.

But suppose there are two lenders in town and you have a choice: you can get a 30-year, $85,000 loan at 10 percent interest and pay two points or you can pay 10.25 percent interest and pay only one point. Which is the better deal?

The answer depends on how long you own the property. The difference between an interest rate of 10 percent and 10.25 percent is $15.75 per month ($745.94 monthly versus $761.69 for a 30-year loan). It would take almost 54 months to pay out $850 at the rate of $15.75 monthly. Moreover, paying $850 at settlement means you have lost any possible interest or investment income on that money. (See Table 4.)

The bottom line: If you intend to own the property much more than 54 months, pay the additional $850 charge up front. If you only intend to own the property for a short time then the higher interest rate is a bargain.

The Common-Sense Mortgage

TABLE 4
Points versus Interest

	Loan 1	Loan 2
Loan amount	$85,000	$85,000
Interest rate	10.00	10.25
Monthly payment	$745.94	$761.69
Number of points	2	1
Cash value of points	$1,700	$850
Extra monthly interest cost	None	$15.75
Extra cost for points	$850	None

Borrowers will need to "run the numbers" and calculate the actual cost of various combinations of points and interest. In most cases, deciding whether or not to opt for a higher interest rate or more points—when such options are available—is a function of time. The longer a property is held, the cheaper the one-time cost of points.

Since points are a cost of financing it would seem that they are an expense which "should" be borne by purchasers, but this is not necessarily the case.

- With VA loans, the seller must pay all points at this time.
- With conventional loans, the question of who pays points is a matter of negotiation. If you are the buyer, you can present an offer that has the seller paying all points. If that is unacceptable, try splitting points. Another approach would be to formulate an offer in which the seller pays a set amount to you at settlement, say the first $3,000 of your closing costs or whatever figure might be appropriate.
- If you're a seller you too have a right to negotiate. From your perspective you would certainly argue that points are an expense to be borne exclusively by the purchaser. When sellers feel the cost of points is too high, they often agree to pay all or a portion of the points due if the buyer will accept

a price increase. In effect, the buyer pays such costs over the term of the mortgage.

Since points are a payment for the use of money, interest, they should be tax deductible, and as this is written, points paid for the *purchase* of a new home are fully deductible in the year in which they're paid. Points paid to *refinance* a home, however, must be apportioned over the loan's life.

Suppose you have a property bought many years ago and today it's mortgage free. You want to raise money and refinance the property with an $85,000 mortgage. The mortgage has a term of 30 years and you pay two points, or $1,700, at settlement. The points in this case must be deducted over the mortgage's 30-year life at the rate of $56.67 a year.

But what if you have a 30-year loan but pay it off in 20 years. How should a deduction for points be treated? Why should points for refinancing be treated differently than points paid when first buying a home? Some members of Congress feel points should be deductible in the year in which they're charged, so check with a tax advisor for the latest rules and interpretations.

Questions to ask:

Will your lender allow you the option of paying fewer points in exchange for a higher interest rate?

Will your lender allow you the option of paying more points in exchange for a lower rate of interest?

How long must you own the property to justify a high-interest mortgage with few points?

How long must you own the property to justify a low-interest loan with more points up front?

Can you fully deduct points charged for new loans from federal taxes?

Can you fully deduct points charged for refinancing from federal taxes?

How are points deducted, if at all, when the money is used for education costs, medical expenses or major home improvements?

How are points treated if the loan is used for a business purpose?

WHY LENDERS NEED APPRAISALS

What is the worth of a given property? It may seem as though a sales price, determined by informed buyers and sellers in an open market, would be the best index of value. Yet this is not always the case as far as lenders are concerned.

While buyers and sellers may look at a property as a home or an investment, lenders see the very same real estate in different terms. To lenders, property is security—the ultimate recourse in the event a borrower fails to repay a mortgage. In this sense, lenders must know real estate values to limit their risk.

Consider what would happen if a lender valued a real estate parcel at $100,000 and made an $80,000 mortgage based on that judgment. If the mortgage was not repaid the lender would sell the property at foreclosure, a process which in itself is costly and time-consuming. But if the property could be sold for only $60,000 or any value less than the mortgage balance and the cost of foreclosure, the lender would have a loss.

To limit such risks, lenders want a precise but conservative estimate of value before making a loan. To determine the right numbers an appraiser satisfactory to the lender will be hired to evaluate the property.

The worth of a particular property is represented by more

than bricks and mortar. Here are the major factors appraisers use to determine real estate values:

Occupancy. It is generally agreed that owner-occupants have a clear interest in maintaining property values. Tenant-occupied properties are seen as representing more risk to a lender and therefore investment loans are likely to have a higher rate of interest than residential mortgages.

Transition. Property values which fluctuate as a result of zoning changes, growth patterns and other factors must be noted. Most instances of transition are evolutionary but in some cases there can be dramatic value fluctuations. In one situation, an appraisal was changed from $15,000 to nearly $500,000 because a property was rezoned and incorporated into a rapidly developing urban area.

Predominant Value. Housing patterns tend to be homogeneous. Homes worth $100,000 are in $100,000 neighborhoods; $50,000 properties are in $50,000 areas, etc. For appraisers, it is important for properties to be within the general pricing patterns of their neighborhoods because over-valued homes, even though they may have exceptional features, are difficult to sell or to foreclose at full market price.

Buyers, it is said in the real estate industry, seek the least expensive property they can find in the most expensive neighborhood they can afford. This means that a home with a pool and five bedrooms in a neighborhood of conservative three-bedroom homes will be difficult to market at full economic value and therefore a lender will want to limit the size of a loan made against such property.

Facilities. The existence—or lack—of community improvements, such as sewers and sidewalks, will influence property values.

Improvements. Anything other than raw ground, such as houses, apartment buildings, garages, pools, etc., is regarded as an *improvement*. An appraiser will evaluate each improvement in terms of its age, condition and modernization. The remaining economic life of the improvement will be estimated. Extra value will be given for modernized baths and kitchens, additions, and energy-efficient items such as enhanced insulation, wood-burning stoves and even landscaping that reduces energy usage.

Once all the variables have been considered (the items above are but part of a far longer list), an appraiser will calculate a property value using one of three systems. With the *market data* approach an appraiser will compare the subject property with other neighborhood sales. This is the most common form of appraisal for residential property.

The *income* system can be used to determine values for investment properties. Here the analysis is based on revenues and rates of return.

A third type of approach, *cost valuation,* estimates the value of materials and labor needed to erect a similar improvement on comparable property. This form of appraisal is valuable for specialized structures, such as churches and synagogues.

Using one or more forms of analysis, an appraiser will provide an estimate of value to the lender who may then elect to make a loan commitment. However, since the lender views the property as economic security, a conventional, uninsured loan for the full value of the property will not be granted.

Instead the lender will provide a loan for only a portion of the property's value, say 80 percent, and the purchaser will put up the balance in cash, as a second trust or both. For the lender, a limited loan commitment plus the equity contribution of the buyer both have the effect of reducing risk.

Not everyone can put up sufficient cash or secondary financing for a property purchase. In such situations a lender may

provide more than 80 percent financing when there are promises of repayment by a third party, such as the VA, FHA or a
private mortgage insurer.

KNOWING THE PLAYERS: WHO MAKES LOANS, WHO HELPS

There are a variety of players within the mortgage-lending
system—individuals and institutions with which both buyers
and sellers should be familiar. While all players participate in
the lending process, each has a different role and motivation
and these distinctions often provide important clues when looking for the best financing arrangement.

Savings and Loan Associations.   S&Ls are specialized financial organizations which are the largest single source of residential mortgages. By 1985, S&Ls had generated mortgages worth
$431 billion—more than half of all private loans for one-to-four-
unit residential properties.

(These and other figures are taken from '86 *Savings and Loan
Source Book,* a publication of the United States League of Savings Institutions. While the numbers may vary over time, they
are presented here for the purpose of showing the relative
position of different lenders in the mortgage market, positions
which are unlikely to change to a significant degree.)

It is not surprising that S&Ls are so active in the mortgage
market. Historically they have been able to attract savings from
the general public because governmental regulations once
gave them the right to pay slightly more interest than commercial banks. Federal rules have also guided the use of those savings: to get maximum tax benefits S&Ls must invest 82 percent
of their available funds in mortgage loans.

Commercial Banks.   Mortgages are an important, but secondary, activity for commercial bankers. Commercial banks
developed residential mortgages worth $214.3 billion by 1985,

a not inconsiderable sum but significantly less than S&Ls. Unlike S&Ls, the prime focus of commercial banks is demand deposits (checking accounts) and short-term loans, particularly business financing.

Mutual Savings Banks. About five hundred such institutions, located largely in New England, are something of a hybrid between banks and S&Ls. While a large portion (72 percent) of their loans must be in the form of mortgages to get maximum tax benefits, mutual savings banks can also issue checks—a traditional barrier for S&Ls. Mutuals had $122.1 billion in residential mortgages outstanding at the end of 1985.

Whether the classic differences between banks, S&Ls and mutual savings banks will continue is an open question. The development of NOW accounts effectively gives S&Ls a checking capability. However, the price of this new authority has been the creation of highly liquid, interest-bearing demand deposits which may not be a reliable underwriting resource for long-term loans.

The movement toward more liquid deposits as well as the growth of alternative interest-bearing accounts—notably money market funds—suggests that if present trends continue relatively fewer dollars will be available for long-term, fixed-rate mortgages. Money which once would have been destined for use as real estate financing may now wind up elsewhere. Conversely, financing for cars and consumer goods may become plentiful because highly liquid deposits are best used to underwrite short-term loans.

Life Insurance Companies. The nation's insurers loaned $13.5 billion in residential mortgages by 1985 but their major interest is in commercial financing. Loans for commercial projects—often large office buildings, shopping centers and apartment complexes—totaled $122.9 billion.

Credit Unions. Until 1978, federal regulations prevented credit unions from offering mortgages but in that year new rules allowed credit unions to make such loans, but with one important stipulation: the size of the loan was limited by prevailing housing prices in given areas. The loan size limitation (which was removed in 1982) as well as rapidly rising interest rates at that time held back credit union activity in the mortgage area. Between 1979 and 1983, credit union mortgages totaled less than $1.5 billion per year, according to the Credit Union National Association. In the future, however, credit unions are likely to become a larger factor in the mortgage marketplace because of their substantial assets and broad membership.

Mortgage Bankers. Individuals and institutions who represent funding sources such as pension plans and insurance companies. Mortgage bankers locate borrowers who meet standards established by loan investors and then service loans for lenders. "Servicing" the loan means making monthly collections and, if necessary, foreclosures.

Mortgage Brokers. Individuals and institutions who match those who need money with interested investors. Commercial real estate brokers often perform this function.

Sellers. There are always deals available in which some sellers will hold financing; however, when interest rates soar, the character of seller financing changes. In such times seller financing is not an occasional matter—it is a wholesale substitute for the commercial lending system. In 1980 and 1981, for example, it was estimated that when interest rates exceeded 16 and 17 percent, more than 60 percent of all residential resales involved some seller financing.

Real Estate Brokers. Brokers and their agents have several important functions within the lending system even though they are not lenders per se:

First, brokers are a central source of mortgage information. Buyers and sellers commonly depend on brokers to locate real estate financing and to advise them on current rates, points and loan formats.

Second, brokers look at the finances of prospective buyers to determine, in general terms, the level of financing they can afford. While this basic qualifying process does not guarantee financing, it does provide valuable information and guidance to buyers.

Third, brokers keep abreast of the mortgage market and may be able to locate "special" investor funds, money at below-market rates or with other advantageous terms. Knowing where the money is often spells the difference between a sale and no deal.

Lawyers. Attorneys play an important role in the lending process because of the complex rules which govern mortgages.

Lawyers are commonly employed to review real estate agreements prior to final acceptance and to write specialized legal language required for the sale. Attorneys often conduct *settlement (closing)* and in those cases where lawyers do not conduct settlement they frequently review settlement papers for a client, either the buyer or the seller, to assure that settlement follows the understandings described in the contract between the parties.

In the lending process directly, lawyers write and review agreements between buyers and sellers, such as equity-sharing arrangements. They also write and review mortgage documents for lenders generally and for sellers in those cases where a seller *takes back* financing (makes a loan directly to) a buyer. An attorney would want to assure that the loan conforms with all appropriate rules and regulations—items such as usury limits, payment terms, the naming of trustees (if any), insurance requirements, etc.

SECONDARY LENDERS: WHO THEY ARE AND WHAT THEY DO

Anyone who has ever applied for a mortgage is familiar with primary lenders—local institutions such as S&Ls, mortgage bankers and commercial banks that make loans and collect monthly payments. Less well known are secondary lenders, multi-billion dollar organizations that play a key role in the mortgage financing system.

Suppose a local lender has $5 million available for mortgages. Fifty home buyers, each in need of a $100,000 loan, apply for financing and every loan application is approved. This is great news for the first fifty people, but what about future borrowers? Has the primary lender run out of money?

To service additional home buyers the primary lender needs more money and new funds can be raised by selling local mortgages, such as the fifty loans above, to secondary lenders including the Federal National Mortgage Association (Fannie Mae), the Government National Mortgage Association (Ginnie Mae) and the Federal Home Loan Mortgage Corporation (Freddie Mac).

Fannie Mae was originally a governmental agency that was spun off to the private sector. The publicly held organization maintains a loan portfolio which, at the end of 1985, included four million mortgages worth $98 billion. In addition, Fannie Mae has created $100 billion in mortgage-backed securities that may be purchased and resold directly by investors. Fannie Mae buys conventional, FHA and VA mortgages as well as second trusts and adjustable rate mortgages.

Ginnie Mae, which is part of HUD (Department of Housing and Urban Development), assembles and guarantees pools of FHA and VA mortgages. Investors may participate in such pools by purchasing *pass-through* certificates on which they receive monthly payments for both interest and principal. At the end of 1985, pass-through certificates worth $212.1 billion were outstanding.

Freddie Mac is a part of the Federal Home Loan Bank Board, the regulatory agency that oversees federally chartered savings and loan associations. Freddie Mac purchases conventional, VA and FHA loans that meet its standards and finances such purchases through the sale of mortgage-backed bonds to private investors. Between 1971 and the end of 1985, Freddie Mac had made commitments to purchase mortgages worth nearly $181 billion.

In addition to the three major secondary lenders, there are smaller firms as well. The advantage of having a variety of players in the secondary market is that each is likely to have somewhat different loan standards. This means that local lenders can have more flexible loan policies than might otherwise be possible because a mortgage which does not conform to the requirements of one secondary lender may be acceptable to another.

While the sale and ownership of residential property is usually seen as a local matter, real estate financing is clearly within the stream of interstate commerce. The mortgage on a small house in Houston may well be owned by a pension fund in Boston, a situation that is plausible because secondary lenders have effectively created a national market for mortgage-backed securities and through those securities a market for mortgages themselves.

To have a national mortgage market investors must be able to buy, sell and trade standardized loan products, the value of which can be measured against alternative investments. The secondary lenders have created such products by developing guidelines that define which mortgages they will accept from local lenders.

To have an acceptable, or "conforming," loan which can be resold, primary lenders will tailor their lending practices to meet the standards established by secondary lenders. For instance, one guideline may suggest that no more than 28 percent of a borrower's gross monthly income can be devoted to mortgage payments. Such a guideline might then have a series of exceptions which would allow local lenders some flexibility.

While there are major differences between secondary lenders—for example, one is private (Fannie Mae), one deals only with FHA and VA loans (Ginnie Mae) and only one has a major loan portfolio (Fannie Mae)—the national mortgage market collectively created by these secondary lenders has profoundly influenced the entire process of real estate financing. Here's why:

First, the existence of a national mortgage market means that money can readily move from capital surplus areas to regions and lenders that require additional funding. A national mortgage market prevents the "Balkanization" of the housing industry, a situation where mortgages could be available in one region or state but not others.

Second, the guidelines established by secondary lenders for conventional loans have proven to be in the public interest. Financial qualification standards, for example, protect borrowers, sellers, lenders and mortgage investors alike, since they assure that loans will be made only to financially able purchasers. In contrast, it is worth noting that so-called creative financing arrangements—in which similar guidelines are generally not employed—have resulted in significant numbers of foreclosures and, it can be surmised, substantial numbers of "house poor" homeowners, individuals who can afford to pay for little more than their mortgage.

Third, a national marketplace creates an element of liquidity, the ability to quickly convert mortgages to cash at a reasonable value. Without a national marketplace, a common ground to buy and sell standardized products, an equal level of liquidity would not exist.

Fourth, a national mortgage marketplace allows local lenders to view their mortgage portfolio as a potential profit center, since loans may be regarded as a commodity to be bought, sold or held advantageously. Moreover, primary lenders can also reap profits by servicing the loans of others—collecting monthly payments for a fee, usually three-eighths of a percent of the remaining principal balance. The servicing business can be highly profitable and in some cases local lenders may offer loans at especially attractive rates to build up service portfolios.

HOW TO APPLY FOR FINANCING

As complex as the mortgage system may seem, its inconsistencies are largely superficial. Mortgage lending actually proceeds on a predictable basis which is governed by observable principles. By knowing the rules and understanding how the system works, buyers and sellers can develop both money-making and money-saving strategies.

Determining who qualifies for a new mortgage is a difficult problem for both borrowers and lenders, since, by itself, a large income alone is not enough to guarantee a passable loan application. In the strange world of mortgage financing, it often happens that individuals with lesser incomes are more likely candidates for loans than wealthier applicants.

Getting a mortgage is a relatively simple task, particularly for those who are prepared. When making applications, be certain to have the following information in hand to speed the loan processing.

- Identification numbers for savings and checking accounts and the names of those institutions where they are maintained.
- Account numbers for money market funds and security accounts and the value of such holdings as of a recent date.

- Account numbers and current balances for each credit card you hold.
- Lists of all installment debts, such as auto loans currently outstanding, showing the amount and number of payments remaining on each loan.
- If you currently have a mortgage list the name of the mortgage holder, account number, monthly payment, original loan size and current balance.
- A notation if you are the beneficiary of any trust, estate, IRAs or Keogh plans indicating the number of dollars or other assets involved.
- An explanatory statement if you are the recipient of substantive cash gifts on a regular basis.
- A description of any private income you may have such as money from stocks, bonds, partnerships, etc.
- A letter, as appropriate, describing any law suits you anticipate or to which you will be a party.
- A letter, as appropriate, detailing any outstanding legal judgments.
- A statement of net worth showing the present market value of major holdings such as your current home (less marketing costs and outstanding mortgages), the resale value of your car, stock holdings, the cash surrender value of insurance policies and other items. List major debts such as mortgages, car loans, credit card balances, etc. The difference between the value of what you own and what you owe is your net worth.
- If you are self-employed list business assets and liabilities and be prepared to provide tax returns for at least two years.
- Help your lender and yourself. Write a cover letter describing your current financial position—where you've been and where you're going.

The list above may seem somewhat lengthy but it will greatly assist lenders when they evaluate your application. The fact that you have treated a mortgage application in a businesslike manner will be regarded as a plus by virtually all mortgage loan officers.

In addition to the information you provide directly, lenders will also obtain a credit report at the time you apply for financing. This outside reference source will help lenders evaluate your past history of loan repayments. However, borrowers should review their credit history at local credit bureau offices to assure that the information is accurate and timely. Matters of dispute should be clearly noted.

WHAT LENDERS LOOK FOR

With all the information being supplied for a loan application you may well wonder how lenders are going to evaluate the material they receive. In essence, lenders will consider objective criteria such as income ratios and net worth as well as subjective issues that may not show up on paper, matters such as the potential of a borrower to bring in additional business. Here are the key items that lenders normally consider when reviewing a mortgage application:

Income Ratio. A lender will want to know not only the amount of an applicant's income but that not more than a certain portion is devoted to the payment of *principal, interest, taxes and insurance* (PITI).

Suppose that PITI totals $700 a month for given property. If a lender allows an income ratio of up to 28 percent of an individual's gross monthly income for housing costs, it means that an annual income of $30,000 would be required to support a $700 payment. If PITI were limited to 25 percent of gross monthly income, an annual wage of $33,600 would be needed.

Income-ratio requirements may vary among lenders, so it pays to find the loan source with the best income-ratio standard.

Since income ratios are inverse relationships, the lender with the highest income ratio will have the most liberal loan standard.

Secondary Income. The wages that many people earn do not represent their entire income. Many individuals have secondary incomes from part-time jobs, dividends, trusts, etc. As long as such income is regular and continuing, lenders are likely to regard it as part of a person's income base.

Debt. In addition to housing costs, most of us have other continuing obligations such as auto payments, alimony, credit card debt or child support. Lenders are likely to set a ceiling here, saying perhaps that no more than 36 percent of an individual's gross monthly income may be set aside for ongoing expenses. To fall within the guidelines, it may be necessary for an applicant to reduce credit card bills or finish monthly auto payments ahead of schedule.

Employment. Steady employment is a major concern of all lenders. By "steady," lenders do not mean holding a single job for forty years. Job changes are considered normal and healthy as long as they provide a consistent pattern of upward income growth.

Lenders are also concerned about job obsolescence and self-employment. In the first case, a meteoric rise to the top of the buggy whip industry, unlike a good career in computers, medicine or whatever, is not likely to enthrall many lenders. In the second case, self-employment raises questions about income regularity and size. Most lenders require tax returns for at least two years before they will consider an application from a self-employed individual.

Net Worth. One index that lenders value is a strong *net worth*, that is, the value of assets over liabilities. By definition, borrowers who have accumulated extensive holding of property, stock, cash and other resources while holding down their debts have demonstrated a basic credit-worthiness.

Credit History.   Having a sound income is of little benefit to a lender if a borrower's funds are not used to meet credit obligations. A lender will want a credit report showing that a borrower has repaid monthly debts on a timely and regular basis.

While the categories above describe general areas of interest to lenders, they do not discuss exceptions. The reality is that many borrowers fail to meet one or more criteria, yet obtain financing anyway. This happens because lending is as much art as science.

An individual may not earn enough to meet a lender's income-ratio requirement but that same person may be a physician completing a residency or a couple, with one spouse returning to the work force. On paper such individuals may not qualify for financing but in the real world they are likely to have rising incomes which lenders cannot ignore.

Despite these guidelines, it should be understood that lending criteria change, sometimes overnight.

Suppose you apply for a loan when interest rates are 10 percent and during the few weeks when the lender is processing your application rates rise to 11 percent. While your income may have allowed you to borrow $100,000 when rates were at 10 percent, a higher interest level will cut your ability to borrow. It may be that at the higher rate a lender will lend only $92,150—a big enough difference to kill many deals.

WHAT ARE THE POLICIES OF THE LENDER?

Few people would search for a new car by visiting only one automobile dealer and the same concept holds true for mortgage financing: to get the best deal one must shop around. This is an enormously useful activity because the mere process of speaking to mortgage loan officers, real estate brokers and others is by definition both educational and potentially profitable.

To market their product—the rental of money—lenders disseminate vast amounts of information through advertising, direct public contacts, advisories to the real estate community and general press coverage. While the availability of information should certainly be regarded as beneficial to the general public, the sheer volume of data is often difficult to absorb or fully analyze. Not only is there a lot of information but it is forever in flux—today's interest rates and terms at fifty different community lenders could easily change by tomorrow.

The information problem is compounded by the issue of imprecise definitions. What, for example, is an *adjustable rate mortgage* (ARM)? Basically it is a mortgage in which the lender has the right to change the rate of interest in accordance with a specific index. But the number of ARM formats, each with its own distinctions, is virtually endless.

Not all loans, even those with identical labels, have identical terms and the differences can be financially significant. As an example, Fannie Mae has defined several standard—"conforming"—ARM formats but the huge secondary lender has also purchased at least 125 non-standard mortgage products.

Information on new financing is available from loan officers at S&Ls, commercial banks, mortgage bankers, credit unions and other lenders as well as local real estate brokers, who are usually familiar with current market information.

Keep a notebook with a separate page for each lender contact and record the phone numbers and names of each loan officer with whom you speak for future reference. While some information will remain current, some will change. If you are in the market for financing over several months it will be necessary to check with lenders on a regular basis, say once every week or two, to keep current.

Questions to ask loan officers:

Are you making new mortgage loans? If not, can you recommend any local lenders who are now active?

What is your current rate of interest for conventional financing, that is, a loan for 80 percent of the purchase price on the property?

In general terms, given an annual income of so many dollars, how much mortgage can I afford? Tell the loan officer that you are looking for a general figure only and that you understand that individuals can be qualified only after the lender has had a chance to review written applications. The answer will usually be couched in a formula such as 1.6 times annual income, 2.0 times annual income or yearly mortgage payments equal to 25 or 28 percent of an individual's gross (pre-tax) income.

Is the rate quoted the nominal level of interest or the annual percent rate (APR)? Use the APR, a figure which tends to be higher because of compounding, as a standard when comparing rates.

Does the APR figure include the value of points? Note that in those cases where the expense of points is divided between buyers and sellers, the effective loan cost to purchasers should be calculated only on the basis of points actually paid.

Does the lender offer FHA or VA financing? Graduated payment loans? Growing Equity Mortgages (GEM)? Adjustable rate mortgages? Other formats?

As a matter of policy, does the lender reserve the right to change the rate of interest between the time the loan application is received and the date of settlement? Are the rates locked in or does the lender reserve the right to change the rate of interest between the time a loan is approved and the date of settlement? Some lenders closely follow the market, while others guarantee that the rate quoted at the time of application or approval will be in effect at settlement. There are lenders who also have a limiting policy; that is, the rate of interest will be no higher than the rate established at the time the application was made or approved. If the market rate drops, so does the interest level on your loan but in no case does it go higher.

Is there a prepayment penalty if the loan is repaid early? Is the lender currently enforcing prepayment clauses?

Is the loan assumable? FHA, VA and ARM mortgages are usually assumable, while other loans, particularly those issued after 1978, are generally not assumable at all or only with the consent of the lender.

Does the lender offer *private mortgage insurance* (PMI)? This is a form of insurance in which a third party guarantees partial repayment of the loan to the lender. This guarantee plus the equity value of the property and the borrower's down payment reduce the lender's risk and for this reason a smaller down payment, say 5 to 15 percent, will be acceptable to the lender. For its part in the transaction, the private mortgage insurer is paid a fee by the borrower.

Will the lender *escrow* money—hold money in trust—to assure payments for property taxes, PMI fees or other liabilities? Escrow funds must be paid at settlement and represent an additional cash expense to borrowers. Lenders commonly escrow money to assure the payment of local property taxes, a claim which takes precedence over any mortgage obligations. Questions to ask about escrow accounts: What rate of interest is paid on such funds? When are escrowed monies refunded?

What fees are required by the lender? For example, what is the cost of a mortgage loan application and is all or part of the money returned if the application is not accepted? In addition to an appraisal, which is required for virtually all mortgage loans, will the lender need a survey or photos of the property? If buying a condo or co-op, will the lender require a legal review? If so, at what cost?

Note that these questions concern lender policies and they are important because different lenders approach loan applications independently. The policies of one lender may make you ineligible for financing, while those of another may allow you to borrow far more than you need.

Many borrowers feel somewhat uncomfortable about asking direct questions of a lender but the reality is that real estate financing is a business deal and direct questions must be asked to get the best terms. If asking tough questions is uncomfortable consider the alternative: higher mortgage payments for the next 15, 20 or 30 years.

3
Financing and Ownership

When looking at real estate we often associate a form of property with a type of ownership. Townhouses, for instance, are frequently seen as condominiums when they could be cooperative units or part of a planned unit development (PUD).

For lenders, and consequently for owners, buyers and investors, ownership is a central financial issue. It is entirely possible to have two identical apartments in two identical buildings in a single city, each worth $100,000, yet because one is a condominium and the other a co-op, the ability to readily finance or refinance each property will vary dramatically. Different forms of property ownership mean more or less risk for lenders and thus a greater or lesser willingness to lend.

The ownership of real estate may be compared to a shopping basket of rights and the biggest shopping basket is associated with the outright possession of property, real estate which is held in *fee simple* ownership, or *severalty*. Some of the basic rights associated with fee simple ownership include:

- You can sell your property to anyone at any time.
- You have the right to finance your property in any manner you choose, refinance it at any time or pay off all liens and own the property free and clear.

- You pay property taxes directly. If a neighbor does not pay his or her taxes there is no possibility that your property will be foreclosed.
- You can rent all of your property or you can rent a part of it.
- You can paint the front door cherry red and your neighbors will have no right to complain (though they do have a First Amendment right to snicker).
- You can sell individual rights, such as mineral rights or a right-of-way.
- You can have pets, or children or both.

What you can't do is violate *zoning codes*, public policies established for the benefit of the general community. If you live in a suburban area, for example, you may own the backyard outright but you can't turn it into a shooting gallery.

Fee simple ownership does not necessarily mean that only one person holds title. Fee simple ownership, as well as other ownership interests, may be held by several people or by entities such as partnerships or corporations. Ownership groupings can include:

- Lone individuals.
- Husbands and wives as *tenants by the entirety,* a form of ownership reserved exclusively for married couples. With this form of ownership there is an automatic right of survivorship; that is, with the death of one spouse title to the property automatically passes to the other.
- Unmarried individuals. There are times when unmarried individuals wish to own property with a right of survivorship and they can do so in many states by establishing a *joint tenancy with a right of survivorship.* In the event of death, title to the property can pass automatically to the surviving owner.

- General owners. A *tenancy in common* can be formed in those cases where joint ownership is merely a business deal. Each owner has an undivided interest in the property which can be sold, exchanged or willed. There is no automatic right of survivorship.

- Entities. Property rights can not only be held by people but by entities as well. Real estate can be owned by partnerships, corporations and trusts. Thus it is entirely possible to have 20 people or 20,000 people through a single corporation owning real estate on a fee simple basis.

Additionally, an endless number of ownership combinations —corporations and individuals, partnerships and trusts, trusts and corporations, etc.—can join together to form *syndicates*, which are organized to buy, sell and manage real estate generally, and *joint ventures*, which are established for a specific real estate deal such as the construction of a particular shopping mall or the ownership of an apartment complex.

Holding title is a potentially complex matter that is made even more complicated by the fact that ownership rules vary in each jurisdiction. Because holding title to real estate is complex, and because real estate ownership is related to a variety of other matters such as taxes and estates, consult with an attorney about any title questions you may have.

For example, what happens if husband and wife die simultaneously in a car crash? Who gets the property if there are no children? The relatives of the husband? The relatives of the wife? The state? A correctly drawn will is necessary to properly resolve such potential issues which, as odd as they may seem, do occur. Speak to your lawyer for complete information regarding wills.

While fee simple ownership is the ultimate form of real estate possession because it gives owners the largest number of rights, it is not the only way to own property. You can also possess property through other ownership formats: condominiums, PUDs, cooperatives and timesharing—forms of ownership with unique characteristics and thus separate financing requirements.

CONDOS, PUDS AND CO-OPS

In the 1960s few people had ever heard of condominiums and almost nobody owned one. Today the situation is different. Condos are everywhere and what had once been a wrinkle in the marketplace is now an accepted and popular alternative to fee simple ownership.

What is condominium ownership and what makes condos unique in the eyes of a lender? Condos have these characteristics:

- Condo ownership means that you possess a specific unit within the condominium project plus an interest in the common areas—possibly the land under the condo, the pool, the hallways, etc. You may also have an interest in certain limited common elements such as a balcony or patio. Limited common elements are owned by the condo but their use is reserved exclusively for a particular unit owner.
- There is a separate recorded deed for each condo unit.
- Condo units are bought, sold, taxed, financed and refinanced independently. This is important to lenders because it means that the failure of one condo owner to make mortgage payments will not cause the foreclosure of other units.
- All unit owners are voting members of the condominium association, often called the "council of unit owners," and may be elected to the association's board of directors.
- The condo association as well as all common costs are funded by a monthly condo fee levied against each owner. Failure to pay this fee can result in foreclosure.

While a condo owner does have exclusive title to and possession of a given unit, condos do not offer the same shopping basket of rights as sole ownership. To assure the comfort and safety of all owners, there must be certain rules, understandings, compromises and financial allocations which govern the condominium regime, information contained in these key documents:

Declaration.   Describes the condo and how it works, including such matters as the location of units and the definition of common areas. Shows how voting will be conducted, usually one unit/one vote or votes based on the square footage of each unit—the bigger the unit the bigger the vote. Once in place matters established in the declaration are almost impossible to change. The declaration is usually packed with an engineering report, paid for by the developer, which describes the physical characteristics of the improvements being sold.

By-Laws.   Outline the general management of the condo; for example, how often the board of directors is required to meet. By-laws can usually be changed by majority vote.

Rules and Regulations.   Directives established by the board of directors, items such as how long the pool will be open and how much the monthly condo fee will be increased next year.

Budgets.   A condo budget is developed each year to show projected expenditures based on past projections and experience. Included in the budget is a reserve fund, money set aside for future capital needs such as the repair of a cracked pool or the replacement of a new roof.

Public Offering Statement.   When a condo is first offered for sale to the public the developer must provide a public offering statement, a lengthy document which usually includes the declaration, by-laws, a projected budget, the terms of any maintenance or management agreements and an engineer's report describing the condition of the project and estimating future repair and replacement requirements.

Even though condo units are owned and financed independently, lenders generally view condos as representing more risk than fee simple ownership. You may be a wonderful person and well entitled to a mortgage but what about other condo members? Will a lender be able to get full value for your unit at a foreclosure if the condo association decides to save money and defers needed maintenance? What happens if a large portion of owners rent out their units? Will investors want to allocate association money for elective expenses such as fixing up the tennis courts or redecorating the lobby? If there is a large portion of investor/owners, is the lender then making a loan for residential or investment property? Investments represent more risk to the lender than owner-occupied units.

When you buy a condo (or a PUD or a co-op, for that matter), in the eyes of the lender you will have fewer dollars to support a mortgage.

Suppose you can afford monthly mortgage payments of $800 for a single-family house. At 10 percent interest that $800 can underwrite a 30-year conventional mortgage for $91,160. But if you bought a condo there would be a monthly condo fee which is a lien against the property. If the condo fee was $100, lenders might figure that you could only set aside $700 a month for mortgage interest and principal. In turn, $700 would only underwrite a 30-year, 10 percent mortgage worth $79,765.57.

Condos also present another dilemma for lenders: all those documents. Is there something in the by-laws or rules that will reduce the lender's security? The only way to find out is to have the papers reviewed by the lender's attorney—an additional loan application cost.

New condo buyers can generally get financing through the

lender who financed the project's construction. Since the lender is familiar with the project there is little if any need for a new review of the condo papers.   .

Resale unit buyers can eliminate the documents problem by talking to lenders who previously financed units at the project. Such lenders have already reviewed the basic papers, so there is no need for an additional review. Real estate brokers and condo association officers can name those lenders who have made loans at the project.

All forms of financing may be used to finance condos but borrowers may find that processing is more complex than with fee simple properties. Get a list of lenders who already have made loans to unit owners since they will be familiar with the property but don't hesitate to contact other lenders who may offer better terms and rates.

However, the additional cost of application for a new lender must be viewed in context. If it costs an extra $100 to process a loan but you can save one-fourth of a percent interest, it pays to spend the additional $100 to get financing from a new lender. With a 30-year, $50,000 loan, the difference between a 10 percent rate and a rate at 10.25 percent is $9.26 per month, a difference which means that the $100 extra fee will be saved within a year.

A second type of "corporate" ownership is a *planned unit development,* or PUD, a cross between condo and fee simple ownership with these characteristics:

- With a PUD you may own a townhouse, condo or single-family home.
- You and the other project members belong to an owners' association that takes care of mutual needs such as the mowing of common areas, snow removal, pool management, etc.
- PUD units are taxed and financed separately.
- Since PUDs are owned separately they have separate utility meters.

- The level of financial risk represented by a PUD unit is usually equated with that of a condo.

PUDs have proven popular in many suburban areas because they often combine planned growth with a variety of housing styles. Some PUDs are actually entire "new communities" where the owner's association is nearly the equivalent of a town government. Other PUD projects are quite modest. For instance, one stand of PUD townhouses consists of only 11 units, and the sole common activities of the owners' association are snow removal and lawn cutting. The monthly PUD fee is just $5.

Co-ops, a third form of "corporate" ownership, are generally perceived as a far more restrictive form of possession than fee simple, condo or PUD ownership. If you own an interest in a co-op you do not own real estate directly. Instead, you own stock in a corporation and that corporation owns the entire project. In addition to stock, you also have an exclusive right to the use of a particular unit as well as a right to use all common facilities.

Because it is an organization rather than an individual which actually owns the property, the co-op has great power over the day-to-day operations of the project.

A co-op—much like a selective country club—has the right to assure that new members are compatible with current owners. New buyers must be approved by the co-op board, a process that can be tinged with highly subjective criteria. Thus to sell a co-op one must not only find a purchaser who is ready, willing and able to buy the property but one who is also acceptable to the co-op. Conceivably, if no buyer is acceptable to the co-op, one's interest in a co-op would not be marketable. Co-ops also have these unique features:

- The sources of authority in a co-op include the articles of incorporation of the cooperative association, the association by-laws and the house rules. These documents should be reviewed by prospective buyers to determine how the co-op is organized.

- Co-op projects are financed with an underlying, or blanket, mortgage. For instance, a single project may be built with 200 units and financed with a $10 million mortgage. Assuming all units were the same size, each unit would then have a pro rata mortgage obligation of $50,000. If the underlying mortgage is not paid the entire project can be in default, in which case all units may be foreclosed.

- Co-op units are not taxed individually. The co-op project, since it is a single corporate entity, receives a single property tax bill. If this bill is not paid, the entire co-op is in default and all units can be foreclosed.

- Because co-op ownership is in the form of stock, co-op buyers and sellers may be able to avoid property transfer taxes when they buy or sell units.

- If the co-op conforms with IRS regulations, deductions for mortgage interest and property taxes may be passed through to individual unit owners.

In terms of financing, lenders—except for those in the New York area, where co-ops are widely accepted—have not been rushing to make resale co-op loans. Here's why:

If you are a lender and someone applies for a condo or PUD loan, it is clear that a definable property will be pledged as security for the mortgage. The actions of other unit owners, such as the non-payment of taxes, will rarely, if ever, affect the unit you finance.

With a co-op the situation is different. If 10 percent, or whatever number, of the co-op members do not pay their taxes, then ownership of the entire project is threatened. Since a lender has no right to check the credit of other unit owners, there is no way of knowing the overall financial condition of the shareholders as a group—an important consideration, since the actions of other owners can have a direct bearing on the borrower's interest. Moreover, the borrower is pledging a stock certificate rather than property as a security for the loan, a certificate which is bound to the fortunes of the entire corporation.

Co-ops also present interesting financial questions when resold.

Suppose you buy a unit when a building is first built or converted to co-op status. Your unit costs $55,000 and of that amount $50,000 is represented by the underlying mortgage. Five years later your unit is worth $85,000 and you want to sell your interest. What do you do about financing? Since the underlying mortgage is for all the units at the project, your buyer cannot simply get a new first trust.

One approach is to have the buyer assume your portion of the underlying mortgage and to then pay the difference between the underlying mortgage and the sales price in cash. A second choice is for you to become a lender, to *take back* some financing above the value represented by the underlying mortgage. However, if you take back financing from a buyer, where will you get the cash to buy a new residence for yourself?

While buying for cash and seller take-backs represent traditional approaches to co-op refinancing, new lending practices have made buying and selling co-ops far easier than in the past.

So-called "share" financing, essentially second mortgages for co-ops, is now available. If a unit is worth $100,000 and the underlying mortgage has a $60,000 balance per unit, then a $20,000 share loan would mean that 80 percent financing is available; a $30,000 share loan would give 90 percent coverage. Share loans are now attractive because lenders can sell them to investors in the secondary market, something which was impossible several years ago. For a free booklet entitled "A Consumer Guide to Financing a Cooperative Unit Using Share Loan Financing" send a stamped, self-addressed legal-sized envelope to the Share Loan Service Corp., 1630 Connecticut Ave. NW, Washington, DC 20009 (phone: 202-745-4713).

Another approach to co-op financing has been through the use of so-called recognition agreements. With recognition financing, ownership documents are assigned to lenders who then have certain rights in the event borrowers default or the unit is sold. Check to see if a co-op in which you are interested has recognition agreements.

Lastly, borrowers might ask about the FHA 203(n) program, which can be used to insure co-op loans for individual units. This program is so obscure, and so complex, that as of January, 1987, there is not one known example of an individual unit financed under this program. Still, it's on the books. . . .

Because of their corporate nature, condos, PUDs and co-ops raise a variety of questions that in many cases would not be asked when buying or financing fee simple real estate.

Here are some of the critical issues to review:

What is being sold? In some cases, certain parts of the property, such as pools or underground parking spaces, have been retained by developers and the result is that these facilities are available only at extra cost.

What is the current condo fee? Condo fees are subject to change and normally go up over time. Look at past budgets and see if there have been radical fee increases from year to year. If so, it may be that the budget is not well planned.

What is the current co-op fee? Note that the co-op fee will include a payment for the underlying mortgage. With a condo or PUD unit, monthly fees and mortgage payments are paid separately.

If you are considering a new project, how was the condo, PUD or co-op fee estimated? What other projects has the developer completed? Visit past projects and speak to unit owners there. Has the developer made a good-faith effort to keep all promises? Has all promised work been completed? What would the owners do differently?

Are any major capital repairs expected within the next two years? If so, are adequate reserves being built up to handle repair costs? Be aware that public-offering statements contain a wealth of information regarding potential repairs. For instance, an engineer's report may say that unit air-conditioning systems have a projected life of 15 years. If the building is 12 years old you can expect to make replacements fairly soon.

To cite another example, a public-offering statement may show that a roof has a life expectancy of 20 years and the building is 23 years old. In such cases the developer has honestly and openly declared where a potential cost may be found. In the event of a claim against the developer because of roof leaks, the developer could justly say that the problem had been disclosed to purchasers and that the units were bought by informed buyers. The moral: It pays to read condo, co-op and PUD documents closely.

Have reserves been set aside? Check the budget to assure that reserves are being collected for future repairs and improvements. The alternative to reserves are special assessments, possibly huge, budget-wrecking fees charged to each unit owner when an emergency repair must be funded. Failure to pay a special assessment could result in foreclosure.

Has there been a special assessment in the past two years or are any expected within the next two years? If you are a buyer and a large special assessment looms in the near future you should adjust any purchase offer downward.

How are utility bills paid? In many projects utility costs are included in the fee. The problem with paying utilities as a group is that individual unit owners are not directly responsible for their gas and electric costs and utility expenses at such projects tend to be far higher than at condos or co-ops with separate meters. Also, it invariably happens that while you are willing to conserve fuel, a neighbor runs a sauna or model steel smelter twenty-four hours a day. Resolve the problem before it develops by avoiding projects without separate meters.

How large is the unit? The size of a unit is generally expressed in terms of square feet but the definition of a unit may vary. Some developers measure from the middle of one common wall to the middle of the next common wall, while others measure wall to wall. Some developers include balconies and patios in their calculations.

What is standard? Are the appliances in the model the ones being sold with the unit or are they extra-cost options? What about carpets, tiles and kitchen floor cabinets? Do they come with the unit or are they extra-cost options? Items sold with the unit are items which will not have to be bought or upgraded later.

How much parking is available? Are spaces assigned? Do you pay extra for parking?

If you are buying a co-op unit, is the sale contingent on the approval of the co-op board? If so, on what criteria is approval based?

Are there any new law suits or judgments currently outstanding against the condo association or co-op? If so, what is your potential responsibility as an owner?

Are there now or have there been any law suits by the condo association, co-op, PUD or individual owners against the developer? Suits can arise for many reasons, not all of them justified, but in many cases they concern allegations of incomplete work, which should be of interest to prospective borrowers because they may require special assessments if not settled.

Is there any alteration or improvement to the unit which violates condo declaration, master deed, by-laws, rules, regulations or insurance coverage? Is there any alteration or improvement that violates any aspect of the co-op's rules, regulations or insurance coverage?

Are there any outstanding building or health code violations against either the unit or the project? In particular, ask whether pools have been shut down for health code violations.

Is the unit now leased? If so, what are the terms of the lease? Leases remain in effect even when ownership changes, unless the lease provides otherwise. If the property is in an area governed by rent control, does the tenant have an automatic right of first refusal to purchase the property? Consult with an attorney when buying leased property.

Are many units rented? Are large blocks of units owned by investors? This can be a serious problem, since resident owners may be more willing to make repairs and improvements than non-resident investors. Also, lenders may not be overjoyed by the prospect of making a loan in projects with a large portion of investors, a factor that may reduce resale values.

Is the project on a land lease? With a land lease the ground under the project is leased for a given term, perhaps 75 or 100 years. At the end of that period title to the improvements on the property—the entire project—revert back to the owners of the land lease. With some land leases, the leases can be renewed at a rate to be decided by the land owner or the owner may have an option to lease or not lease. In all cases, the unit owners face the possibility of new costs and the loss of their lease and thus their unit.

A land lease may be attractive initially because acquisition costs are reduced—you are buying a unit but not the ground under it. The problem is that as time goes by there is less and less incentive to maintain the project. After all, why repair the roof ten years before the reversion date? Also, a land lease is much like an apartment rental. At the end of the rental period not only may you be required to leave but you will have no equity in the property.

Much can also be learned about condos, co-op and PUDs by speaking with past and current presidents and treasurers of owner associations. Also, why not speak to prospective neighbors? They would certainly have an interest in meeting a potential owner and it would be a good opportunity to evaluate the project on an informal basis.

TIMESHARING

Few of us vacation year-round so why own or pay for resort property fifty-two weeks a year or hassle with ever-increasing resort rental costs?

That basic question is behind the new and growing "timesharing" concept, an idea which involves some 1,000 projects and one million owners nationwide. Timeshare sales in 1987 are expected to total $1.8 billion—up 180 times since 1972, when units worth only $10 million were sold.

Until recently most property was sold on a fee simple basis, you bought a home or vacation property and owned it outright. Within the limits of zoning and public safety you could rent it or keep a dog the size of a heifer and answer to no one about your taste or style.

As choice locations in both urban and resort areas grew in value, condominiums increasingly replaced fee simple ownership. While people paid more per square foot for condo units than for fee simple property, condos had fewer square feet and thus cost less per unit.

One result was that condos made the ownership of real estate more affordable for buyers who were otherwise unable to purchase. Higher prices per square foot also meant more dollars per project to developers, an economic factor that should not be overlooked.

Timesharing goes a step further. A timeshare project is not only a condo, it is a condo where multiple owners have access to a given living space, albeit at different times. With the timeshare concept, what you get is the use of a furnished condo unit for a specific period of time, say the first week of February in Miami or the second week in December in Aspen. Units are available year-round, however, which means that prices for timeshares in a single project can vary extensively. The National Timesharing Council, an industry association, reports that the average unit price in 1986 was $7,500, although some weeks sold for as much as $25,000.

The timeshare concept raises four central questions: What are you buying? How do you pay for it? What happens if you can't use your unit? and, are timeshare units a good investment?

Timeshare units are sold in two formats. Many projects sell units on a fee simple basis; that is, the full ownership of a condominium interest. These units may represent a recorded, legal interest that, within the condo's rules, can be sold, rented, traded or willed.

Timeshare units are also marketed on a *right-to-use* basis, where purchasers are not actually buying real estate. Instead, they receive one of three types of right-to-use leases, including *club memberships,* which allow for the use of facilities but are not generally easy to re-sell, *vacation leases* that can be sold or rented, and *vacation licenses,* which cannot be sold but typically give access to hotel facilities. Right-to-use programs generally have a set time frame, say 12 to 40 years, after which the unit reverts back to the developer.

If you're interested in purchasing a timeshare unit don't expect to get a mortgage from your nearby, friendly lender. Since

1980, savings and loan associations have been able to make loans for timeshare purchases, but only as unsecured (personal) consumer credit loans.

According to Charles R. Wolfe of Gaithersburg, Maryland, a consultant to timeshare projects nationwide, most timeshare purchases are paid for this way: The developer first finances the entire project through a commercial lender. Individual purchasers, in turn, put down 10 to 20 percent of the cost of their units in cash and the balance is then financed by the developer. The interest rate for such financing, according to Wolfe, is usually at a slightly higher level than currently available second trusts.

In many cases, timeshare units are purchased on an *installment loan* or *land contract* basis; that is, ownership in the property is not conveyed until all or most of the loan has been paid. Conceivably, if a single payment is missed the loan could be in default but most developers, according to industry sources, have a liberal late payment policy.

The "advantage" of the installment loan system, at least to developers, is that lengthy foreclosure procedures are avoided. This is necessary because a single timeshare project may encompass thousands of interval units, each with a relatively small mortgage balance. For instance, a project with 50 units could sell 2,500 intervals (50 units × 50 weeks)—as many transactions in a single building as may occur in small cities!

Foreclosure in such circumstances is costly and impractical, so installment sales are often used to reduce the developer's financial risk. If a buyer won't pay the mortgage, at least the developer can re-sell the unit without too much difficulty.

Foreclosure may also result if annual maintenance fees are not paid. This is a charge for the management and upkeep of both the project and the unit, particularly cleaning between intervals. Maintenance fees typically range from $150 to $250 per unit week.

Since the developer will be managing the project and providing financing, many states now require developers and sales organizations to be registered and bonded. For more information about a particular developer, contact such authorities as consumer affairs offices, real estate commissions and state attorneys general.

Because timeshare units provide rights only during specific time periods they may seem useless if you are not free for a given week. However, units may be exchanged, one of the unique attractions of the timeshare concept. It works this way:

You register your unit with an exchange service at least ninety days before your use interval. They will then suggest possible units for which you can trade, units that may be in different parts of the country or even overseas. In general, like units are traded for like units but it is sometimes possible to trade an inexpensive unit in one location for a prime unit elsewhere. In addition, many units are exchanged within projects.

Whether or not timeshare units are a good investment is a matter of opinion and the view here is that right-to-use units have little profit-making potential and are best viewed as a hedge against future vacation costs. As the National Timesharing Council says, "Consider your timesharing unit a vacation purchase, not a real estate investment. Buy with the intent to save disposable income otherwise budgeted for vacations."

Fee simple units, however, may have considerable value, particularly as the timeshare movement becomes more widely accepted.

While the timeshare industry has grown significantly in the past few years there is little resale experience. Because units are financed largely by developers, resale mortgages—in the conventional sense—are not available. Moreover, because units represent the ownership of specific time intervals, there is an argument to be made that resales will be rendered more difficult by the need to find someone with an urge to vacation during a particular time slot.

As Wolfe, a former president of the National Association of Real Estate License Law Officials and a past chairman of the Maryland Real Estate Commission, notes, "I don't think you'll lose any money on it. They've gone up in price in the last ten years and I think they're still going to go up in price."

The American Resort and Residential Development Association, of which the National Timesharing Council is a part, publishes "Resort and Urban Timesharing: A Consumer's Guide." Copies may be obtained by sending a stamped, self-addressed business envelope with $2.00 to ARRDA, Suite 510, 1220 L Street NW, Washington, D.C. 20005.

Questions to ask:

What form of timesharing ownership is being sold?

If a lease interest is for sale, how long is the lease?

Are there any resale intervals available in addition to intervals available through the developer? If so, at what price and at what terms?

How is the interval unit financed?

If installment financing is used, what happens if a payment is late? Is there a penalty or does the loan automatically terminate?

Would your local lender, or a lender where the project is located, provide a personal loan to cover the cost of the unit?

What is the current maintenance fee?

What is included with the unit (furniture, dishes, etc.)?

Does management have an in-house exchange program? If so, is there a fee to unit owners? How much?

Have there been complaints to the Better Business Bureau, local consumer offices or the state real estate commission concerning either the project or the developer? If so, what are the complaints about and how have they been handled?

How is timeshare financing treated under tax reform? Ask a CPA or tax attorney whether interest on timeshare financing can be deducted if the mortgage is a personal loan not secured by real property.

Knock on a few doors and ask current unit owners what they think about the project and the developer.

4

How to Pick the Right Mortgage

The most difficult problem in real estate financing is not in finding a mortgage. Real estate financing is always available in every market and in every community—if you are willing to pay the price. Simply stated, there is no shortage of people and institutions that will gladly loan all the money you need at premium rates and terms.

The real dilemma is choosing one loan from among the essentially limitless number of financing options that are available at any given time. The issue here is not confined merely to interest rates and monthly payments, rather there is the broader problem of finding the best financial package within the context of your needs, income, assets, financial potential and personal goals.

Many of the questions regarding loan selection are academic in the sense that borrowers often have few realistic choices. It would be great, for instance, to have a zero-interest loan but if you don't have the up-front cash such financing is out of the question.

Since we must each work within the bounds of our financial positions the best way to find a loan is to see which mortgage format best meets our needs. If we lack cash we will want financing that requires little money down. If we lack income we will want financing with small monthly payments. If our financial position is stronger we could opt for a loan with a low interest cost but high monthly payments. Here is how common lending forms can be divided according to borrower requirements.

Benchmark.   Since borrowers are going to compare loan rates and terms we need a standard against which mortgages can be measured. The best benchmark is the "conventional" loan, financing which features a 30-year term, self-amortization, market interest rates, 20 percent down and level monthly payments.

Although conventional financing is the most consistent benchmark, FHA ARM loans are useful when comparing adjustable rate mortgages since they offer uniform terms nationwide. Rates and fees, of course, may differ.

Low Down Payment.   Many buyers cannot afford to make a 20 percent down payment and so there is a need for financing that requires few dollars up front. Such loans include FHA, VA, no-cash deals and loans backed with private mortgage insurance (PMI). In addition, growing equity mortgages (GEM) often require small down payments because they represent relatively less risk to the lender than many other loan formats. *Pledged account mortgages* (PAM) and *reserve account mortgages* (RAM) do not require much cash in the form of a down payment, but someone, possibly the buyer, must deposit funds with a lender.

Much Cash Up Front.   All cash deals mean 100 percent of the purchase price must be paid up front. Zero-interest loans usually require one-third down. The 20 percent down required for conventional financing seems high in today's market. Also, it should be said that buyers can elect to put down additional cash when financing property with any loan format.

Low Initial Monthly Payment. As monthly payments drop it becomes easier to qualify for financing and several loan formats—graduated payment mortgages (GPMs), front-loaded interest-only plans (FLIPs), GEMs and buy-downs—all have low initial payments. Adjustable rate mortgages (ARMs) and *graduated payment adjustable rate mortgages* (GPARMs) usually feature low monthly costs at first but, unlike the other loan formats in this category which have programmed monthly increases, future ARM payments may rise or fall in a random manner.

Random Variable Payment. When loans, such as ARMs and GPARMs, have monthly payments that can rise or fall according to an index they require more budget planning than loans with set monthly costs.

Low Rates and Terms. Blend loans feature below-market interest rates. Assumed loans, except for ARMs and financing requiring lender "consent" for assumption, will have both below-rate interest and a shortened term. Second trusts and wraparound mortgages can have both low rates and terms, depending on the particular deal. (See Table 5.)

Low Interest Cost. Low interest "cost" does not necessarily mean a low interest "rate." Instead these are loans which over their terms require relatively few dollars for interest expenses. *Zero-interest plan* loans (ZIP) have—not surprisingly—no direct interest expense. GEM mortgages are programmed to have short terms and low interest costs. Second trust and wraparound loans, depending on individual rates and terms, can often cut interest costs significantly.

Short Loan Terms. If 30-year financing is a "standard" loan term, then shorter mortgages would include 15-, 20- and 25-year loans, GEM mortgages (15 years or less), and virtually all second trusts. Wraparound loans are less than 30 years, depending on the remaining term of any existing financing.

TABLE 5
Finding the Right Loan

Principal Benefit	Prime Loan Choices	Second Loan Choices
Benchmark	Conventional financing	FHA ARM (for ARMs only)
Low down payment	FHA, VA, private mortgage insurance (PMI), no cash	Growing equity (GEM), pledged account (PAM) and reserve account mortgages (RAM)
Much cash up front	Zero-interest (ZIP), all cash	Conventional loans
Low initial monthly payment	Graduated payment (GPM) and front-loaded, interest-only plan (FLIP), buy-downs and growing equity mortgages (GEM)	Adjustable rate (ARM)
Random variable payment	ARM, graduated payment ARM (GPARM)	
Low rates and terms	Assumable loans and blend loans	Second trusts and wraparound loans
Low interest cost	Zero-interest (ZIP), growing equity mortgages (GEM), blend loans, bond-backed mortgages and assumptions	Second trusts and wraparound loans
Short loan terms	15-year loans, growing equity mortgages (GEM), second trusts	Wraparound
Assumable loans	ARMs, FHA, VA mortgages	Older conventional loans
Monthly payment to borrower	Reverse	Home equity loans
Balloon payments	Second trusts, ARMs, roll-over loans	Some graduated payment loans

TABLE 5 *(Continued)*

Principal Benefit	Prime Loan Choices	Second Loan Choices
Loans to avoid	Land contracts, roll-over loans, 40-year mortgages	Some ARMs

Assumable Loans. ARMs, FHA and VA financing can be assumed in most cases. Older conventional loans are frequently assumable at original rates and terms.

Monthly Payment to Borrower. A home can be seen as a storehouse of value and one way to get cash from that storehouse is with a reverse mortgage. Another approach may be to have regular withdrawals with a home equity loan.

Balloon Payments. Balloon payments are a common feature of second trusts, ARMs and roll-over loans. Some GPMs also have balloon notes.

Loans to Avoid. There are three loan formats that are difficult to justify from the borrower's perspective: land contracts, roll-over loans and 40-year mortgages. The first two mortgage formats are hazardous, while the latter is needlessly expensive. In addition, certain ARMs—those without interest caps, those with negative amortization or those that feature monthly payment changes—should be avoided.

HOW TO COMPARE LOAN FORMATS

Because needs differ there is not a single, magical mortgage formula that will somehow resolve the loan problems of all borrowers. Different strategies work well for different people and it is therefore necessary to have a sound selection process before one can have a sound selection.

Variety has always been part of the real estate financial system because conventional loans simply don't work for all purchasers—too much down is required, initial monthly payments are too high, financing is too long and total interest costs are too great. To get around these problems, and in many instances to simply make a better deal, buyers routinely use alternative mortgage formats.

Just because a sale is not based on conventional financing does not mean that a deal is "abnormal" in some way. Alternative mortgages are perfectly legitimate forms of financing that can cut interest rates, reduce monthly payments, lower down payments, and drop overall mortgage costs. Alternative mortgages can also feature large down payments, negative amortization, changing monthly payments and interest rates that rise and fall randomly during the term of the loan.

The fact that alternative loans are different from conventional financing does not mean that such distinctions are necessarily negative. All loans are merely financial tools which are useful in some cases and inappropriate in others. Deciding whether or not to use a particular loan format depends on the needs of the buyer, the facts and circumstances in each sale.

Loans should be compared individually—the second trust of one lender versus the second trust of another—as well as format against format—zero-interest mortgages versus graduated payment loans. Here are thirteen central points of comparison.

1.   Does the loan require fewer dollars down or more dollars down than other mortgage formats? Small down payments mean maximum leverage—the use of OPM to finance as much of the property as possible. Unless mortgage rates are "high" relative to other investments, it pays to seek leverage when buying. Once a loan is in place you can then look at restructuring and refinancing opportunities. FHA and VA loans are examples of financing that require few dollars up front.

2. Are monthly payments subject to change during the term of the loan? If changes occur, are they pre-planned or random? Preplanned changes, such as monthly payment increases found in graduated payment loans, allow borrowers to budget their incomes. Random changes, such as those associated with ARM financing, are more difficult to project. How often are changes permitted?

3. Are the initial monthly payments larger or smaller than other mortgage formats? The lower the initial monthly payments the easier to qualify for a loan of any given size. Graduated payment loans are attractive because they often feature significantly lower initial payments than would be required for conventional financing. In many cases loans offer below-market interest rates initially as an inducement to borrowers. ARMs, for example, usually have initial rates below conventional financing levels but such rates are not guaranteed for the life of the loan.

4. Are monthly payment changes limited? Is there a cap on the amount your monthly payments can rise, say, not more than 10 percent annually?

5. Is there a cap on the maximum amount of interest that can be charged? Is there a minimum? If there is no interest cap, it means rates can rise with the market. Would the lender agree to an interest cap in exchange for an up-front fee? Note that if increased interest costs are not passed through to borrowers through higher monthly payments or occasional cash injections, negative amortization may be permitted.

6. Is negative amortization allowed? If negative amortization occurs early in the term of the mortgage is it automatically corrected later with higher scheduled payments, that is, without additional infusions of cash?

7. If negative amortization occurs, can the loan term be extended? With adjustable rate loans there is often a provision

---

Basic Mortgage Checklist

What is the down payment required compared to other loan formats? Larger_____Smaller_____

Are monthly payments subject to change during the term of the loan? Yes_____No_____

How often are payment changes permitted? Monthly_____ Semi-annually_____Yearly_____Biannually_____Other_____

If changes occur, are they pre-planned or random? Preplanned _____Random_____

Are initial monthly payments larger or smaller than other mortgage formats? Larger_____Smaller_____

Is there a cap on monthly payment changes? Yes_____No _____

Is there a cap on the maximum amount of interest that can be charged? Yes_____No_____Is there a minimum? Yes_____No _____

Is negative amortization allowed? Yes_____No_____

If negative amortization occurs, can the loan term be extended? Yes_____No_____

If interest payments are related to an index, which index is used? Name of index:_____

Can the loan be assumed at its original rate and terms by a qualified purchaser? Yes_____No_____

Can the loan be prepaid in whole or in part at any time without penalty? Yes_____No_____If not, what are the conditions of prepayment?_____

---

to extend the loan term from 30 to as many as 40 years. This provision benefits the borrower in the sense that it is not necessary to refinance the property if any loan balance remains after 30 years. It also means larger interest payments and slower amortization over the life of the mortgage.

8. If interest payments are related to an index, which index is used? The longer the span of events being measured the better the index from the borrower's perspective.

9.   Can the loan be assumed at its original rate and terms by a qualified purchaser? This may be of value in the future when today's borrower becomes tomorrow's seller.

10.   Can the loan be prepaid in whole or in part without penalty? This is a key question because if a loan can easily be prepaid in part and without penalty it means the borrower can unilaterally restructure the loan at any time.

11.   What are the tax consequences of the loan? Speak to a CPA or tax attorney for advice.

12.   When all factors are considered, which loan format is best within the context of your needs today?

13.   Which loan format will best meet your needs five years from today? Ten years? Will your income decline as a result of retirement or a job change? If so, be wary of loans with rising monthly costs, such as graduated payment mortgages, or loans which may have random monthly increases, such as adjustable rate loans.

COMPUTERS AND THE SEARCHING PROCESS

When searching for real estate financing it pays to consult as many local lenders as possible—savings and loan associations, mortgage bankers, credit unions, banks, insurance companies and even relatives and employers. Use the questions found in the section on lender policies (Chapter 2) as a guide and keep careful notes showing how each potential lender responds to your call.

In addition to local lenders, we are now at the beginning of a new phenomenon: the computerized mortgage information service.

Mortgage information can be easily assembled, digested and

displayed with a computer. In fact, the fast turnover of rates and terms makes computers ideal for keeping up with industry changes.

If you've ever shopped for a mortgage you know that finding a loan is not a calm or casual adventure. But now computers have arrived and with them the possibility of one-stop mortgage shopping and the chance to find bargain financing from among hundreds of loans.

Ideally, a computer system should allow you to fill in some blanks, press a few buttons and have the best mortgage in town pop up like morning toast. While computers have yet to become that efficient, they are radically changing the way we shop for mortgages and buried within those changes are both new opportunities and potential pitfalls for borrowers.

Borrowers have traditionally sought mortgage money from such sources as savings and loan associations, mortgage bankers (individuals and companies that bring lenders and borrowers together and then "service" loans), commercial banks, insurance companies and, more recently, credit unions. Multiply the number of loan sources in a given community by the variety of available mortgage products and one can see that hundreds of loans are available at any time.

Although in theory there are many choices, few borrowers have the time or stamina to contact every local loan source. Choices are often made on the basis of recommendations from real estate brokers, proximity to a lender, long-standing financial relationships or in response to advertisements.

Once a lender has been found, it is necessary first to choose the right mortgage instrument and then apply for financing. The lender will have the property appraised, get a credit check, verify the application and complete all necessary paperwork, a process known generally as "origination." Application charges to borrowers usually total $100 to $150 while the total cost of originating a mortgage is generally calculated as 1 percent or more of the loan's value, a fee that is incorporated into the up-front charges paid at settlement (closing).

How do computers change the system? On a basic level, computers can be seen as an electronic shopping mall where lenders hawk their latest products. Want an adjustable rate mortgage (ARM)? Feed in the amount needed and the computer could show interest rates, monthly payments, adjustments and caps for every ARM in the system. How will an ARM compare with VA financing or a conventional loan? The computer can make point-by-point comparisons within a few minutes.

As an electronic shopping center, a computer is really nothing more than a glorified database which cuts the number of phone calls borrowers need to make. Since information about various loan options is in one place and in a single format, it is possible to compare hundreds of mortgages. Looking at so many loans provides some sense of market trends and helps distinguish the good deals from the dogs.

Just as important, information in the electronic shopping center is current. A lender offering a new loan or changing a rate can update the computer at any time.

By itself, a vast amount of data may be incomprehensible. How do you sort through so many loan choices? Should you just pick the mortgage with the lowest initial rate or are there other factors to consider?

Mortgage choices today can be fine-tuned to mesh with changing incomes, retirement programs, tax brackets and alternative investments; in other words, mortgages can be part of a complete financial planning effort. Trained advisors can explain how different mortgages work, the meaning of industry terms such as "negative amortization" and "wraparound" financing, as well as the relative costs of various loan alternatives.

Joining a database with the services of a loan advisor is a big help for most borrowers but knowing about loans does not assure financing. Our terminal needs a keyboard so we can enter information about ourselves and the property we want to buy or refinance and our information must go to someone who can originate financing, either a lender or a mortgage banker.

Combine the elements of a database and counseling service, add on an electronic application system and tie the whole package together with an authority to originate loans and presto: one-stop mortgage shopping, the kind of service home buyers have been dreaming of for years.

Computerized mortgage services are no longer a dream. Thousands of terminals are now in place at real estate offices, lenders and mortgage bankers throughout the country.

The National Association of Realtors, for example, offers a system to member boards called "Lend" which provides mortgage information in conjunction with a local multiple listing service (MLS). With Lend, an MLS member can quickly sort through a variety of mortgage options to find the best available financing for a purchaser. A broker, for example, can see which lenders are offering 30-year mortgages, who has the lowest rates and the fewest points.

One major attraction of the Lend system is 24-hour access to lender information. Many real estate deals are pulled together at night and on weekends, and so it's advantageous to have loan information available during off hours.

Another advantage is the ability to make comparisons. Not only do brokers, buyers and sellers get to compare loans, but lenders can also see what the competition is offering.

While Lend is an information program, the association has also developed a loan origination system called "Rennie Mae," shorthand for "Realtors National Mortgage Access." Now exclusively marketed by American Financial Network (OTC, or over the counter) of Dallas, Texas, Rennie Mae has been described as a "public utility" that connects brokers and lenders, provides current mortgage rates and allows lenders to take applications directly from broker offices.

With Rennie Mae, a purchaser/borrower searches the system to find the best combination of rates and terms for a particular loan format and then uses the same terminal to apply for a loan. The application, in turn, is then electronically transmitted to the lender selected by the borrower.

The Rennie Mae system offers three major attractions: speed, choice and cost. First, even as the details of a home purchase are being worked out, a buyer can see if appropriate financing is available. Second, because many lenders list loan products on the system, consumers can select from a wide variety of options. Third, under Rennie Mae there is no charge to the consumer for either searching or applying for a loan. Instead, the broker pays $50 for each application transmitted over the system and $75 when the mortgage closes.

To cover the costs associated with the system, the broker is paid half the origination fee, money which otherwise would go to the mortgage officer who processed the application. In effect, there is no additional cost to the consumer through the Rennie Mae system.

A third approach to computerization is offered by Shelternet, a subsidiary of First Boston, Inc., an investment banking organization. Shelternet connects 100 loan originators to mortgage bankers, savings and loan associations and banks, with more than 1,000 offices in 30 states.

To understand what Shelternet does you have to envision a mortgage pipeline. At one end are borrowers who need mortgage money. At the other end are investors such as pension funds and insurance companies who have money and want to invest it in home loans. In effect, Shelternet is a "wholesale mortgage banker," that can move huge amounts of money throughout the country with electronic speed.

The way the system works is that each day at the private First Boston trading floor on Park Avenue in New York, mortgage-backed securities worth from $5 billion to $7 billion are bought and sold. In some cases one investor sells to another. In other cases First Boston, through Shelternet, gathers individual mortgages together from local lenders to create a package of loans with a certain value (say $5 million) and a certain yield (say 10 percent interest). The package can then be sold to investors on the trading floor.

On the local level, a mortgage banker, savings and loan association or banker—in Florida, California or wherever—has a steady stream of money through Shelternet which can be offered to local home buyers. The local lender can quote rates and specify mortgage formats because he knows what's currently available on the system.

A related Shelternet product is the company's "Point of Sale" program. This is essentially a computer-based tool that allows a loan originator or even a consumer to analyze a variety of loan choices. The program not only has value in picking the right mortgage, but is also structured so it can be used as a teaching tool for loan originators.

To get the name of a local Shelternet originator call 800-822-5587. New York residents should call 914-332-4500.

The idea of a nationwide mortgage market means we are likely to see homogenized interest rates. Capital will flow from surplus areas to needy ones with electronic speed. Borrowers, in turn, will no longer be forced to rely on local loan sources. If your nearby friendly lender limits mortgages to $200,000, someone in the system will surely be willing to make a larger commitment.

On a localized basis, the process of homogenization will become more pronounced as a result of computerization. By having hundreds of loan choices in one place, lenders will quickly see how their products match up with the competition. If others are offering lower rates, high-priced lenders will need to drop rates to remain competitive. Alternatively, lenders with rates that are "too" good will raise interest levels to capture additional profits. In the end, computerization will have the effect of moderating loan variations.

In addition to the programs mentioned above, computerization is also being seen more often within individual companies. For instance, a brokerage firm may computerize current mortgage information as a sales aid for agents. Another approach would feature a mortgage lender who automatically generated updated loan materials for area brokers. A third concept uses computers to automatically prepare loan applications at realty offices.

The growing use of computer systems has already begun to influence the mortgage market and their growing acceptance raises a question: How can you get the best deal with an electronic loan service?

From the borrowers' viewpoint, it is advantageous to have several hundred loan choices displayed in one place. But as many loans as a given system may contain, no system contains all available mortgages and it is entirely possible that the best loan is not in the system. For this reason borrowers may still benefit by calling various local lenders if only to assure they are getting the best deal.

Computer systems also present the problem of rigidity. Loans may be processed within guidelines: if you need so much income to afford a certain mortgage, you may not get financing if your income is marginally low or your debts are marginally high. In contrast, a lender you know may be more flexible, particularly if you are a long-time client with a respectable credit history.

Although computers produce copious volumes of information, one has to ask about utility: How useful is the data you receive? For example, when comparing ARMs it is not enough to look at interest rates. There is a considerable potential difference between two ARMs with equal interest rates when one permits negative amortization while the other does not. Clearly the latter loan is a better deal.

Lastly, there is the issue of locking-in rates. Mortgage rates change constantly and if you apply for a loan July 1, the interest rate could be 2 percent higher by the time you settle in August. Some lenders guarantee rates as of the date of application, others as of the date of approval and some only as of the moment of settlement. Borrowers would do well to see if rates quoted as of the date of application can be locked in; otherwise interest quotes have little, if any, value.

5
No-Cash
and All-Cash Deals

Buying real estate would certainly be much easier if no cash was required up front. Not only are such deals possible but they are commonplace—millions of veterans have bought property with 100 percent financing, and similar deals by non-vets are made daily.

Properties can be bought without cash in a number of ways and a short list of alternative approaches might include purchases in which:

- The seller or a third party takes back a self-amortizing mortgage for the entire value of the property plus all closing costs.
- The purchaser assumes a first trust and the seller or a third party finances the balance with a second trust. At the end of the term a balloon payment is due.
- The purchaser gets a new mortgage and the owner or a third party takes back a second trust with a balloon payment.
- The buyer assumes or gets a new first mortgage, a second trust from the seller and a third trust from still another source.
- The purchaser assumes a first trust or gets a new loan and trades a 1947 Rolls-Royce in mint condition for the balance due.
- The purchaser is a veteran and gets 100 percent financing with a VA-backed mortgage.

- A rich aunt pays for the property.
- The buyer trades a house in Tampa for the seller's home.
- A property is bought and before settlement the purchaser resells the house to another buyer at a profit.
- A property is bought and, coincidentally with settlement, a portion is sold to pay all costs above financing.

In every case the term *no money down* can be substituted for the words *deferred liability*. The buyer owes money in the future or paid money in the past (for the purchase of the Rolls, the house in Tampa, public service to earn VA benefits or the psychological cost of his aunt's good will) or devalued the property by selling off a portion.

Deals with no money down make great sense in those cases where enormous balloon payments can be avoided and purchasers can afford monthly carrying costs—the precise arrangement used by the VA. The problem is that some borrowers equate the idea of "no cash" with "no responsibility." They forget that not everyone can afford high monthly mortgage payments or raise enough cash to pay off balloon notes. (See Table 6.)

TABLE 6
No-Cash Deals

Money down	None.
Loan size	100 percent financing.
Monthly cost	Largest possible for property.
Balloon note	None with VA but balloon payments are common with conventional no-cash deals.
Loan term	30 years with VA but often far shorter with investment deals, say 3 to 5 years.
Pros	No-cash deals allow borrowers to acquire property with no initial capital. Large loans mean large tax deductions for interest payments, no points and reduced settlement costs.
Cons	No-cash deals mean high monthly mortgage bills and the possibility of huge balloon payments.

The best time to make a no-cash deal is when interest rates are low, because there are probably better places to invest money. When mortgage rates are high purchasers are often best advised to invest in their own mortgage. If rates later fall the property can be refinanced.

No-cash financing is often used by investors and in such cases monthly mortgage payments often exceed rentals, a situation known as "negative cash flow." This polite term means that each and every month the investor must make cash payments to keep the property. Negative cash flow is not a serious problem for many investors because they can afford to pay the negative cash flow from their general income and the tax and appreciation benefits of ownership offset monthly cash losses.

For example, suppose Harding buys a four-unit apartment which produces rentals worth $2,000 a month. Harding's costs for first and second mortgages, property taxes, repairs, maintenance, etc., total $2,250 per month. Harding thus has cash losses of $250 per month, or $3,000 a year, a sum Harding can readily pay from other income.

Where Harding benefits in this deal is that his income tax deductions for mortgage interest, property taxes, electricity, depreciation and other items total $15,000 annually. In his tax bracket, these deductions reduce Harding's tax bill by $4,200. In addition, each month the mortgage is being paid down and so the equity in the property rises even if market values remain stagnant.

Moreover, Harding takes steps to reduce his losses. He paints the hallway and plants new shrubs to make his property more attractive. Rather than raising rents directly at first, he invests $4,000 and installs individual utility meters so that electric bills are paid directly by the tenants. With the new meters in place Harding air-conditions each unit. A year after he bought the property, Harding raises monthly rentals by $35 per unit but the tenants stay. Why? Because the property is a better place to live.

The problem is that not every Harding—or Smith or Brown —can afford $250 in cash each month. Not everyone can invest an additional several thousand dollars in a rental property or is in an income bracket that will produce the same tax savings as Harding's.

To be successful, investment deals with no money down must be affordable in the event property income does not rise, vacancies occur or major repairs are required. Buyers must also have a clear, reasonable plan to both carry and repay all debt, particularly short-term balloon payments, which are a frequent feature of investment no-cash sales. Without such planning no-cash deals are a sure prescription for financial disaster.

Questions to ask:

What is the interest rate for conventional financing?

What is the interest rate for the first trust? Second trust? Third trust? Etc.

Does the no-cash deal include financing to cover the cost of closing?

Are balloon payments part of the deal? If so, exactly how will they be repaid?

Are you making a no-cash investment with the expectation of raising rents? If so, why is it that you will be able to raise rentals, while the present owner has not? How will a rent increase affect vacancy rates?

Do you have sufficient income to cover negative cash flow?

Do you have enough capital to make repairs or cover vacancy losses, if any?

Is it possible to subdivide the property? Since the property is security for at least one loan, will the lender(s) allow you to subdivide?

How will a no-cash deal affect your tax position? Speak with a tax advisor for further advice.

Is your financing assumable?

Can your financing be repaid in whole or in part without penalty at any time?

BUYING FOR CASH

The least cumbersome way to buy real estate is to pay cash. If you've got the money, paying cash will save dollars by eliminating loan discount fees *(points)*, mortgage application charges and origination fees (generally 1 percent of a mortgage). Settlement costs will also be reduced, since there is no need to set aside escrow funds for the payment of taxes, FHA, VA or private mortgage insurance or other expenses.

But if buying a home with cash has attractive aspects, there are also problems. The most basic difficulty is that few people have the dollars needed to buy a home without financing. But even when the dollars are available, buying for cash is not always a sound financial choice. A home without a mortgage is a home without a major tax deduction. A home without a fixed-rate mortgage is a home which cannot fully profit from inflation.

Given the balance of benefits and problems, when should real estate be bought for cash? The answer depends on alternative investments and your personal situation.

First, have you devised a personal financial strategy? Have you set aside funds for retirement plans, placed cash in a savings account or other liquid asset and bought sufficient health and life insurance? Are you making high-interest credit payments for credit cards, cars or furniture? If so, paying cash for property is not likely to be your best financial choice.

Second, are you about to retire? Selling a large home may generate enough dollars to buy a retirement property for cash. Buying for cash, in turn, will cut monthly living costs. If you pay cash will you have enough income from other sources to live in the style to which you are accustomed?

Third, what is your tax situation? When you sell a personal residence and buy another personal residence of equal or greater value, any tax on the profit made from the sale of the first property is deferred. Note that buying a house of "equal or greater value" does not mean you must pay cash for the second property—you could get a mortgage and invest cash from the sale of the first home. Also, after age 55 you are entitled to a one-time profit exclusion from the sale of a personal residence of up to $125,000 at this writing. (This means if you only claim $100,000 you forfeit the right to claim the balance.) Check with a CPA or tax attorney for an update on current tax regulations and for advice concerning your specific situation.

Fourth, what about liquidity? Traditionally it has been difficult to get cash out of a house without selling or refinancing. This tradition has changed with the ready availability of home-equity loans. Still, real estate is not a liquid investment in the sense of a savings account or mutual fund where access to your assets is ultimately guaranteed. After all, you could apply for a home-equity loan and be rejected.

Fifth, how does a mortgage look as an investment? If mortgages are available for 10 percent, paying cash means you are getting an effective, pre-tax return of more than 10 percent; the exact return will depend on your tax bracket. How does investing in a mortgage compare with stocks, bonds, mutual funds, and retirement plans in terms of both return and risk?

One attraction of paying cash for real estate is that you can finance property at a later date, perhaps when rates have come down or you have a specific need for capital. However, paying cash requires some element of crystal ball gazing. What if you pay cash today and interest rates rise? Will you qualify for all the new financing you need or want at a later date?

Paying cash for real estate is a strategy which assures control

TABLE 7
The All-Cash Deal

Loan size	None.
Interest rate	None.
Monthly payment	None.
Down payment	100 percent of the purchase price.
Pros	No monthly payments, lender fees or interest charges.
Cons	No tax deduction for interest payments and no leverage.
Central issue	Is your money best invested in a house to avoid mortgage payments or in other "investments" such as lower credit card debt? Is your money put to better use with stocks, bonds, retirement plans or other investments?

over real estate dollars. Some people who would never pay cash for investment property have homes that are free and clear of any debt. Why? Because home ownership—as distinct from investment real estate—implies certain psychological values. It may be that buying for cash is not a sound financial choice in many cases but it is an alternative which some people find more comforting than high rates of return, a feeling that cannot be measured in dollars and cents. (See Table 7.)

Questions to ask:

What is the prevailing interest rate for conventional mortgages in your community?

What is the current return you can expect from the conservative investment of your funds?

How large is the one-time profit exemption from the sale of a personal residence? (Speak to a CPA or tax attorney for current information.)

Do you anticipate reduced income as a result of retirement in the next decade?

Do you expect to move to smaller housing within the next ten years?

Do you believe that home mortgage rates will generally rise or fall from current levels over the next several years?

As a matter of personal preference would you want to own a home which is free and clear of all mortgage debt? While this may not be the best choice in terms of dollars and percentages, it is a choice that comforts many people.

6

The Conventional Loan

Until the mid-1930s, the most common form of real estate financing was the *straight,* or *term,* mortgage with a five-year life and semi-annual interest payments. Straight loans were attractive years ago because interest rates were low and plenty of cash was available when refinancing was necessary.

But the Depression and harsh weather in the Midwest—the Dust Bowl—brought out the worst features of the term loan system. People who were unemployed could not make semi-annual interest payments, farms where crops no longer grew were not acceptable collateral for new financing and many lenders failed, shutting off valued sources of community cash and credit. The inevitable result was a rash of foreclosures and calls for a new system of home financing.

That new system arose in the 1930s when the Federal Housing Administration popularized the long-term, self-amortizing home loan, a concept we today know as *conventional* financing.

A conventional loan is the benchmark against which all other mortgage concepts should be measured and such loans are distinguished by five central features:

Set Monthly Payments. Each month the borrower makes payments which are substantially equal during the life of the mortgage.

Set Interest Rates.   The interest rate is established at the time the loan is first created and remains unchanged during the life of the loan.

Fixed Loan Term.   Most conventional loans are designed to be repaid over an extended period of time, usually 30 years.

Self-Amortization.   Conventional financing is arranged so the entire loan, including all interest and principal, will be completely repaid during the term of the mortgage. As a result there are no *balloon* payments—huge sums of money due at the end of the loan term—associated with conventional loans, so refinancing at the end of the mortgage is not necessary.

Coverage.   Conventional loans are equal to 80 percent of the purchase price. A buyer must put down cash or additional financing for the balance.

With these factors in mind, a conventional sale might look like this: Buyer Stevenson purchases a new home for $106,250. Of this amount, $21,250 is represented by the cash down payment paid by Stevenson at settlement, and the remaining $85,-000 is in the form of a 30-year mortgage from a local lender. At the end of 30 years, Stevenson owns the property free and clear of any mortgage debt.

Conventional loans are appealing to lenders because such financing assures limited risk. The buyer's down payment creates a deep cushion which protects the lender in the event of foreclosure. With the $106,250 home above, for instance, the buyer has invested $21,250, leaving the lender with an $85,000 liability secured by the value of the property. If the house must be foreclosed, the lender's interest will be completely protected if the property sells for $85,000 plus the cost of the foreclosure action. Since $85,000 is considerably below the property's market value, the lender has only the most limited financial exposure. (See Table 8.)

TABLE 8
The Conventional Loan

Sale price	$106,250
Cash down	$21,250
Loan size	$85,000
Loan term	30 years
Monthly payments	Level, $745.94
Balloon payments	None
Interest rate	Fixed, 10 percent
Total payments	$268,537
Total interest	$183,537

Conventional loans are a useful index against which individual lenders can be compared. Unlike other forms of financing, conventional mortgages are commonly offered by all community lenders and since the terms and conditions of conventional loans are standardized, it is an easy matter to determine which lender has the best available rates and terms.

However, conventional loans raise a serious issue today: Is a 30-year loan the best mortgage format? For some portion of all borrowers, conventional loans remain the best deal in terms of interest rates, monthly costs and down payments. But for many borrowers, conventional financing is far from the best arrangement. Other mortgage formats, as we shall see, feature less money down, smaller initial monthly payments, and interest savings that can top $100,000 for loans of comparable size. While conventional financing may have been a great idea fifty years ago, it is the mortgage of choice for fewer and fewer people today.

Questions to Ask:

What is the current rate of interest for conventional financing? (This question should be asked when considering any loan format, since it provides a baseline from which to measure alternative mortgages.)

What portion of the home can be financed with a conventional loan?

Can I get conventional financing if a second trust is used to finance a portion of the purchase?

In addition to the current interest rate, are "points" or loan discount fees being charged? If so, how many?

In general terms, how much income will I need to qualify for a conventional loan of X dollars?

7
Second Trusts

Real estate sales which are not made entirely for cash involve the use of at least one mortgage or deed of trust. However, a large number of transactions involve more than one loan and in those cases where a single property is used to secure multiple loans an important question arises: Who gets paid first?

An order of repayment among private lenders is established in the loan papers created between property owners and lenders. Claims will be fully settled in order; that is, the claims of the first mortgage or first trust holder will be completely repaid before any claims by a second loan holder are addressed. In turn, the claims of the second mortgage or second trust holder must be fully satisfied before the debt of a third lender can be addressed, and so on.

The catch for junior trust holders is that there may not be any cash remaining once prior claims have been satisfied. Second trusts and mortgages thus represent more risk than first loans and therefore command higher interest rates. Here is an example illustrating why secondary financing has inherently more risk than primary loans.

A home is bought for $106,250 and Cleveland, the buyer, knows he can get a conventional, 30-year loan for $85,000 at 10 percent interest. The rest of the money will come from Cleveland, who has $8,000 in cash, and a $13,250 loan from Uncle

Bob. It's agreed that the $13,250 will be in the form of a second trust secured by the property, that the term of the loan will be five years and that there will be no balloon payment.

Cleveland, with Uncle Bob's money in hand, gets an $85,000 first mortgage from a lender. After two years, Cleveland defaults and the property is sold at foreclosure for $85,000. The first mortgage holder takes the $85,000, leaving nothing for Uncle Bob. (See Table 9.)

TABLE 9
Second Trusts: Mr. Cleveland's Loans

Purchase price	$106,250
Cash down	$8,000
First trust	$85,000 at 10 percent interest
First trust term	30 years
First trust monthly payment	$745.94
Second trust	$13,250 at 12 percent interest
Second trust term	5 years
Second trust monthly payment	$294.74
Total monthly payment	$1,040.68
Balloon payment	None in this example

Note that the first trust holder had no economic incentive to sell the property for more than $85,000 plus foreclosure costs. Thus, while a lender with a second trust can seek to foreclose on a property in the event his loan is in default, consideration must be given to the idea that by triggering a foreclosure a second mortgage holder may do little more than satisfy the claims of a prior lender. In effect, the threat of foreclosure by a second trust holder, and the protection offered by foreclosure, is greatly reduced by the prior claims of another lender.

Also, it should be said that Cleveland had steep monthly payments totaling $1,040.68 in this example. His monthly payments could have been lower if he had a second trust with a balloon payment. In that case, his cost for a second trust could have been, say, $100 per month rather than the $294.78 he agreed to pay his uncle. Perhaps with lower monthly costs he could have avoided foreclosure.

If second trusts represent enhanced risk why are so many sellers, lenders and investors willing to hold such paper? One answer might be that the element of risk is offset by a higher rate of return. Another response is that some sales are possible only with second trusts. For example, when interest rates are high borrowers may not qualify for financing from local lenders and if sellers don't take back second trusts their properties won't be sold.

It is possible that a junior loan can resemble a first trust in all particulars but this is not likely. In a typical situation, several distinctions are common.

Loan Term.   While conventional loans may have a term of 30 years, second trusts are generally for a shorter term, say 2 to 10 years with most loans being 5 years or less. If you are a borrower you will want the longest possible term because long terms mean lower monthly payments for self-amortizing loans and more time to refinance if a balloon payment is due at the end of the loan.

Amortization and Monthly Payments.   Because secondary loans have a short term they can only be self-amortizing if they have large payments. For example, a 30-year, $85,000 loan at 10 percent interest requires monthly payments of principal and interest of $745.94. A 10-year, 10 percent self-amortizing loan for this amount would require monthly payments of $1,123.28, and a 5-year note would call for payments of $1,806.00 per month.

Instead of being self-amortizing, however, secondary financing is likely to feature relatively small monthly payments. Such payments have two effects: they make the loan affordable to a borrower and they create a balloon note, a huge final payment at the end of the loan term. Indeed, if the interest rate is sufficiently high and the monthly payments are sufficiently low, *negative amortization* may occur, a situation in which the balloon payment will be larger than the original debt.

Coverage.   With a conventional loan, the purchaser typically makes a 20 percent down payment in cash, while a lender puts up the rest of the sales value in the form of a mortgage. With a second trust, the buyer's cash contribution is frequently less than 20 percent. For example, if a buyer puts down 10 percent of the purchase price in cash and gets a second trust for 10 percent then the balance of the purchase price, 80 percent, can be financed with a conventional loan. A conventional lender is likely to be satisfied with this arrangement as long as the buyer is financially qualified.

Questions to Ask:

What is the interest rate for conventional financing?
What is the interest rate for second trusts?
Can you get a lengthy second trust, say 10 or 15 years? If you're a buyer, the longer the second trust the better.
Will second trust financing involve a balloon payment? If so, how large a payment?
If you are getting a new first mortgage will the lender allow second trust financing to be used in the acquisition of the property? This is a question that should be satisfied before being committed to a purchase agreement.

HOW TO CUT HOUSING PRICES WITH SECOND TRUSTS

Second trusts can be regarded as a kind of financial ball of putty, loans that can be stretched, compressed, pulled and flattened into any shape acceptable to both borrower and lender. In those cases where it is the seller who becomes a lender by taking back a second trust, second trusts can be molded to favor either buyer or seller.

Imagine a situation where the prevailing rate of interest for a conventional loan is 10 percent while second trusts are available for, say, 12 percent interest. In a particular sale, a property is sold for $120,000. By adjusting the cost, size and terms of a second trust different results—and advantages—can be produced from a single core transaction.

▪ **Case 1.** The property is sold for $120,000 and a lender puts up $80,000 for a first trust. The seller takes back a $16,000 second trust at 12 percent interest and the buyer puts up the balance ($24,000) in cash. In this illustration there is market financing for both the first and second trusts, 80 percent of the deal is financed and 20 percent of the sale will be paid in cash by the purchaser. This is an essentially neutral deal with no advantage to either buyer or seller, assuming the property has a market value of $120,000.

▪ **Case 2.** The property is sold for $120,000 and a lender puts up $80,000 at 10 percent interest for a first trust. The seller takes back a $16,000 second trust at 10 percent and the buyer pays the $24,000 balance in cash. Here the buyer has an advantage because the interest charge on the second trust is less than the prevailing market rate for such financing. Alternatively, a deal with the same financial result could be arranged by lowering the sales price.

▪ **Case 3.** The property is sold for $120,000 and a lender puts up $80,000 at 10 percent interest for a first trust. The seller takes a $40,000 second trust at 14 percent. In this example, the buyer is trading costlier financing for the opportunity to purchase property with no money down. This scenario works for buyers with enough income to support enlarged monthly mortgage payments and who are in the upper tax brackets, a factor which partially offsets high mortgage costs. The seller here is getting $80,000 in cash (the proceeds of the first mortgage) plus a note with an above-market interest rate, a good deal for owners who don't need the cash represented by the second trust, $40,000 in this illustration.

Second trusts can be manipulated in terms of size as well as interest. It often happens that a buyer or seller has an intense ego commitment to a particular dollar figure. For example, a seller may want $120,000 for a given property, not because the home is worth that much but because the owner feels the $120,000 figure conveys a certain social status. Similarly, a buyer may not want to purchase real estate for more than a particular dollar value, say $110,000.

- **Case 4.** A property is sold for $120,000 and a lender finances $80,000 with a mortgage. The buyer is willing to pay the $120,000 price, which he feels is excessive, only if the terms of the deal can be negotiated. In this instance the buyer asks for, and gets, a $30,000 second trust from the seller at 9 percent interest and pays $10,000 in cash at settlement. The true economic value of this transaction is far less than the recorded price of $120,000 may indicate.

- **Case 5.** A home is marketed for $120,000 but a buyer will only offer $115,000, his "limit." The seller agrees to a deal with an $80,000 first trust from a local lender, $10,000 in cash from the buyer and a $25,000 second trust at 16 percent interest held by the seller. The buyer has not exceeded his paper limit, but the value of this package is worth more than a cash deal for $115,000.

- **Case 6.** A home is marketed for $120,000 with $20,000 in cash from the purchaser, $80,000 from a local lender and a $20,000 second trust from the seller at 12 percent interest. If the second trust is self-amortized over three years, the payments would be $664.29 per month. If the payments were set at $200 monthly, a far more affordable figure for most purchasers, there will be a huge balloon payment due at the end of the loan. To avoid a balloon payment and still have reasonable monthly payments, the term of the loan could be extended. For instance, a 15-year second trust (a rather long second trust) would only require monthly payments of $240.03 to be self-amortizing.

To negotiate second trust alternatives it is necessary to calculate the costs, benefits and disadvantages of a series of possible loan arrangements. One useful way to make such comparisons is to create a table showing monthly payments, the length of the loan, total cost of the loan (the number of payments × the monthly expense plus the value of any balloon payment. To find total interest, subtract the value of the original principal balance), the value of any balloon payments, interest rates and principal balances. Using such a chart will allow you to compare second trust alternatives to see which is best for you. (See Table 10.)

SELLERS AS SECOND TRUST LENDERS

The concept of "real estate financing" usually implies that an institution such as a savings and loan association, mortgage banker or bank will somehow be involved in the mortgage process. However, it often happens that second mortgages are seller "take backs," direct arrangements between buyers and sellers in which sellers make loans to purchasers and thus assume a new role, that of lender.

While commercial lenders are in the business of processing loan papers and making mortgages, individual sellers rarely have an equal level of expertise. For this reason sellers who wish to hold second trusts should examine such financing carefully before making commitments. Buyers too should review loans

TABLE 10
Comparing Second Trusts

	Deal 1	Deal 2	Deal 3
Sales price	_____	_____	_____
Cash down	_____	_____	_____
First trust	_____	_____	_____
Interest rate	_____	_____	_____
Term in years	_____	_____	_____
Monthly payments	_____	_____	_____
Second trust	_____	_____	_____
Interest rate	_____	_____	_____
Term in years	_____	_____	_____
Monthly payments	_____	_____	_____
Total monthly payment for both loans	_____	_____	_____
Balloon payment	_____	_____	_____
Points	_____	_____	_____
Total cost*	_____	_____	_____
Total interest	_____	_____	_____

*It is probable that the first and second trusts will have different terms; to figure total loan costs multiply first and second trust monthly payments by the number of months each will be outstanding. For example, a 30-year first trust will have 360 payments, a 5-year second trust will have only 60 payments.

from sellers with care to assure that they do not contain unworkable or unfair provisions.

The rules governing second trusts are established in the jurisdiction where the property is located. Different jurisdictions have vastly different approaches to second trusts and both buyers and sellers should investigate such financing with care before ratifying a real estate sales agreement. Here are the major areas to consider:

Interest. What is the proposed rate of interest? Many states have usury laws which establish maximum rates of interest for various kinds of financing. If the interest rate exceeds the usury level, the lender may suffer severe penalties. In some cases, a distinction is made between the rate that is allowable for residential second trusts and for second trusts that are part of an investment purchase and so the purpose of a loan may influence the rate allowed.

When money is tight, market conditions may require high interest levels to justify a second trust. But what happens if the usury limit for second trusts is 20 percent and a fair market return is 22 percent? In such instances either the loan will not be made or the terms of such financing will be adjusted so that usury rules are not violated. For example, rather than having a $20,000 loan at 22 percent, buyer and seller may agree to other terms, perhaps a $23,157.90 loan at 19 percent interest ($20,000 × 22 percent equals $4,400; $23,157.90 × 19 percent also equals $4,400).

Payment. Second trusts are usually designed so that borrowers can make relatively small monthly payments. These payments, plus the short term which second trusts generally feature, often require a balloon payment at the end of the loan term. How much is the monthly payment? How large is the balloon payment? Where, specifically, will the borrower get the money to repay the balloon payment? By refinancing? Through an inheritance? Savings? If savings, why not structure a self-amortizing loan initially and avoid the whole issue of a balloon payment?

Format. Standardized real estate contracts commonly call for the precise wording and terms of a loan to be "in the lender's usual form." This means commercial lenders get to make the rules. If you are a seller/lender, then surely you should insist on the same right, which means, in effect, that your attorney should draw up or approve loan documents.

Servicing. Commercial loan payments can be made at the institution where the loan originated, by mail, or electronically from one commercial lender to another. But what about loans which are made by property owners? In many cases, borrowers simply mail monthly payments to second trust holders, a system that may be disrupted if payments are delayed or lost in the mail. To assure that payments are being made—and received —in a timely manner, it may be best to make payments to a local lender who can date and verify the payment and then forward the money to the second trust holder. For more information about establishing such accounts, speak to officers at local savings and loan associations or banks.

Restrictions.   Local rules concerning second trusts may contain a variety of conditions, requirements and restrictions. In the District of Columbia, for example, the right to make a second trust with a balloon payment may vary according to whether or not the seller is an owner/occupant or a non-occupant (investor) owner.

Insurance.   Sellers making second trust loans should be concerned with two insurance issues:

First, commercial lenders insist on title insurance, of which they are the beneficiary, to at least the value of their loan so they will be protected in the event title to the property is faulty. Junior note holders often require similar protection so they can be repaid in the event of a title dispute.

Second, commercial lenders routinely require property owners to maintain adequate fire, theft and liability insurance. Second trust holders can have the same requirement, which means that seller/lenders should also get copies of the original policy (at settlement) as well as updates showing that the policy remains in force and that timely premium payments are being made.

Continuation.   If a situation develops where a borrower cannot repay a balloon note, serious questions arise for both the buyer and seller/lender. Should the property be foreclosed? Is there a way the note can be refinanced or extended? One approach to this problem has been developed in Maryland, where certain borrowers who made balloon notes after July 1, 1982, may unilaterally extend the term of their notes for up to two years, a situation which means that monthly payments would continue but the balloon payment would be postponed.

Default of the First Trust.   Since first and second mortgage holders are often paid separately, the maker of one note may not know if payments on the other loan have been missed. Many second trusts contain a provision that they are automatically in default if the first mortgage is not properly paid.

Taxes.   Seller/lenders will certainly want to know that taxes on the property are being paid in a timely manner, and borrowers may be required to present proof of payment.

Trustees.   If the junior note is a "trust" and not a "mortgage," then the owner/lender should have the right to name the trustee or trustees.

Credit.   The willingness of an owner to hold a second trust should be contingent on a review, satisfactory to the owner/lender, of the borrower's finances and credit. This means that a lender should have the right to see a borrower's credit report and, if the borrower is self-employed, past tax returns as well. It may be wise to have all credit information evaluated by a CPA.

The areas above clearly suggest that second trusts contain a host of potential problems for the unwary. To avoid needless difficulties, it is essential to consult with an attorney familiar with such financing in the jurisdiction where the property is located. Note also that many of the issues which concern second trusts are also important in those instances where sellers are creating first mortgages.

Questions to ask:

What is the rate of interest for conventional financing?

What is the interest rate on savings accounts and money market funds?

What interest rate is available if you make a second trust?

What is the usury rate in the jurisdiction where the property is located?

Will the second trust be a self-amortizing loan or will it require a balloon payment?

What portion of the purchase price is in the form of cash from the buyer?

Are there legal restrictions which limit the use of a second trust in your transaction? Speak to an attorney for complete advice.

Can you meet your financial needs in the event your borrower fails to make timely payments?

Can you meet your financial needs in the event your borrower stops making all payments?

Can you meet your financial needs if you must spend several thousand dollars in a foreclosure procedure?

Can you meet future obligations, perhaps a balloon payment of your own, if your borrower fails to make his or her balloon payment to you?

Does the buyer have a unilateral right to continue the note and not make the balloon payment? Does this type of regulation govern balloon notes in your area? If you are a seller, how would the deferral of a balloon payment affect your personal finances? Would such a regulation make a second trust unworkable?

What will a local lender charge to service your loan?

What are the tax implications of deferred payments? Speak to a CPA or tax attorney for complete information.

HOW TO SAVE $100,000 WITH SECOND TRUSTS

Second trusts can be used effectively both to acquire real estate and to refinance property. When compared with 30-year conventional loans, second trusts are often a bargain even when they have higher interest rates.

Second trusts can be surprisingly cheap in terms of actual interest costs because they have short terms. Combined with an assumable first trust in a sale, or added to an existing loan when refinancing, second trusts can save borrowers thousands of dollars in many cases.

Suppose Hansen has an assumable, 6 percent mortgage with 15 years to run. He needs $45,000 to pay his daughter's college tuition and so he looks at refinancing alternatives.

The Hansen home is worth $100,000, the present mortgage balance is $25,000 and monthly payments are $210.96. (The original loan balance was $35,187.)

Hansen could go out and refinance the entire property by getting a $70,000 loan at the current rate—10 percent in this example. That loan would require 360 payments of $614.30 each. Or Hansen could get a $45,000 second trust at 12 percent interest. If this was a 10-year second trust, 120 monthly payments of $645.62 would be needed for a self-amortizing loan. Table 11 shows how Mr. Hansen could cut his interest bill by $105,701.

In addition to interest costs, one must also consider up-front fees. If a single point is charged in each case, a point for the $45,000 second trust will cost $450, while a point for a new $70,000 first mortgage will cost $700. Loan origination fees are likely to be far less expensive with the smaller second trust. Fees for appraisals and credit reports should be identical.

For Hansen, the use of a second trust will save more than $100,000 in interest costs. If the additional cost per month,

TABLE 11
Mr. Hansen's Loan Choices

	New First Trust	First Trust/Second Trust
Loan principal	$70,000	$25,000 loan balance $45,000 new financing
Interest rate	10 percent	6 percent old loan 12 percent new loan
Monthly payment	$614.30	$210.96 old loan 645.62 new loan $856.58 Total
Number of payments	360	180 old loan 120 new loan
Total payment	$221,148	$37,973 old loan 77,474 new loan $115,447 Total
Total interest	$151,148	$45,447
Interest saved	none	$105,701
Points	700	450

$242.28, is more than he can afford, Hansen could work out some arrangement to offset the expense, such as postponing the purchase of a new car or eliminating a vacation. Alternatively, his daughter could agree to pay the additional money by working part-time.

Notice that Mr. Hansen would have been just as far ahead if he were buying rather than refinancing property under similar circumstances. For example, suppose a house was available for $85,000 and that a $25,000 first trust at 6 percent interest was assumable. Hansen could pay $15,000 in cash and get a conventional loan for $70,000, or he could assume the existing mortgage and get a second trust for $45,000. If the rates and terms were the same as with the refinancing example, Hansen would save more than $100,000 in interest costs by choosing the second trust.

8

How to Pay
Off a Balloon Note

Whenever balloon loans are discussed great attention should be paid to the risks of such financing, mortgages that feature huge payments at the end of their terms. Borrowers who fail to make this large final payment may lose their property through a foreclosure action. Yet, despite the potential risk, balloon payments are a common feature of many real estate transactions because they offer advantages to savvy borrowers.

While balloon notes have traditionally been associated with second trust financing, they are becoming more common with first mortgages as well. Roll-over loans have huge balloon payments. Graduated payment mortgages (GPMs) and adjustable rate mortgages (ARMs) can have balloon payments also.

Balloon payments result from one of two situations. In the first case, monthly payments are too low to amortize the loan. For example, it would cost $703.93 a month to have a $50,000 loan at 10 percent interest amortized over 9 years. If the monthly payments are only $400, Table 12 shows what happens.

With this loan there is no amortization whatsoever because monthly payments are always less than $703.93. After 9 years, a borrower would owe $52,900.90.

In the second case, balloon payments can develop when monthly payments are large enough to produce a self-amortizing loan but the loan term is too short. For example, to amortize an $85,000 loan over 30 years at 10 percent interest would require monthly payments of $745.94. Table 13 shows what happens to the loan if the payments were set at $745.94 but the term of the loan was only 5 years:

TABLE 12
Low Monthly Payments

End of Year	Principal ($)	Interest ($)	Loan Balance ($)
1	−209.43	5,009.43	50,209.43
2	−231.36	5,031.36	50,440.78
3	−255.58	5,055.58	50,696.36
4	−282.34	5,082.34	50,978.71
5	−311.91	5,111.91	51,290.62
6	−344.57	5,144.57	51,635.19
7	−380.65	5,180.65	52,436.35
8	−420.51	5,220.51	52,436.35
9	−464.54	5,264.54	52,900.90

TABLE 13
Short-Term Balloon Schedule

End of Year	Principal ($)	Interest ($)	Balance ($)
1	472.50	8,478.73	84,527.50
2	521.97	8,429.26	84,005.53
3	576.63	8,374.60	83,428.90
4	637.01	8,314.22	82,791.89
5	703.72	8,247.51	82,088.17

In this case the principal balance at the end of 5 years is $82,088.17, an amount somewhat lower than the size of the note originally. With payments large enough to produce self-amortization, the principal value of this loan—or any loan—will always decline.

Borrowers should distinguish between balloon arrangements that result in smaller principal balances and those which actually increase the size of the debt. Growing balloon payments take more money to refinance from borrowers who have not made—or who have been unable to make—amortizing monthly payments. Such borrowers may require more income to refinance their property than to acquire it initially because they are seeking larger loans, depending on interest rates. In addition, as the size of the debt rises one has to wonder if there is enough value in the property to justify a growing loan.

The balance between the risk and benefit of a balloon payment must be carefully weighed by individual purchasers and lenders. Buyers without adequate financial means, discipline or planning should clearly stay away from balloon financing. Those who do use balloon loans must develop a rational repayment strategy, possibly one of the eight listed below.

Strategy 1.   Loan term. In general, borrowers should seek the longest possible term when using balloon financing. More years mean more potential opportunities to renegotiate loans, refinance property or sell real estate if necessary.

Having the longest possible term does not necessarily mean that borrowers should wait to the last minute before refinancing. As time passes interest charges accrue and balloon payments grow. More dollars, even dollars devalued by inflation, will be required to satisfy the note and so the problem of repayment should be examined as soon as the loan is made.

Strategy 2.   Refinance in part. In those situations where the first mortgage has a balloon payment it may be possible to raise needed cash by obtaining a second mortgage, hopefully a loan without a balloon requirement.

Strategy 3.   Get a new balloon note. This may not resolve the ultimate problem of a balloon payment but at least it will defer the issue for a while. With the new balloon financing at least try to get better terms, that is, a longer note if possible, lower interest or better monthly payments.

Strategy 4.   Refinance completely. If you have been making regular payments on your current mortgage and have a good credit record you may be able to refinance with a new, self-amortizing loan from a commercial lender.

Strategy 5.   Get an extension. If you have a good payment record, a lender may want to continue the loan, particularly if the rate of return is at or above current market levels. Borrowers will have the most leverage if they couple an extension with an interest increase long before the balloon payment is due.

Strategy 6.   Sell part of the property. It may be possible to subdivide your property and sell off some portion to meet a balloon payment. Beware that many first trust loans restrict the ability to subdivide, so if you have both a first trust and a second trust it is the first trust loan which must be checked to determine if subdivisions are permissible.

Strategy 7.   Sell an interest in the property. Enter into an equity-sharing arrangement with a cash-rich buyer. This will result in eliminating the balloon payment while diluting your interest in the future profits, benefits and losses associated with property. Again, check the first trust to see if an equity-sharing arrangement is permitted.

Strategy 8.   Sell the property. Investment buyers will frequently acquire property that is financed with a balloon note with the intention of marketing it before the balloon payment is due. The proceeds from the sale can then be used to pay off all liens against the property, including the balloon note. In considering this approach, one must wonder what happens if the value of the property does not appreciate or if the cost of marketing eliminates all profit.

Questions to ask:

How large is the balloon payment? (Always get an amortization schedule to determine principal and interest costs.)

What is the rate of interest?

When is the balloon payment due?

How long will the process of refinancing take? Be certain to allow extra time in case an application is delayed or rejected and additional weeks or months are needed to process a new or revised application.

What are the tax implications of subdividing property, particularly land which is part of a personal residence? What are the tax implications of entering into a shared-equity arrangement? Speak to a tax consultant for current advice.

Can you subdivide property while keeping the first trust? In many instances subdividing is prohibited by the terms of the first trust.

9
How to Save Money with Assumable Mortgages

The largest single source of below-market financing is the multi-billion-dollar pool of existing mortgages, where payments may be continued by real estate buyers without a change in interest rates or other conditions. Known broadly as *assumable* mortgages, such financing is available in every community and represents a source of significant dollar savings for many purchasers. An assumable loan situation could look like this:

Mr. Pace likes a $45,000 house in the country and offers to buy the property with $5,000 down. The rest of the sale would include assuming a first trust with a $20,000 balance and getting a $20,000 second trust from the seller.

The reason Pace wants to assume the first trust is that it has a 6 percent interest rate. His payments on the note total only $150 per month and the loan has a little more than 18 years to go. The second trust, a 10-year, self-amortizing note at 12 percent interest, costs $286.94 per month.

As an alternative, Pace could get a 30-year, $40,000 first trust at 10 percent interest. The monthly payments would total $351.03. While the assumption/second trust arrangement costs $85.91 extra per month when compared to new financing, Pace will save $58,897.50 by using the combined financing package. (See Table 14.)

TABLE 14
Mr. Pace's Loan Choices

	New Loan	Assumption and Second Trust
Money down	$5,000	$5,000
Loan balance	$40,000	$20,000 first trust
		20,000 second trust
		$40,000 Total
Interest rate	10 percent	6 percent first trust
		12 percent second trust
Number of payments	360	$220.27 first trust
		$120 second trust
Monthly cost	$351.03	$150.00 first trust
		286.94 second trust
		$436.94 Total
Extra monthly cost		$85.91
Total payments	$126,370.80	$33,040.50 first trust
		34,432.80 second trust
		$67,473.30 Total
Extra cost	$58,897.50	

Assumable mortgages offer three major advantages to borrowers.

First, assumable mortgages offer the possibility of below-market financing. When you can take over a loan with 6 percent interest in a 10 percent market, you're ahead.

Second, buyers who might otherwise be frozen out of the real estate market by high interest rates can often find affordable housing when they locate property with assumable financing.

Third, assumable mortgages produce faster equity growth. In their first years, monthly mortgage payments are heavily tilted toward interest costs and only a limited number of dollars remain to reduce the principal balance of a loan. Over time, the balance between interest payments and principal reductions changes, with more and more money going to pay down the principal balance of the loan.

Since loans are typically assumed several years after they originate, it means that buyers who assume benefit from larger equity reductions each month. For example, a 30-year, $85,000 mortgage at 10 percent interest will require monthly payments of $745.94. Of this amount, only $37.60 will be used to reduce the principal balance in the first month. If such a loan were assumed after 60 payments, the monthly cost would be the same but the principal reduction would be $61.36.

Within the pool of assumable mortgages are loans with interest costs of 4, 5 and 6 percent. As a rule, the lower the rate of interest the older the loan. Older mortgages, in turn, have smaller remaining principal balances, which means that buyers will need more cash or secondary financing to obtain such loans. A $100,000 home may well have an assumable loan at 6 percent interest but the principal balance may be just $20,000. To buy this property a purchaser will have to come up with $80,000 in cash or credit, financing which is not available to everyone and which may be better invested elsewhere even when it is available.

While low interest assumptions are clearly something for which buyers should search, the benefits of assumable financing are not always certain.

Consider a situation where a property is available for $100,-000. There is a $50,000 assumable first trust at 9 percent. The buyer has $20,000 in cash and asks the seller to take back a $30,000 second trust. The seller will do this, but only if the buyer pays 12 percent interest.

If accepted, the result of this arrangement would be a blended overall interest rate of 10.12 percent. The question is whether the combined rate and monthly payment required for the two loans is a better or worse deal than simply refinancing the property on a conventional basis. It is entirely possible that an assumption with a second trust will have both a higher interest rate and a higher monthly payment than a new loan.

In addition to comparing interest rates and monthly payments, financing costs must also be weighed. Is there a modest assumption fee or is a large payment required? How does the expense of an assumption compare with the expense of new financing, including loan application fees, points, and origination costs?

The element of time must be considered when comparing assumptions with alternative financing arrangements. An assumed mortgage plus a second trust may have higher monthly costs than a new conventional loan but the combination package may have a term which is considerably shorter. This means that if you intend to hold property for many years, the higher payments may actually be a bargain if there are fewer of them.

Questions to ask:

What is the remaining mortgage balance of the assumable loan?

What is the interest rate of the loan to be assumed?

What is the remaining term of the assumable mortgage?

How much cash is required to take over an assumption?

What is the prevailing interest rate for conventional financing?

What is the prevailing interest rate for a second trust?

How large is the assumption fee?

In comparison, what is the cost of new financing in terms of a loan origination fee, points, title insurance, legal fees, etc.?

WHERE TO FIND ASSUMABLE LOANS

For many years home loans were freely assumable because interest rates were relatively stable and the value of money was not rapidly eroded by inflation. Lenders who paid 4 and 5 percent for savings accounts and other short-term deposits could profitably loan money for 30 years at 6 and 7 percent interest. Assumptions, in such conditions, were practical because the interests of neither lenders nor borrowers were harmed.

This system worked well until the late 1970s. At that time the cost of short-term borrowing began to rise above the return lenders were receiving from mortgage portfolios and huge losses were the natural result.

Why did the system change? Inflation meant that the public could no longer preserve the spending power of its dollars by making short-term deposits at low rates. Mortgage interest rates went up as lenders were forced to pay more interest to attract short-term deposits and accounts.

Just as important, dollars which at one time would have been deposited with mortgage lenders were now diverted elsewhere. The "lending" industry was transformed into the "financial services" industry, where more players competed for the public's money. Billions of dollars, for example, were shifted from banks and savings and loan associations to money market funds and other new investment choices, a process known as "disintermediation" in the jargon of the financial community.

The fact that short-term funding costs rose meant that lenders had multi-billion-dollar mortgage portfolios paying 4, 5, 6, 7 and 8 percent interest which were underwritten by short-term borrowing at rates of 12, 13 and 14 percent and even higher. As part of their strategy to limit losses, lenders began to restrict the assumability of new loans. New mortgages made in the "lender's usual form" began to commonly include a *due-on-sale* clause (also known as an *alienation* clause), which provided that the entire loan would be payable at the time the property was sold or, alternatively, that mortgages could be assumed but only with the prior written "consent" of the lender.

As restrictive clauses became more common, lenders were able to reduce their portfolio of outstanding assumable mortgages and thus lower their exposure to changing market conditions. While original borrowers with fixed-rate mortgages could get loans at current market rates, such rates could not be freely passed along to future buyers. In effect, the burden of inflation had been shifted from lenders to borrowers.

Not surprisingly, due-on-sale clauses raised and continue to raise a number of issues. Are such clauses in the public interest? If not, can lenders enforce them? Are there ways to evade due-on-sale restrictions? A variety of law suits have resulted from efforts to avoid such limiting clauses. What must one do to get the "consent" of a lender? In many cases lenders will not agree to an assumption under any conditions, while in other situations lenders will approve assumptions when interest rates are raised or new fees are charged or both.

While new mortgages routinely contain due-on-sale clauses, the pool of loans which are assumable encompasses millions of mortgages. Here, in general terms, is a catalogue of loans that are commonly assumable:

FHA Mortgages.   Some five million loans with a face value of more than $135 billion have been insured by the Federal Housing Administration. FHA mortgages, including those being made today, are assumable at their original rates and terms. A lender, according to the FHA, cannot charge more than $500 for processing when a loan is assumed.

Two FHA exceptions: First, when FHA financing is less than two years old, buyers must be financially qualified to assume. Second, about 100,000 FHA-insured loans made through state and local financial agencies in recent years can only be assumed by purchasers qualified to participate in state housing programs, usually low- and moderate-income households that have not owned property in the past three years.

VA Mortgages.   There are more than four million loans, with a face value of nearly $125 billion, that have been guaranteed by the Veterans Administration. Such loans, including those made at this time, are assumable at their original rates and terms, except for loans made recently through state and local housing programs where a selective due-on-sale feature is in force. Note that you need not be a veteran to assume VA financing.

Silent Loans. Conventional loans not containing due-on-sale clauses or language to the contrary should be freely assumable at their original rates and terms.

Due-on-Sale Loans. In some circumstances a lender may elect not to enforce a due-on-sale clause. For example, the Federal National Mortgage Association (Fannie Mae), which has bought pools of home mortgages worth billions of dollars, will not enforce due-on-sale clauses for loans it purchased before November 10, 1980.

ARMs. Adjustable rate mortgages are commonly assumable at current rates by qualified buyers.

State Bans: In some jurisdictions due-on-sale clauses are prohibited. For specific information, contact a knowledgeable real estate attorney in the jurisdiction where the property is located.

Consent Loans. In those instances when a loan is assumable with the consent of the lender, such consent may be given, often in exchange for an increase in interest to the current rate, charging fees up front or issuing new mortgage documents that entail certain payments to the lender.

The question with both consent loans and ARMs is whether or not assumable mortgages with market interest rates are bargains. Since the rates for both conventional and assumed loans with current interest rates will be substantially the same, one must weigh the expense of an *assumption fee* (a charge made by a lender at the time of an assumption to at least cover the cost of paperwork and frequently to raise the lender's yield from the mortgage) and all other charges versus the cost of new financing, including items such as loan application fees, origination charges, points, etc.

Questions to ask:

Is the loan freely assumable?

If the loan is assumable, is there an assumption fee? (As a matter of negotiation try to get the other party to pay this cost or at least share this expense.)

If there is a due-on-sale clause, will it be enforced?

What actions will be required to satisfy a lender whose "consent" is needed for an assumption? Will interest levels rise? Are new mortgage papers required?

ASSUMPTIONS AND RESPONSIBILITY

While the term *assumption* is used generally to describe mortgages that are passed from seller to buyer, more specific definitions are required to resolve an important issue: Who is responsible to the lender if loan payments are missed?

To determine the precise obligations of buyer and seller one must see if a property has been purchased "subject to" the mortgage or if the loan has been "assumed."

In those cases where property is purchased "subject to" the mortgage it is understood that the buyer is not responsible to the lender for the repayment of the loan. If payments are not made by the buyer the lender will seek compensation from the original borrower. While the buyer may have little direct responsibility to repay the loan, it would take a truly irrational person to not recognize that default means foreclosure, the loss of any equity invested in the property and the total improbability of future mortgage borrowing. These are powerful financing considerations which no purchaser can reasonably overlook.

When mortgages are *assumed* and the buyer agrees to be responsible for the entire debt, the lender can pursue both the original borrower and the purchaser in case of default.

Properties purchased with assumed financing or bought "subject to" the mortgage represent deals between buyers and sellers rather than lenders and borrowers, except when the "consent" of a lender is given. This means it is possible for freely assumable financing, such as most FHA or VA mortgages, to be passed from seller to buyer even when the purchaser is totally unknown to the lender.

Lenders may not be able to prevent the take-over of freely assumable mortgages but, in turn, they are not required to release original borrowers from the obligation to repay their loans. After all, if sellers could merely pass on the responsibility to repay mortgage debts it would be a simple matter to hurt the lender. Here's what could happen in the worst case.

Wainwright bought a property 10 years ago for $100,000 that was financed with $20,000 in cash and a freely assumable $80,-000 mortgage. Because of flooding, the value of Wainwright's property has dropped substantially and to reduce his loss, Wainwright sells his home to a vagrant who agrees to assume the original loan. The vagrant makes no payments on the mortgage and the bank soon forecloses. The mortgage balance is $75,000, the foreclosure value is only $40,000 and so the lender suffers a loss of $35,000 plus foreclosure expenses.

How much liability, in real terms, do original borrowers have when a loan is assumed or payments are continued "subject to"? Since the overwhelming majority of all mortgages are never in default, there is only the most limited possibility that a lender will pursue an original borrower for compensation. Even when a loan is defaulted, original borrowers still benefit from several practical considerations.

First, the innate value of the property is generally far greater than the balance of assumed financing.

Second, in those sales which feature large down payments and second trusts, the original borrower's liability for the first trust is well defended because all proceeds from a foreclosure sale would first be applied to the repayment of that debt before any payments would be made for a second trust or to the purchaser. In "no cash" or "cash plus" sales, however, the seller's protection would be limited if non-existent.

Third, there are some who argue that it is a good strategy to remain liable for a mortgage. If the buyer defaults, it is suggested, it may be possible to get the property back at discount by repurchasing it from a buyer faced with foreclosure.

Whether or not it will be possible for original borrowers to get a release depends on the policies of the lender. Lenders, however, have little incentive to release original borrowers except in those cases where mortgage terms can be structured more favorably in their behalf. Several incentives may encourage lenders to release original borrowers, including:

Higher Interest. A lender may authorize a release for the original borrower if the interest rate on the loan can be raised.

Buyer Qualification. Lenders have a clear and understandable desire to assure that new borrowers will be credit-worthy individuals. Raising interest rates is a useless exercise if the new borrower cannot afford monthly mortgage payments.

New Papers. In some instances lenders will release original borrowers if they can issue a new mortgage with the exact same terms as the first loan. A new mortgage, rather than a mere continuation of the old loan, will generate additional fees to the lender.

Fees. *Assumption fees* are charges made by lenders to cover the cost of processing new paperwork. However, some lenders see such charges as profit-centers and exact substantial payments to permit a release.

In addition to getting a release directly from a lender, original borrowers may also require a release from other parties. See Appendix B for detailed information regarding VA and FHA release policies.

Questions to ask:

If you are a buyer, are you assuming old financing or purchasing property "subject to" an old loan?

If you are a seller and your loan is assumable do you want a release?

What are the lender's release policies?

10
Assisted Loans

Cash is a key ingredient in many real estate sales and yet money up front is not always necessary to cement a deal; indeed, a number of real estate strategists recommend buying without cash if possible.

What happens if you're a buyer without dollars, someone with enough income to support mortgage payments but too little currency on hand? Or, how can you boost your credit standing if you have saved your dollars but have limited earnings?

A large portion of all real estate transactions may be described as *assisted* sales, deals in which a buyer without sufficient cash or adequate credit receives material aid from an individual or institution that has no claim against the future appreciation of the property. Families, friends, the VA, FHA and private mortgage insurers are among those that may be clustered in a discussion of assisted transactions. In addition, assisted sales could include equity-sharing arrangements, deals which are often made within families.

GIFTS AND CO-SIGNERS

The help of friends and family in a real estate deal most often comes in the form of cash gifts or the extension of credit, acts of generosity that must be viewed with some care.

For the protection of buyers, sellers and lenders, a "gift" should be seen as something more than a passing oral comment by Uncle Willard or whoever to come up with $15,000 if you ever purchase real estate. A gift commitment is truly a gift when it is:

Irrevocable.   A "gift" that can be taken back is not a gift.

Free of Consideration.   A "gift" on which one pays interest, where repayment in whole or in part is expected, or where other valued consideration is anticipated is not a gift.

Available.   A gift which is not in hand by settlement may cause the forfeiture of a deposit because the deal cannot be completed.

Binding.   What happens if a gift commitment is made and the donor dies before the gift is delivered? Gift commitments should be binding on heirs, executors, administrators, successors and assigns.

Contingent.   A purchase which is dependent on the delivery of a gift should be structured so that if the gift is not received by a given time and date, the sale is off and the deposit of the purchaser will be returned in full. Conversely, if it is the intent of the donor to provide a gift for the purchase of a particular property, that gift should be returned if for some reason the sale falls through.

Carefully Thought Out.   Sizable gifts may involve significant tax questions which should be reviewed by an attorney and/or tax authority prior to any commitment. For instance, will the donor be forced to pay a gift tax? How will a gift affect the recipient's tax basis in the property? It may be that an outright gift is not the best approach in certain cases. Rather than providing a large bundle of cash up front, some donors instead take back a mortgage which they then partially forgive each year.

There are some buyers who have managed to accumulate enough cash for a real estate purchase but lack sufficient income, at least on paper, to qualify for a mortgage. In such situations, co-signers with good credit may participate in a sale.

A lender will want a co-signer to repay any portion of the loan which is in default above the value represented by a foreclosure sale. In many instances, lenders will not only want a credit-worthy individual to be a co-signer but also to be on the deed as a co-owner. The reasoning is that in the event of default the lender can pursue the co-signer for foreclosure costs, which often amount to several thousand dollars, as well as any portion of the loan that is not satisfied in the sale.

The possible problem with a co-signer as co-buyer is that this is not truly the relationship which many families or friends envision. Also, a co-signer on the deed may endanger the ownership of the property—and the lender's interest—if the co-signer goes bankrupt or is forced to pay a liability claim. With a co-signer as a co-owner, both buyer and co-signer would be wise to have an attorney draw up an appropriate agreement outlining the relationship between the parties and resolving potential estate issues as well.

As with gifts, sales that depend on co-signatories should be made contingent on performance: that is, there is no deal if the co-signer refuses to sign documents, provide credit information and to take such other steps as may be required to complete the sale. In addition, the actions of co-signers should be binding on heirs, executors, administrators, successors and assigns.

In the case of both gifts and co-signers, borrowers should be aware that not all prospective donors and co-signers can be regarded as capable individuals. The ability of habitual alcoholics, the legally insane, those with certain drug dependencies, minors, senile individuals, and bigamists to make gifts or co-sign documents may be subject to future challenge even when such personal difficulties are not immediately apparent. Be certain to obtain advice from an attorney in the event of competency questions.

Questions to ask:

Can you reasonably expect a gift from any friend or relative? If so, are there any conditions?

Is the donor willing to sign all requisite forms?

What are the tax implications of a gift? Speak to an attorney or CPA for specific advice.

If friends or relatives are willing to act as co-signers will the lender also require them to be co-owners? If they are co-owners, what is your relationship? Is it an equity-sharing deal? Speak to an attorney about co-ownership issues.

VA FINANCING

By their nature, programs developed by the federal government tend to be large and the no-money-down VA mortgage program is no exception. There are four million VA-backed loans outstanding and together they represent some of the best financing around.

What makes VA financing unique? There are several major factors:

- The VA is not a lender. Instead, the VA acts as a co-signer to assist qualified individuals who need home mortgages.
- Unlike conventional loans which require 20 percent cash down, there is no VA requirement for a down payment unless the purchase price of the property is greater than the VA's estimate of reasonable value or if a lender requires a

cash down payment as a condition of the loan. Many VA buyers, however, elect to make a down payment even when one is not required to reduce their monthly payments.

- There is no VA limitation on the size of a mortgage. Lenders, however, may elect to limit the size of VA financing they will process.
- Historically, the VA mortgage program has been seen as a loan "guarantee" rather than insurance on which individuals pay premiums. However, the VA now charges a one-time "funding fee" equal to 1 percent of the face value of a loan, money which is paid to the agency at settlement. Whether a "funding fee" is different from an "insurance premium" in anything other than name is a matter of debate.
- VA loans are generally assumable at their original rate and terms, a bargain for many buyers. There is an exception for a small percentage of loans made through state and local housing agencies that may be assumed only by individuals otherwise qualified to participate in such programs.
- VA financing is self-amortizing over a long term, thus there is no balloon payment.
- VA-backed loans may be prepaid without penalty.

VA loans are available to those in the armed services today as well as most veterans with active duty experience since World War II, generally individuals with 90 days of continuous active duty service during wartime or 181 days of such service in peaceful periods. In addition, certain other individuals, such as officers in the Public Health Service, qualify for VA benefits.

The VA mortgage program embodies a guarantee on which lenders rely to reduce their risk. The VA promises at this time to repay up to 60 percent of a loan or a maximum today of $27,500, a figure which represents each veteran's "entitlement."

When the VA program was first established during World

War II the initial entitlement was $2,000. By the end of the war the entitlement figure was raised to $4,000 and it has gradually risen ever since. For VA-qualified buyers the rise of entitlement means that it is possible to have purchased a home many years ago and still have some entitlement remaining. A purchaser who bought a home for $25,000 in 1960 when the entitlement level was $12,500, for instance, would now have a remaining entitlement balance of $15,000, essentially an unused line of credit from Uncle Sam.

It may be possible for a vet to have his or her entitlement reinstated in certain circumstances. A veteran's entitlement could be restored to the full current level when a previous VA-backed loan has been completely repaid as part of a sale or when a VA-qualified purchaser assumes a VA mortgage and substitutes his or her entitlement for that of the original buyer.

If VA interest rates decline, an owner/occupant vet can refinance an old GI loan without using any additional entitlement. The size of the new GI mortgage, however, can be no greater than the value of the old loan balance plus any settlement fees required to obtain the new financing.

The size of an entitlement becomes important when one considers that lenders usually seek a four-to-one ratio of entitlement credit to mortgage debt. With the $27,500 guarantee, a lender will generally loan $110,000 to a financially qualified buyer. However, the $110,000 figure is not a legal limit and a lender could—and many do—make far larger loans.

To qualify for VA financing, a veteran must possess DD Form 214, a form given out when leaving the service, and VA Form 26-1880, "Request for Certificate of Eligibility." These forms are used to get a "Certificate of Eligibility." For current information visit VA regional offices, write the VA, or call via toll-free phone lines.

VA loan rates as of 1986 were established by the federal government and are not always equal to prevailing interest levels for conventional financing, a situation that can cause problems for unwary buyers and sellers. Suppose that a lender receives two $100,000 loan applications, one from a VA applicant seeking a loan at, say, 9 percent and a second applicant looking for conventional financing at 10 percent interest.

Clearly the lender would prefer to loan money at the higher rate; but rather than not make a loan to a veteran, the lender will instead require more up-front charges for VA financing to raise his yield. The lender, for instance, may charge both the veteran and the conventional applicant a 1 percent loan origination fee. In addition, the lender may want one "point" for the conventional loan but four or five points for VA-backed financing in this example.

The catch here is that while VA rules will allow the veteran borrower to pay a loan origination fee, a charge which is not considered interest, the VA will generally not approve a loan that "shows" the veteran paying points, a fee regarded by the VA as interest. This means that all points for VA financing must be paid by sellers.

Thus while buyer and lender may be willing to finance a home with a VA-backed loan, many sellers are not too thrilled at the prospect of paying points. By paying points, homes are effectively being sold at discount because owners are receiving something less than the recorded sales price. Many sellers are not willing to pay what they regard as excessive financing costs for VA loans when conventional financing is equally available, and some owners will place a cap on the number of points they are willing to pay—a tactic that can effectively prevent VA-qualified purchasers from buying their property. Alternatively, some sellers will pay points only if vets agree to higher prices.

As this is written the FHA has removed its requirement that only sellers can pay points. If the new FHA arrangement is successful, then it is probable that VA rules will also be changed.

While VA mortgages would seem to be limited to veterans

alone, the VA program actually benefits a far broader scope of the population. Non-veteran purchasers can assume VA mortgages at their original rates and terms, a significant financial advantage in many cases.

Non-veteran sellers can participate in the program by offering their homes to VA-qualified purchasers. To get VA financing, a home must be evaluated by the VA to determine its economic worth. This means sellers must obtain a "Certificate of Reasonable Value," an appraisal that may be ordered by contacting regional VA offices.

The VA points out that its Certificate of Reasonable Value is for financial purposes only and is not intended to be a structural inspection. It is therefore possible to buy a VA-financed house that is in something less than pristine physical condition.

The question of when to order a VA appraisal is an issue that should be of some importance to sellers. Clearly an appraisal will be required to get VA financing, but should an appraisal be sought earlier in the marketing process, before there is a purchaser with whom to deal?

By getting an appraisal just before a home is offered for sale sellers will at least have the VA's view of what their property is worth. This can be a valuable selling tool if the appraisal meets the expectations of the seller, since property advertising can then be directed toward VA buyers ("VA appraised at $109,000"). But what happens if the appraisal is low? Sellers in such situations have spent money for an appraisal they are not likely to publicize.

Sellers are best served by having the buyer get and pay for an appraisal as part of the loan application process after an offer on the property has been made. An offer is a product of the marketplace and is surely an important benchmark by which the value of the property can be measured, one that cannot be totally ignored in the appraisal process.

If it should happen that the VA appraisal is less than the sales value of the property, the VA will guarantee a loan equal only to the estimated worth of the home. When an appraisal is below the sales value, the VA requires that purchasers have the option to withdraw from the deal, in which case their deposit must be returned in full.

In the event of a low appraisal there are also two other strategies which can be employed. First, a buyer can pay the difference between the sales price and the estimated value in cash. Second, the seller can reduce the sales price to the appraised value. As a matter of negotiation, buyer and seller may meet somewhere between these two choices.

In looking at VA programs, prospective borrowers should be aware that veterans' benefits are not only an economic issue, they're a political matter as well. In 1987, for instance, the President's budget proposed raising the VA funding fee from 1 percent to 2.5 percent, a figure below FHA insurance levels but high enough to make VA financing far less attractive than in the past.

With the funding fee now established in principle, it's possible that it may rise above the 1 percent level. However, any effort to raise the funding fee is likely to encounter severe political opposition, and not just from veterans' groups and real estate organizations. The benefits of the VA mortgage program extend beyond veterans because the loans can be assumed by anyone and because such financing can be used to purchase homes from sellers generally. Excessive funding fees will effectively kill the program and with it the re-election hopes of many congressmen.

Questions to ask:

What is the current VA interest rate?
Is the VA interest rate set by the government or is it al-

lowed to "float" with the market? A floating rate would reduce the need for points.

What is the largest VA-backed mortgage offered by most
local lenders?

What is the current number of points sought by lenders
making VA loans? Check with different lenders, as this figure
may vary. When VA interest rates are similar or equal to
conventional levels there should be few, if any, additional
points.

What is the current VA entitlement?

If you have used your VA entitlement in the past do you
have any remaining entitlement? Check with your local VA
office.

If you are a seller do you want a Certificate of Reasonable
Value? If so, how much is such an appraisal?

Can you substitute an FHA appraisal for a Certificate of
Reasonable Value? This may be possible in some areas, so
contact your local VA office for more information.

If you are a buyer, do you have a Certificate of Eligibility
in hand? How long will it take to get one?

Is there a funding fee being charged at the time you apply
for VA financing? If so, how much?

What course of action will you take if the VA appraisal is
less than the agreed sales price for a property?

Are there new VA rules which will affect your ability to get
VA financing? Check with your local VA office.

FHA LOANS

The Federal Housing Administration (FHA) is one of the oldest
and largest sources of mortgage assistance available to the general public. While VA mortgages can be seen as a reward for
public service, FHA-backed loans are an outgrowth of a different public policy, the view that readily available mortgage

funds will stimulate the economy in general and the housing industry in particular.

The most popular FHA program, loans insured under Sec. 203(b), offers many advantages to home buyers, particularly those with few down payment dollars. Here's how the Sec. 203(b) compares with conventional or VA-backed loans.

- FHA mortgages feature low down payments, usually 5 percent or less, compared with 20 percent down for conventional loans and no-money-down VA financing.

  FHA loans have traditionally been freely assumable at their original rates and terms except for mortgages made through state and local housing authorities, loans which could only be assumed by individuals qualified to participate in such programs. In 1986, however, the FHA changed its free-assumption policy: loans cannot be assumed automatically for a period of two years after origination. From now on, buyers in this two-year period must be financially qualified to borrow. And, to make the policy change even more sulfurous, lenders can charge up to $500 for processing new paperwork related to assumptions.

  The new FHA policy stems in part from the role of TV gurus and seminar oracles. Some want *sellers* to refinance homes with FHA mortgages so that *purchasers* can immediately buy the property and assume the loan. Until the FHA rule changed, this approach was perfectly proper. It allowed buyers to purchase property with mortgages in place and without requiring borrowers to qualify for financing. No more, says the FHA, but some industry groups are fighting the new rule.

- Residential FHA loans may be prepaid in whole or in part without penalty. This means you can make prepayments at any time during the loan term; however, if a payment is not made on the monthly due date, it will be credited to the next due date. For complete information on FHA prepayment planning consult with your lender. In some situations it may be best to make prepayments with two checks: one for the value of the mortgage payment and a second check for any additional monies. With two checks, borrowers will have a record of all prepayments.

- Unlike VA or conventional financing, there is an FHA loan limit. This limit is established by the federal government and varies according to whether or not a region is considered a "high cost" housing area. As this is written, for example, the current FHA limit for single-family housing is $90,000 in Washington, D.C., $67,500 in West Virginia and $135,000 in Alaska and Hawaii.

- While VA loans have been historically regarded as a loan "guarantee"—at least before the imposition of a "funding fee"—FHA loans have always been viewed as a form of insurance.

- Traditionally, both VA and FHA interest rates were set by the federal government. In 1983, however, the government decided to let FHA rates "float" with the market.

The advantage of a floating rate is that FHA interest costs will no longer lag behind conventional rates. For example, suppose the government said the FHA rate was 9 percent but lenders could get 10 percent financing for conventional loans. Why should the lenders make FHA loans at the inferior rate?

The answer is that they shouldn't—and didn't. What they did was charge 9 percent interest for FHA financing plus points. The problem with points under the old regulations, aside from cost, was that only the seller was allowed to pay them. Sellers, not surprisingly, sought to avoid the points problem by not accepting FHA deals or by passing the cost through in the form of higher prices. Under the new rules, however, buyers can now pay points.

By having a floating rate, FHA interest costs will parallel conventional loan rates and so the need for points will diminish if not vanish, depending on market demand. This change, coupled with the "right" of buyers to pay points, should make FHA deals fully competitive with other loan formats. Also, if floating rates work for FHA loan programs the concept will undoubtedly be extended to VA financing as well.

For many years, the insurance premium of the most popular FHA single-family program, Sec. 203(b), was equal to .5 percent of the remaining mortgage balance, insurance that stayed in effect as long as the loan was outstanding. Since loan balances decline over time, FHA insurance costs also dropped each month.

Now, however, the FHA is using a different approach to insurance funding. Rather than paying a .5 percent premium on a monthly basis, the FHA requires instead a single, lump-sum insurance payment up front, an amount equal to 3.8 percent of the mortgage balance. With an $85,000 mortgage, for instance, the up-front fee would amount to $3,230. While a purchaser could pay this sum in cash at settlement, it's more likely that most buyers will opt to increase the size of their mortgage by the value of the up-front insurance fee and make somewhat higher monthly payments.

How does the new insurance payment plan compare with the old formula? If the FHA interest rate for a 30-year, $85,000 loan was 9.5 percent, the monthly payment would be $714.73. Add a 0.5 percent insurance fee and the effective cost to the borrower is 10 percent, or $745.94 the first month.

With the lump-sum program, a purchaser would most likely borrow $88,068. This amount is equal to the $85,000 mortgage plus 95 percent of the insurance fee, or $3,068. Not all of the insurance premium can be financed through the mortgage because 5 percent of the insurance fee must be paid in cash at settlement, a total of $153.40 in this case. At 9.5 percent interest, the buyer would pay $740.52 per month plus $153 extra up front—a minimal difference in the context of a house sale.

An important aspect of the up-front insurance premium is that borrowers who pre-pay their loans can apply for a partial premium refund. The size of the refund depends on the remaining number of years left on the note at the time of repayment.

Sec. 203(b) is designed to help families acquire real property by reducing down payment requirements. The basic down payment formula under Sec. 203(b) is 3 percent of the first $25,000 and 5 percent of the balance. With an $85,000 FHA mortgage the down payment would be $750 ($25,000 × 3 percent) plus $3,000 ($60,000 × 5 percent), or a total of $3,750. In this example, the down payment is equal to only 4.4 percent of the mortgage. (See Table 15.)

TABLE 15
FHA versus Conventional Financing

	FHA	Conventional
Loan size	$85,000	$85,000
Percent down	3% × 25,000	20 percent
	5% × 60,000	
Cash down	$3,750	$18,750
Loan term	30 years	30 years
Self-amortizing	Yes	Yes
Assumable	Yes	Not likely
Insurance fee	3.8 percent	None
Insurance cost	$3,230	None

Loans under Sec. 203(b) can be used to acquire not only single-family homes but also structures with two, three and four units as well. As the number of units increases, so does the base mortgage that the FHA will insure. As this is written, for instance, the basic limit for a single-family FHA 203(b) loan is

$67,500; $76,000 for a duplex; $92,000 for a three-unit structure; and $107,000 for a four-unit building. In areas with a higher base, perhaps $90,000 for a single-family loan, the maximum loan amounts for multiple-unit buildings would be greater.

When used for the purchase of multiple-unit buildings, FHA loans can be an attractive financing tool, particularly for individuals with limited capital. As an owner occupant, a purchaser can acquire property with only the most minimal down payment, thus preserving his or her capital for the repair and upgrading of the property. While occupant-owners can get FHA loans at established interest rates, non-occupant investors cannot get the FHA's preferential down payment terms. Instead, the FHA will permit investor loans equal to only 85 percent of the mortgage amount available to owner occupants.

To obtain FHA-backed loans buyers must be financially qualified and the property evaluated by an FHA-approved appraiser. If it is found that the FHA appraised value is less than the selling price, then either the sales price must be lowered or the purchaser must be willing to cover the difference in cash. The FHA will not permit the use of a second trust to bridge the difference between the sales price and the appraised value of the property. The FHA will permit the use of second trusts as long as the combined value of the first and second trusts does not top FHA loan limits or required loan-to-value ratios.

Like the VA program, FHA financing is a political product subject to the whims and wiles of Washington. In 1987, the President's budget proposal suggested raising the FHA up-front insurance premium from 3.8 percent to a full 5 percent. In addition, families with incomes greater than $40,000 per year would face stiffer down payment requirements.

Why these proposals? One reason is that the FHA program has had high foreclosure rates in recent years. Another reason is that many consider the FHA program a mere duplication of services readily available from the private sector. Given this last viewpoint, why should the FHA exist, much less make loans to middle- and upper-income borrowers?

The FHA program has enabled millions of people to buy homes, and even today, with thousands of loan sources throughout the country, the FHA continues to guarantee a large portion of all mortgages. Raising the insurance premium to 5 percent will drastically reduce demand for the FHA-backed loans, a situation which might then rationalize ending the entire program. Because politics are involved, however, it seems unlikely that the FHA program will be dismantled. A more likely scenario is that application standards will be toughened to favor low- and moderate-income borrowers while funding fees rise modestly.

(*Note to readers:* Check index as well as Appendix C for other specialized FHA loan programs, such as ARMs and graduated payment mortgages, which are discussed separately.)

Questions to ask:

What is the current FHA interest rate?

Are FHA interest rates set by the federal government or are they allowed to "float" with the market?

What is the current FHA loan limit for single-family housing under Sec. 203(b)?

What is the current FHA down payment schedule for Sec. 203(b) loans?

What is the current FHA insurance premium? Is it due at settlement?

If you do not want to pay the FHA insurance premium in cash at settlement can you get a larger loan? If you elect to finance the premium, how much will your mortgage increase? What portion of the premium can be financed through a larger mortgage? How much additional cash will you need at settlement to cover the FHA premium, since less than the full value of the premium can be financed?

If you are selling an FHA-financed property on which you have paid the premium up front, will the buyer give you a credit equal to the remaining value of the insurance premium when you sell?

How many points, if any, are lenders generally seeking for FHA 203(b) loans today? How many points, if any, are being charged for other FHA programs? Contact several local mortgage loan officers to compare costs.

Can you use a VA appraisal when seeking FHA financing?

Are FHA loans freely assumable, freely assumable only after two years, or not freely assumable at all? If FHA mortgages are not freely assumable, what qualifications must be met by a new borrower? How much will it cost to assume?

PRIVATE MORTGAGE INSURANCE (PMI)

There are hundreds of thousands of sales each year that would not occur except for the availability of FHA or VA financing, loan programs that provide financing with little or no money down. Yet FHA and VA programs are not for everyone. Many buyers are not VA qualified and a large portion of all home sales require more money than can be insured by the FHA.

The FHA and VA programs, however, are not the only sources of institutional mortgage assistance or even the largest. When the success or failure of a sale depends on a small down payment, many buyers turn to a unique financial product called *private mortgage insurance*, or *PMI*, as it is known in the real estate industry.

PMI is nothing more than the promise of a private insurer to repay a lender in the event a low down payment mortgage is in default. Without this promise a lender would not make a low down payment loan, because such financing represents an excessive level of risk.

If conventional financing is available at 10 percent interest with 20 percent down plus 2 points, conventional financing with PMI would also be available at 10 percent interest plus two points but with only 5, 10 or 15 percent down plus the PMI premium. It is the combination of conventional financing rates plus reduced down payments that make PMI loans popular. Indeed, in recent years more PMI loans have been issued than either FHA 203(b) mortgages or financing backed by the VA, and in some years more than both government programs combined.

Because interest rates for conventional and PMI mortgages are identical, there are no additional points to pay at settlement as is often the case with FHA or VA financing. And, unlike the VA program, PMI has no regulations which require sellers to pay all points. With PMI, deciding who pays points is a matter of negotiation.

The cost of private mortgage insurance is based on the size of the loan, the type of loan (fixed or variable payment), the type of policy, the length of coverage and the proportion of the property's value represented by the down payment.

Private mortgage insurance can be purchased on either an annual basis or as a multi-year policy. With annual policies, buyers pay premiums monthly on the remaining balance of the loan, whereas multi-year coverage is paid in a lump sum at settlement. Of the two policies, annual coverage is preferred by purchasers nearly 20 to 1.

For many years PMI premiums have been determined by the size of the down payment. A larger down payment means less risk to the lender, so there is a correspondingly lesser need for insurance coverage. With 10 percent down, for instance, there is usually 20 percent PMI coverage. With only 5 percent down, there is 25 percent insurance coverage. Thus if someone puts down 5 percent on an $85,000 property and has PMI coverage, the lender will be insured initially for at least $20,187.

In general, more coverage means larger premiums and that's exactly the case with private mortgage insurance. For fixed-rate loans with multi-year policies, figure a premium equal to 3.2 percent of the loan value if you put down only 5 percent, a 1.8 percent premium with 10 percent down, and a 1.65 percent premium with 15 percent down. For variable payment loans, the premiums are likely to be 3.9 percent of the total loan value if you put down only 5 percent, 2.35 percent for financing with 10 percent down, and a premium of 1.9 percent with a 15 percent down payment. Thus for a fixed-rate, 30-year $85,000 loan with 10 percent down, the up-front would be $1,530, or $1,955 for a variable payment loan of the same size.

For the vast majority who pay for PMI on the basis of their monthly balance, the rates might look like this: With 5 percent down, a typical PMI annual premium for a fixed-rate loan would be 1.25 percent the first year plus .44 percent for each renewal year. For an ARM, the rate would be 1.5 percent the first year and .54 each following year.

How often are the policies renewed? Since PMI is required by lenders as a condition of granting low down payment loans, and since lenders are the beneficiaries of such policies, lenders decide how long the policy will remain in force. In general terms, policies are usually in effect for seven years—fewer years during good times when property values rise and more years during rough times when properties are more difficult to sell.

In 1984, for the first time in 30 years, private mortgage insurers began seeking rates based not only on the size of a down payment but also according to whether or not the loan payments were fixed or variable. The reason, according to John Ochotnicky, a vice president with MGIC of Milwaukee, the nation's largest mortgage insurance firm, is that loans without fixed-payment schedules, such as ARMs and GPMs, represent more risk, 34.7 percent more risk to be exact, a figure based on a study of 30,000 loans.

The risk represented by the new loan formats can be divided into two problems for insurers: loans in default and delinquent mortgages. More defaults obviously means more claims while more delinquencies raises a different problem: a larger number of delinquencies are a sign of increased future claims, and so insurers must set aside additional reserves to protect against expected losses. More risk also means higher insurance rates, and that is exactly what has happened.

How does PMI insurance compare with FHA and VA coverage? The VA charges a simple 1 percent "funding fee" at settlement. The FHA has a funding fee, which depends on the term of the loan. For a 15-year loan, for instance, the funding fee would be 2.4 percent of the loan's value, payable at settlement. A 30-year mortgage would have an up-front funding fee equal to 3.8 percent of the total loan. These funding costs can, in some cases, be financed over the term of the mortgage.

Lenders are willing to accept a lower down payment with PMI-backed loans because they have less risk. If a PMI buyer defaults, the lender faces one of two choices, either of which is far more attractive than an uninsured foreclosure.

A PMI insurer may pay off the entire loan and thus gain title to the property. This happens in 30 to 40 percent of all PMI defaults.

Alternatively, the insurer will pay 20 to 25 percent of the total claim. The "total claim" can include not only the outstanding mortgage balance but also such items as accrued interest, foreclosure costs, attorney's fees, and property tax payments made after the loan is in default.

It may seem that with only 20 or 25 percent PMI coverage that the lender would still have considerable financial exposure but this is not the case.

First, the original size of the loan was less than the sales value

TABLE 16
Insurance Premiums Compared for 30-Year Financing

	PMI	FHA	VA
Loan size	$85,000	$85,000	$85,000
Down payment	$ 4,250 (5 percent)	$ 3,750	None
	$ 8,500 (10 percent)		
	$12,750 (15 percent)		
Up-front premiums (fixed-rate loan)		$ 3,230	$ 850
5 percent down	$ 2,720.00		
10 percent down	$ 1,530.00		
15 percent down	$ 1,402.50		
Up-front premiums (variable rate loan)		$ 3,230	$ 850
5 percent down	$ 3,315.00		
10 percent down	$ 1,997.50		
15 percent down	$ 1,615.00		

As an alternative to up-front, lump-sum payments, most PMI borrowers pay their premiums on a monthly basis. Here is a typical PMI premium schedule.

	Fixed Rate	Variable Rate
Down payment	5 percent	5 percent
Coverage	25 percent	25 percent
First-year premium	1.25 percent	1.50 percent
Renewal rate	.44 percent	.54 percent
Down payment	10 percent	10 percent
Coverage	20 percent	20 percent
First-year premium	.50 percent	.60 percent
Renewal rate	.34 percent	.54 percent
Down payment	15 percent	15 percent
Coverage	17 percent	17 percent
First-year premium	.35 percent	.35 percent
Renewal rate	.34 percent	.39 percent

of the property. The difference between the loan amount and the selling price is represented by the purchaser's down payment.

Second, over time the buyer has paid down the original loan balance with each monthly payment, except in the case of negative amortization loans where the value of the principal balance actually increases over time. As the principal balance declines, the proportion of the property's worth represented by the outstanding mortgage balance declines as does the level of the lender's risk.

Third, there is the possibility that the value of the property has increased over time. Again, as the gap between the loan balance and the market value of the property is enlarged, the lender has less risk.

Fourth, the property has a foreclosure value which may be equal or greater than the outstanding loan balance plus related costs. If the foreclosure value covers 100 percent of the money due to the lender, then the lender would have no claim against a private mortgage insurer. If the foreclosure value fell short of the amount of money due to the lender, then the lender could make a claim against the insurer up to the value of the policy.

Although a private mortgage insurance premium is paid by the real estate purchaser, the lender is the beneficiary of the policy and determines whether or not it will be continued. This feature, as well as several others, makes private mortgage insurance and the companies which offer such policies unique. Here's why:

- Although real estate buyers pay the premiums, private mortgage insurance agreements are actually contracts between lenders and insurers. A common provision of such agreements is that lenders must foreclose when monthly payments are four months behind.
- Private mortgage insurance premiums are established at the time a policy is issued and may not be changed.
- Private mortgage insurance may be canceled only in the event of fraud or unpaid premiums.

- Private mortgage insurance is not sold through general insurance brokers. Instead, policies are marketed directly to lenders who then make such policies available to borrowers as a condition of granting a loan. Lenders may not collect a sales commission for the placement of private mortgage insurance.

- PMI helps lenders re-sell loans in the secondary mortgage market, an important consideration for lenders who continually roll over funds to make new mortgages. Because of the substantial reserves private mortgage insurers are required to maintain, PMI-backed loans are regarded as secure mortgage investments. Secondary lenders such as Fannie Mae, Freddie Mac and private pension funds have bought millions of conventional loans backed with private mortgage insurance—estimated purchases worth $35 billion in a recent year.

- Private mortgage insurers benefit from high inflation rates. The reason: inflation reduces the worth of the dollar, so it takes more cash dollars to acquire a given piece of real estate. Since mortgages are valued in terms of cash dollars, it follows that mortgage insurers face fewer claims as property values rise, regardless of whether or not the increase in value is a product of inflation or real economic appreciation.

Private mortgage insurance is often mistaken for *mortgage life insurance*, a different product. Mortgage life insurance is designed to protect purchasers if they are unable to pay their mortgage as a result of disability or death.

Mortgage life insurance is available through many lenders as well as general insurance agencies. Policies obtained through lenders often name the lender as the beneficiary, while policies placed through brokers allow the buyer to select the beneficiary. For further information about costs and coverage, speak to both lenders and insurance brokers.

Questions to ask:

How much cash down is required?

What is the current premium for the first year of a private mortgage insurance policy and for each renewal year thereafter for loans with 5 percent down, 10 percent down and 15 percent down?

If buying a multi-year policy, how many years of coverage will the lender require? What is the one-time cost of a multi-year PMI policy? Can you add this expense to the mortgage amount you are seeking?

What is the lender's general policy on renewing PMI mortgage coverage? How many years can you expect to pay a premium?

As a condition of obtaining a mortgage, does the lender require the purchaser to place any money in an escrow account to assure that PMI premiums are paid? If so, how much?

EQUITY-SHARING

It is not always so easy to classify mortgages, and equity-sharing agreements are not mortgages in the sense of FHA or conventional loans; yet they can be regarded as a form of assisted financing. Regardless of how they're defined, they're great for families who want to buy property together, and investors may use them also. Here's how they work.

Equity-sharing is an arrangement in which at least two people hold title to a given property. One, the "equity" or "money" investor, puts up part of the cash or credit needed for acquisition but does not live on the property. The second person uses the property as his or her principal residence and also pays in capital to participate in the investment.

Because equity-sharing arrangements are often made within families or between friends one is tempted to classify such financing solely as an assisted loan, something akin to a gift. However, while equity-sharing agreements can be structured so they are extremely favorable to one party or the other, they clearly involve an ownership interest and offer the possibility of profit based on economic appreciation, tax advantages and equity accumulation—benefits not enjoyed by true lenders or by the FHA, VA or private mortgage insurers.

Also, at first glance, it may seem as though there is little which makes equity-sharing arrangements new or different from earlier investment ideas but this is not the case.

For example, equity-sharing deals differ from an earlier concept, the "Shared Appreciation Mortgage" (SAM). With a SAM loan, the lender traded an interest discount for an ownership interest in the property. Suppose interest rates were 10 percent. A lender under a SAM loan might cut the rate by 40 percent to 6 percent, a level which would be a positive bargain. In exchange, the lender would get a 40 percent interest in the property. When the property was sold the lender would share in the profits.

SAM loans, however, are rare today for several reasons.

First, lenders must pay interest on the money they loan. If you pay 6 percent on funds that a lender could lend at 10 percent, the lender has to make up the difference somewhere or lose out on the deal.

Second, there is no guarantee that the value of the property will rise and therefore there is no guarantee of any appreciation to share. If the value of the property remains level or drops the lender will get back his principal but not interest at a market rate.

Third, oddly enough, if the value of the property skyrockets upward a lender could have usury problems. After all, regulated lenders may be prohibited from receiving returns above a certain level and a really profitable deal may be viewed as "unconscionable."

Equity-sharing arrangements are feasible today because of a

recent change in tax regulations. In the past, when two or more people owned property and one resided at the site, no owner could claim a tax loss even if costs greatly exceeded income. With equity-sharing, the non-resident owner can claim a loss and thus reduce taxable income generally.

As an example, imagine that the Franklins and their son, Franklin Junior, agree to purchase an $85,000 house. A $10,000 down payment is required, of which the Franklins contribute $8,000 and their son pays the remainder. The son also agrees to reside at the property and pay a fair market rental. The ownership of the property is then divided equally in this case. (See Table 17.)

TABLE 17
The Franklins' Equity-Sharing Arrangement

	Franklins	Franklin Junior
Down payment	$8,000	$2,000
Payment to lender, repairs, etc.	$500	$500
Payment to Franklins		$500
Total monthly rental		$1,000
Ownership	50 percent	50 percent

The property has a fair market rental of $1,000 per month. The cash costs of the property are also $1,000 for mortgage payments, taxes, etc. Here's how the deal works:

- Franklin Junior pays $500 per month to his parents as rent, since they own 50 percent of the property. He also pays $500 per month directly to the lender for the mortgage and taxes.
- The Franklins receive $500 per month from their son. They then pay the lender $500 per month.
- At the end of the year the Franklins report a taxable rental income of $6,000 (12 × $500). They also deduct 50 percent of all costs for which they are liable and that they actually

pay, including mortgage interest, taxes, repairs, condo and co-op fees. In addition, they get a depreciation credit. The result is a significant tax loss.

- Franklin Junior claims deductions for 50 percent of the mortgage interest and taxes he actually pays and for which he is liable. However, because he resides on the property he cannot claim depreciation, repair, condo or co-op deductions.
- The investors' equity in the property increases as they make monthly mortgage payments. Hopefully, their equity also increases as a result of rising values.
- When the property is sold the profits will be divided according to the ownership interest of each party.

The new equity-sharing rules, according to IRS spokesman Wilson Fadely, were devised to help families buy property together. However it is not too difficult to envision a situation in which potential residential investors such as young families, retirees, college students and others will seek equity investors to assist in a real estate purchase.

Indeed, one can see real estate brokers putting equity and resident investors together and then selling them suitable properties. Not only are the tax shelter possibilities attractive, but the problem of rental management is neatly resolved since there is no need to search for a tenant.

Whether an equity-sharing arrangement is a family affair or a pure investment it is clear that a written understanding between the parties should be developed by a knowledgeable attorney.

Questions to ask:

How much cash down is required from each party?
What is the percentage of ownership of each party? Note

that the percentage of ownership does not have to be related to the cash contribution of the equity investor.

What are the responsibilities of the resident partner in terms of maintenance and upkeep?

How much notice must the resident investor give before moving out?

How will a fair market rental be established? How will rent increases, if any, be determined?

How are disputes to be resolved? Many business agreements contain a binding arbitration clause so that in the event of conflict a neutral party can resolve the issue without going to court.

What rights will each party have to buy out the other?

In addition to having a written agreement prepared by a lawyer, investors should also speak with a CPA or tax attorney to assure that all tax rules and requirements have been addressed. Also, of all things, each investor will need an appropriate will so that potential probate problems are avoided.

11
Alternative Mortgages from A to Z

Hardly a day passes without the introduction of a "new" loan format, yet the reality is that very few loan ideas represent a quantum leap beyond the current frontiers of finance. Instead most "new" loans are variations of older, core ideas.

While it is not practical to examine the endless variety of possible loan alternatives, it is feasible to review the central concepts of given loan formats. For instance, there may be 500 slightly different ARM loan variations built around a single basic concept. One can look at that concept and have a basic idea of how each variation works.

To fully understand the variation, however, it is necessary to know something more than the core idea. Rather than having a guide which would be quickly dated and forever incomplete, we have instead chosen to first describe central lending concepts and then provide checklists which can be used to understand and compare individual plans.

ARM LOANS

Tea leaves, tarot cards and a crystal ball may not seem to have much in common with something as mundane as a fixed-rate mortgage but in a sense they are all used to predict the future. If you get a 30-year loan at 10 percent interest a lender is betting that his cost of funds will stay far enough below 10 percent so that he can profit for the next three decades.

What makes the lender's calculations tricky is that while you have a 30-year debt at a known rate, he doesn't. Instead the lender borrows money on a short-term basis and at short-term rates from such sources as savings accounts and certificates of deposit to underwrite long-term mortgages.

Since the future has a way of being unpredictable, many lenders are trying to get out of the prophesy business by offering adjustable rate mortgages (ARMs), loans where interest rates, monthly payments and principal balances can vary. These loans now represent an important alternative to fixed-rate financing, an alternative which can be the best available choice for certain borrowers.

What is an ARM? If ARMs are good for lenders can they also be good for borrowers? Here's how they work:

Interest. The initial rate of interest is generally below conventional financing levels because borrowers, and not lenders, are now penalized by inflation. Lower initial interest rates mean that buyers can qualify more easily for ARM financing, a major advantage. The initial interest rate can be in effect for as long as several years or as little time as a month.

After the initial rate lapses, interest is then computed on the basis of an index over which the lender has no control, perhaps the weekly average yield on three-year U.S. Treasury securities plus a margin amount. If the index is at 8 percent and the margin amount—a sum added to the index—is 2 percent, then the initial interest rate would be 10 percent. If the index rose to 9 percent, the ARM rate would go up to 11 percent.

Rate Changes. Depending how the loan is written a lender may have the right to change the interest rate as often as every month. This is highly unusual, however, and it is more likely that the lender will be allowed to change the rate only once every several months or once a year. The fact that the interest rate changes does not necessarily mean that monthly *payments* will rise, however, since payment changes may be restricted to once a year, once every six months or whatever.

Rate Caps.   An ARM may provide for an absolute cap on the maximum interest rate that can be charged. Conversely, there is likely to be an interest rate minimum.

Monthly Payments.   ARMs often have set monthly payments for a given period, say one year, two years or five years.

But suppose monthly payments remain stable for three years, yet during this time the interest rates rise. How does the lender get the extra dollars to which he is entitled?

The way some ARMs work is that unpaid interest is added to the principal balance of the mortgage, thus creating "negative amortization" or "deferred interest." Conversely, should the interest rate drop, the mortgage balance would be reduced at an accelerated rate.

Principal Cap.   If there is a payment cap that holds down monthly costs it is possible that the mortgage balance could grow regularly over a period of years. A lender does not want to have an endlessly rising mortgage on the books, so a principal cap is usually established, perhaps 125 percent of the original loan balance. If the original amount of the loan was $90,000 and the balance rose to $112,500 over many years because of negative amortization, the borrower would have to make a lump-sum payment to keep below the cap, refinance the property with another loan or sell.

Loan Term.   Because it is possible that the size of the loan balance may increase, many ARM loans have a built-in extension provision. With the approval of the lender, it is usually possible to extend the loan term from 30 to 40 years. The advantage of a loan extension is that it may eliminate the need to refinance the property.

Prepayment.   Since ARM loans reflect current interest costs, a lender will not lose money if a loan is repaid early. For this reason, ARMs may commonly be repaid in whole or in part without penalty.

Assumptions.   Since ARM rates reflect current market trends a lender is not in the position of having a long-term, 10 percent loan underwritten with 12 percent, short-term financing. For this reason, ARMs are generally assumable by qualified buyers.

With all its specialized provisions and clauses an ARM may seem unusually complex. In practice, however, such loans are not hard to follow. Here's an example:

Willoughby is looking for an $85,000 mortgage. A local lender offers either a 10 percent, 30-year conventional mortgage or an ARM with an initial interest rate of 7.5 percent. The initial conditions of the mortgage include a 30-year term and an interest rate two points above the average weekly yield for three-year U.S. Treasury bills, an index published in most major newspapers.

It is agreed that Willoughby's initial monthly payment of $594.33 will remain level for two years and that the lender can change the monthly payment only once every two years thereafter. If the payment is going to change, the lender must give thirty days' notice to Willoughby.

Willoughby and the lender also agree to several caps. The monthly payments cannot be raised more than 15 percent at any one time. The maximum interest rate will be 12.5 percent and the minimum will be 6 percent. In the event of negative amortization, the loan term may be extended to 40 years if the lender agrees.

After two years the index, fueled by inflation, rises, and the new interest rate is 10 percent. Willoughby's monthly payment is increased by the maximum, 15 percent, and his payment is now $683.48. However, this amount is less than Willoughby should pay with a 10 percent interest rate, and unpaid interest is added to the loan balance.

Two years later inflation is conquered (at least for the moment) and the index falls to 4 percent. That rate, plus the margin, mean Willoughby is now paying 6 percent interest for his loan. Willoughby's monthly payments drop 15 percent to $580.96 ($683.48 less 15 percent [$102.52] equals $580.96).

Not only have Willoughby's payments dropped below his original monthly costs but he is now paying off the negative amortization that occurred in the last two years. If all the negative amortization is repaid he will also begin to repay the original loan principal at a faster rate than a self-amortizing loan would permit. (See Table 18.)

TABLE 18
Mr. Willoughby's ARM versus 10 Percent Conventional Loan

	ARM	Conventional
Loan amount	$85,000	$85,000
Loan term	30 to 40 years	30 years
Initial interest	7.5 percent	10 percent
Initial monthly payments, years one and two	$594.33	$745.94
Monthly payments years 3–30	Variable	$745.94
Frequency of payment changes	2 years	None
Maximum interest	12.5 percent	10 percent
Minimum interest	6 percent	10 percent
Possible negative amortization	Yes	No
Self-amortization guaranteed	No	Yes

In the same way that the cobra and the mongoose are natural enemies, so too are inflation and fixed-rate loans. When the buying power of paper money drops—when it takes three dollars to buy groceries worth two dollars—the value of fixed-rate mortgages also drops.

Adjustable rate mortgages effectively shift the burden of inflation from the lender to the borrower. With an ARM, the interest rate of a loan will rise with inflation, thus preserving the lender's buying power.

ARMs are generally enticing to borrowers because they feature low initial interest rates: say 7.5 percent at a time when conventional loans are available at 10 percent interest. In particular, during periods when interest rates are high, ARMs may well be the best available financing for two reasons: First, with a low initial interest rate an ARM will represent below-market financing at a time when most buyers may not qualify for conventional loans; second, ARM borrowers are not eternally committed to the high interest rates that are in place at the time they make their loans. ARM costs can fall once high market rates pass.

Consider the example of an astute buyer who gets 7.5 percent ARM financing for an $85,000 loan when 30-year conventional loans are not available for less than 10 percent. The 7.5 percent rate is guaranteed for one year, and, after that, interest levels can rise only 2 percent per year. There is a 12.5 percent interest cap on the loan and a 6 percent interest minimum.

One year later conventional loans are still at 10 percent while the ARM rate has risen to 9.5 percent. Even though the cost of the loan has increased, the ARM borrower is still far ahead of the buyer with a fixed-rate loan. Despite the increased monthly expense, here's where the buyer benefited:

- At 7.5 percent interest computed on a 30-year basis, the ARM borrower paid $594.33 per month in the first year or a total of $7,131.96. In the second year, with the interest cost at 9.5 percent, the borrower paid $714.73 per month or $8,576.71. In comparison, a 10 percent fixed-rate loan cost $745.94 per month or a total of $17,902.46 over two years. The ARM buyer paid a total of $15,708.67 ($7,131.96 + $8,576.71). The difference: a savings of $2,193.79.

- The purchaser was able to acquire property in a high-interest, buyer's market—a time when few people qualify for financing because mortgage rates are steep. This means the buyer had a substantial negotiating advantage which potentially could be translated into a lower selling price and thus a smaller mortgage than might otherwise have been possible.
- Only when ARM rates go above 10 percent does the purchaser suffer when compared to others who bought with fixed-rate loans at the same time.
- The ARM borrower had far lower initial monthly mortgage costs and thus qualified for a larger loan than his income would otherwise have allowed.
- If ARM rates drop below 7.5 percent, the ARM borrower will actually see a decrease in monthly costs.
- The people who got conventional loans at 10 percent did not benefit when rates dropped a year later. To pay less interest they would have to refinance their property—an expensive proposition with new settlement costs, title fees, etc. Conversely, conventional borrowers will not be hurt if interest rates go above 10 percent. Indeed, relative to then-current borrowers, folks with 10 percent fixed-rate financing will look both wise and prosperous while people with ARM loans may face far higher monthly costs than were anticipated.

While one can construct situations in which ARMs represent favorable financing, there are many times when ARMs are simply inappropriate. For example, if ARM and fixed-rate financing are available at the same rates the fixed-rate mortgage is arguably the better deal because it places the burden of inflation on the lender. ARMs that permit monthly payment changes should be avoided, since they play havoc with personal budgets.

In addition, while ARMs clearly have a place in the mortgage market—especially when rates are steep—they raise serious issues with which borrowers—and lenders—should be concerned.

First, ARM borrowers cannot anticipate mortgage costs over the life of their loans. Not only are payments subject to change, but if negative amortization is allowed it is entirely possible that the loan will not be paid off in 30 years. ARMs thus make personal financial planning far more difficult than fixed-rate loans. With an ARM, one cannot count on having the mortgage paid off by the time Junior goes to college.

Second, ARMs do not guarantee lender profits. What ARMs do, at best, is shield lenders from the worst effects of inflation and limit losses. Since lender profits are based on the difference between all income and all expenses—how much it costs to borrow money on a short-term basis plus all other business charges such as rent, salaries, etc.—it is entirely possible that a lender's cost of funds could rise above mortgage portfolio returns and thus create losses.

Third, since the whole ARM structure is based on an index it is important to determine which measure is used to set interest rates. In general terms, the longer the span of events being measured the less volatile the index. Thus borrowers should greatly prefer an index based on the weekly average of five-year U.S. Treasury securities adjusted to a constant yield rather than daily stock averages.

Fourth, lenders may have less security with ARM financing than is now believed. If indexes rise substantially it is possible that many ARM borrowers will be unable to meet monthly payments and wholesale foreclosures could ensue. The ability to foreclose in such times may be of limited value, since few people will be able to buy housing. Lenders who do foreclose—in addition to having a considerable public relations problem—may find that they control properties that can be sold only at steep discounts.

Fifth, the opportunity to own a home is one of the most

sensitive political matters existent. If ARMs result, or are perceived to result, in an excessive number of foreclosures one would expect to see immediate regulatory and statutory restrictions.

Sixth, ARMs are likely to supplement but not replace fixed-rate, conventional financing. Fixed-rate financing is important to pension fund managers, who need investments with predictable returns. Each year pensions buy mortgages worth billions of dollars through secondary lenders, so there is a continuing demand for fixed-rate loan products. That demand, in turn, means that fixed-rate financing will remain available in local communities.

When ARMs were first introduced every lender seemed to have a different loan product. Like snowflakes, no two were alike.

The problem with thousands of different loan formats is that it is impossible to sell such loans to secondary lenders such as Fannie Mae. Standardized loan products are easy to evaluate and price whereas non-standard loans are not. Moreover, non-standard products are usually produced in small numbers, which means they are not available in the quantities big buyers demand.

Now with some experience in hand standardized ARM loans are available nationwide. These loans represent more of a compromise between the interests of borrowers and lenders than early ARMs, loans that completely favored lenders in most cases.

In addition to standardized ARM loans hybrid financing has begun to emerge. Already, for instance, a "convertible adjustable rate mortgage" allows the borrower to have a loan that initially acts like ARM financing. After a given period, say three years or five years, the borrower can opt to continue the adjustable format or convert to fixed-rate financing at the then-current rate. The "convertible adjustable rate mortgage" ARM offers features that both borrowers and lenders want and represents a compromise of interests.

Another approach is the graduated payment adjustable rate mortgage, or GPARM. A GPARM is essentially a loan with two phases. In the first phase, perhaps five years, monthly payments are initially set at a low figure. This low monthly payment, plus the initial below-market rates usually associated with ARMs, allow more buyers to qualify for financing.

Each year the payment level is raised by a set amount, say 7.5 percent. Also, while payments are rising but known in advance, interest costs are determined by an index. There is negative amortization during this first phase which is added to the loan balance.

In the second phase, a GPARM behaves like a regular ARM. Depending on how the loan is negotiated, the payments may remain steady for given intervals, one to five years, but interest costs will fluctuate with an index. When the monthly payments are scheduled to change they may be adjusted up or down.

Perhaps the least known yet most interesting ARM has been one developed by the FHA. While not widely accepted by lenders because of its original 1 percent annual payment cap, the FHA ARM offers several interesting features:

- Interest costs could rise or fall 1 percent yearly.
- The maximum interest rate cannot rise or fall more than 5 percent over the initial rate.
- FHA ARM loan rates are based on an index selected by the government, most likely a floating weekly average for 1-year Treasury securities.
- Maximum loan limits are the same as those established under the basic 203(b) program.
- Negative amortization is not permitted.
- The loans can be prepaid in whole or in part without penalty.

- The loans are freely assumable at current rates.
- In a demonstration program, the FHA was authorized to issue as many as 43,000 mortgages nationwide—loans with a potential aggregate value of more than $3.5 billion.

Whether the FHA ARM program will continue is an open question. The FHA program now largely duplicates private-sector financing and may no longer be necessary. Conversely, the FHA program has been a model for private lenders, an alternative which has caused ARM mortgage sources to modify and moderate their terms.

Because there are so many potential ARM formats borrowers should carefully compare programs offered by local lenders. With ARMs, it is not enough to know interest rates, down payment terms or initial monthly payment costs.

Questions to ask:

What is the current interest level for fixed-rate, conventional financing?

How much cash down is required?

What is the initial interest rate for an ARM?

What is the initial monthly payment?

How long does the initial interest rate last?

How long does the initial monthly payment last?

How frequently can the lender change the monthly payment?

How often can the lender adjust the interest rate?

Is there a cap that limits the size of each payment change?

Is there a limit on the dollar amount to which the monthly payment can be reduced at each change?

How much notice must the lender give before each payment change?

What index is used to adjust the interest level?

What is the margin above the index rate?

Is there a cap on the amount by which the interest charge can be raised at each change?

Is there a cap on the loan's maximum interest? Is there an interest minimum?

If the monthly mortgage payment is insufficient to reduce the mortgage principal balance, is negative amortization permitted?

Relative to the original mortgage principal, how much negative amortization is allowed? That is, can the mortgage balance grow to 105 percent of the original balance, 110 percent, 125 percent, etc.?

If you have negative amortization, can the loan term be extended? If so, to how many years?

Is a loan extension guaranteed or is any extension at the option of the lender?

Are there extension fees that must be paid to the lender? If so, how much?

Will the lender refinance the property if you reach the negative amortization limit? If so, are any terms, such as maximum interest levels, guaranteed in advance?

Do you have the right to pre-pay the loan in whole or in part without penalty?

Is the loan assumable by a qualified buyer?

BLEND LOANS: HOW TO FINANCE AND REFINANCE AT DISCOUNT

Many borrowers believe they are at the mercy of the market when it comes time to negotiate loan rates. While this may be true generally it is not accurate in all cases.

If you've got a loan with an ancient interest rate you've got leverage. Lenders want to dump old financing, particularly low-rate mortgages that can be assumed, and that means they would like to get your loan off the books. In many instances lenders will encourage you to trade in your old, low-interest, low-balance mortgage for a new loan with higher interest and more principal. However, while the interest rate on the new financing may be higher than your current rate, it will be less than the going market rate.

What if Mr. Rivera has an assumable mortgage with an 8 percent interest rate and a $45,000 principal balance. The loan has 10 years to go. Current interest rates are 10 percent.

Rivera wants to add a $25,000 addition to his house and he could get the extra money with a new mortgage for $70,000 ($45,000 plus $25,000) or a $25,000 second trust. Another approach would be a $70,000 wraparound loan.

However, what Mr. Rivera would really like is a 30-year loan but at something less than 10 percent interest. So he makes the following agreement with the lender: Rivera will give up his old assumable loan if the lender will give him new, 30-year financing worth $70,000 at 9 percent interest—a "blended" rate below market interest levels but above the old rate on Rivera's current financing. Since the lender wants to purge his books of Rivera's loan, he agrees to the deal.

Note that a blend loan and a wraparound mortgage are essentially the same concept. The major difference is that with blend financing the original loan is wiped off the books, while with a wraparound agreement the old mortgage is retained—usually to the discomfort of the original lender.

Negotiating a blend loan is a contest between borrowers and lenders, and whoever has the better position wins. Sometimes the "better position" is a matter of perception rather than reality. Here are three advantages borrowers need to get the best refinancing deals:

First, the interest rate on old financing must be well below current mortgage levels.

Second, the original loan may or may not be assumable but you will have a much stronger position if the loan can be assumed.

Third, you cannot be dependent on the lender for financing. If you *need* money the lender will have little incentive to offer a bargain rate. This means if you are financing or refinancing you must have alternatives that do not require the repayment of a current loan. Such alternatives might include cash on hand, second trusts, wraparound loans or personal credit.

In those cases where borrowers want a blended rate to buy rather than refinance, the situation is somewhat different.

To start, the current financing must be freely assumable at its original rate and terms. If a loan is not freely assumable the lender has no incentive to bargain. Look for FHA, VA and older conventional loans to meet this requirement.

In addition, the purchaser must demonstrate to the lender that it is possible to acquire the property without disturbing the original loan. This could occur if the seller or third party takes back a second trust or wraparound loan or the buyer can pay cash above the current financing. In essence, if the old loan is assumable and the buyer is not dependent on the lender for financing, then blend loans may be a practical, and money-saving, home financing alternative.

Questions to ask:

What is the remaining loan balance?
What is the interest rate on present financing?
Is the current loan freely assumable?
What are the current monthly payments?
How much additional cash do you need?
What is the current interest rate for conventional financing?

Are local lenders making wraparound mortgages and second trusts? If so, how does a blend loan arrangement compare with a wraparound deal or a combination of the old financing plus a new second trust?

What fees and points will the lender charge in a blend deal? Note that these costs, like interest, are negotiable.

BUY-DOWNS

When interest rates soar, owners are often stuck with unsalable properties. Even though properties are not moving, however, interest costs accrue, taxes continue and owners want to sell as quickly as possible to preserve their profits.

With a buy-down, someone other than the borrower pays a portion of the mortgage, thus making properties more affordable. In effect, buy-downs are a subsidy. When times are tough and properties don't move it is the seller who pays for the buy-down.

Suppose prevailing interest rates are 12 percent and builder Thompson has unsold houses priced at $106,250. With interest rates so high, payments for a 30-year, $85,000 loan total $874.32 monthly. To qualify for such financing, a buyer must make $37,470 yearly if a lender will allocate no more than 28 percent of the purchaser's income for principal and interest payments.

Thompson is paying interest on his construction loans, prime plus two points, 14 percent in this case. He figures it's better to sell the properties at discount than hold on and pay construction loan interest, so he offers this deal: he will pay $100 per month for the first 36 months of ownership to any buyer. (Alternatively, Thompson could pay points to a lender to bring monthly costs down. Whether he pays the buyer or lender directly is not important—the significant idea for borrowers is that their loan costs are being subsidized.)

With monthly payments down to $774.32, an income of $33,-

185 is now required for financing worth $85,000. The effective initial interest rate, at least to the buyer, is just above 10 percent. The lender, however, is being paid the full amount due for a 12 percent loan, $874.32 in this case ($774.32 from the buyer and $100 per month from Thompson).

With lower monthly costs Thompson soon sells one of the remaining units but he must pay out $3,600 (36 × $100) for the buy-down but his actual cost is somewhat less. The reason: he doesn't pay all the money up front. Instead he deposits or invests the money and collects interest.

The second house is sold differently. The buyers, Mr. and Mrs. Poppin, want Thompson to apply the $3,600 buy-down as a credit against the purchase price, bringing the cost down to $102,650. The 20 percent down payment will drop from $21,250 to $20,530—a $720 saving. The mortgage will also drop, from $85,000 to $82,120. A 30-year, $82,120 mortgage at 12 percent interest will require monthly payments of $844.70 and an annual income of $36,200.

During the first three years of ownership the buy-down saves $70.38 per month ($844.70 less $774.32) or $2,533.68 over 36 months when compared to the lower-price arrangement negotiated by the Poppins. However, since the Poppins paid $720 less at closing, the buy-down's true benefit is just $1,813.68. Or is it?

After the first three years the numbers change rapidly. Now the Poppins' mortgage is lower by $29.62 per month, $844.70 versus $874.32. If they own their home another 62 months ($1,813.68 divided by $29.62 equals 61.23) the two deals will be equal—at least in the sense of total mortgage payments to date. After 62 months, the Poppins pull ahead by nearly $30 with each payment.

The Poppins, however, don't need to wait five years to benefit from their decision. By taking a price reduction rather than a buy-down, they've owed $2,880 less to the lender from the day they bought the house. (See Table 19.)

TABLE 19
Buy-down Comparison Chart

	Buy-down	Discounted Sale	Conventional Loan
Sales price	$106,250	$102,650	$106,250
Loan size	$85,000	$82,120	$85,000
Down payment	$21,250	$20,530	$21,250
Monthly buy-down	$100	None	None
Effective interest rate			
Years 1–3	10 percent	12 percent	12 percent
Years 4–30	12 percent	12 percent	12 percent
Monthly buyer payments			
Years 1–3	$774.32	$844.70	$874.32
Years 4–30	$874.32	$844.70	$874.32
Projected interest cost	$226,155	$221,972	$229,755
Potential buyer savings	$3,600	$7,783	None
Qualifying income	$33,185	$36,201	$37,471

Buy-downs are not restricted to any term—one could have a buy-down for the entire length of the loan. However, if the numbers are right, even a short-term buy-down can be a good deal. For example, if you had a five-year buy-down but only intended to own the property three years because of a business relocation, then a buy-down could be attractive.

When considering a buy-down it always pays to review a sale to see if the deal would be better by simply discounting the purchase price. While a buy-down is certainly a better deal than conventional financing, it may be less attractive than a simple discount. When comparing discounts versus buy-downs you must gauge the size of the monthly payment you can afford and consider how long you expect to hold the property. In general, if you have the income, short-term buy-downs go well with short-term ownership; discounts go well with long-term ownership.

Questions to ask:

What is the current rate of interest for conventional financing?

What is the effective rate of a loan with a buy-down provision?

How much cash down is required?

How long will the buy-down remain in effect?

What is the total value of the buy-down?

If the buy-down is to be a monthly mortgage supplement, what happens if the builder or owner goes bankrupt? Is there any requirement to set aside buy-down funds in an escrow account?

If buy-down funds are to be held in escrow who gets the interest? If you are the purchaser you should certainly argue that it belongs to you.

If the value of the buy-down is applied to the sales price of the property, how would down payment, mortgage size, monthly payments and income qualification standards change?

How long do you expect to own the property?

Is the loan assumable by a qualified buyer at its original rate and terms?

Can the loan be prepaid in whole or in part without penalty?

FLIP, OR INTEREST-ONLY, LOANS

While *zero-interest plan,* or ZIP, loans eliminate all interest payments, *front-loaded interest-only plan,* or FLIP, loans take a completely different tack. With a FLIP loan you pay interest but no principal—at least at first.

FLIP loans are reliable, conservative mortgages which fill a niche in the financing market. They offer a fixed interest rate, a known payment schedule and the advantage of marginally lower initial monthly payments.

FLIP loans are typically written so they have two phases. In the first phase, usually 3 to 5 years, the borrower makes monthly payments equal to interest only. During the balance of the loan term, phase two, the payments are sufficiently large to have a self-amortizing loan. However, since phase two is usually 25 to 27 years long, the payments are larger than for a 30-year, fixed-rate mortgage.

Here is how a conventional mortgage would compare with a FLIP loan if the interest-only first phase of the FLIP mortgage was for five years. The principal in both cases is $85,000 and the rate of interest is 10 percent.

Conventional Mortgage: 360 payments of $745.94 with a total interest cost over 30 years of $183,537.

FLIP Mortgage: 60 payments of $708.33 or a total first-phase interest cost of $42,500 plus 300 payments of $772.40 for a total of $231,720. Total payments: $274,220. This sum, less the $85,000 principal, leaves a total interest cost of $189,220. (See Table 20.)

TABLE 20
FLIP versus Conventional Financing

	FLIP	Conventional
Loan size	$85,000	$85,000
Loan term	30 years	30 years
Interest rate	10 percent	10 percent
Monthly payments		
Years 1–5	$708.33	$745.94
Years 6–30	$772.40	$745.94
Total interest	$189,220	$183,537
Balloon payment	None	None

When compared to conventional financing, then, FLIP mortgages require marginally more interest ($5,683) over 30 years.

However, since FLIP loans have smaller up-front monthly payments, buyers who would not otherwise qualify for conventional mortgages may be able to get financing.

If a lender will only allow an individual to use 28 percent of his or her gross (pre-tax) income for principal and interest payments, it means that an income of $26,641.07 would be required to get the $85,000 conventional loan described above. The FLIP financing, with its lower initial payments, would require a gross annual income of $25,297.50—a difference of only $1,343.57 per year.

During periods when interest rates are high and lenders strictly enforce income qualification standards, a FLIP loan could be the difference between home ownership and renting for a marginally qualified purchaser. When compared to conventional financing, FLIP loans should also be considered by individuals who expect to own property for a relatively short time, say three to five years, or who anticipate higher incomes that will make larger mortgage payments easier to handle in the future.

Questions to ask:

What is the interest rate for conventional financing?

How much cash down is required?

What is the interest rate for a FLIP loan?

How long is the interest-only phase?

What are the monthly payments during the interest-only phase?

How long is the amortization period when principal payments are being made?

What are the monthly payments during the amortization period?

Can the loan be prepaid in whole or in part without penalty?

Can the loan be assumed by a qualified buyer?

GRADUATED PAYMENT MORTGAGES (GPMS)

Most of us enter the work force with the thought that our incomes will rise over time. Unfortunately we often buy real estate long before we enter our peak earning years, a situation that creates two problems:

First, because our incomes are limited we can only afford smaller mortgages and less expensive homes.

Second, what mortgage payments we do make are difficult to afford because we are also buying furniture, cars and first trying to support families.

GPMs are designed for people with rising incomes. They feature fixed interest rates plus low initial monthly payments that rise annually during the first years of the loan. Here's how a GPM would work:

The Hunts were married last July and are now looking for their first home. They have a combined income of $24,300. If 28 percent of their income can be devoted to the payment of mortgage interest and principal, they can pay $566.98 a month. At 10 percent interest, a monthly payment of $566.98 will support a 30-year mortgage worth $64,607.84. The same monthly payment, however, would underwrite a GPM loan worth $85,000. (Note that as a practical matter borrowers would have to also pay insurance, taxes and possibly condo or co-op fees, costs that would reduce the number of dollars available for principal and interest.)

Their lender tells the Hunts that with a GPM loan the first monthly payments are lower than those for a self-amortizing, conventional mortgage, while later payments are higher. The size of the monthly payments is determined by a schedule. For example, the Hunts could arrange to have monthly payments rise 7.5 percent annually for the first 5 years of their loan. In years 6 through 30 the payments would be level. Since the Hunts expect their incomes to rise they take the GPM financing. (See Table 21.)

TABLE 21
GPM versus Conventional Financing

	GPM*	Conventional
Loan size	$85,000	$85,000
Loan term	30 years	30 years
Interest rate	10 percent	10 percent
Monthly payment		
Year 1	$ 566.98	$ 745.94
Year 2	609.50	745.94
Year 3	655.21	745.94
Year 4	704.36	745.94
Year 5	757.19	747.94
Years 6–30	813.98	747.94
Year-end loan balance		
Year 1	$86,776.13	$84,527.50
Year 2	88,204.00	84,005.53
Year 3	89,206.98	83,428.90
Year 4	89,697.42	82,791.89
Year 5	89,575.40	82,088.17
Year 6	88,727.00	81,310.77
Year 7	87,789.75	80,451.96
Year 8	86,754.36	79,503.23
Year 30	–	–
Yearly negative amortization		
Year 1	$ 1,776.13	–
Year 2	1,427.87	–
Year 3	1,002.98	–
Year 4	490.44	–
Year 5	122.02	–
Year 6	–	–

*GPM loan with 7.5 percent payment increase annually for five years.
SOURCE: GPM figures based on HUD Transmittal Document No. 4, Appendix 1, Page 3 (Jan. 21, 1978).

Since payments in the first 5 years of the Hunts' loan are not high enough to produce a self-amortizing loan, it means that negative amortization is occurring. This problem could be resolved by making an extra-large down payment at settlement or by having higher payments in the last 25 years of the loan. Since the Hunts do not have the dollars to make a big down payment they opt for larger monthly costs in future years. They make this decision because they assume they will have the income to carry such costs easily.

It should be said that when negative amortization occurs 100 percent of any monthly payment is being used to pay interest and is usually tax deductible. Speak to a CPA or tax attorney to find out if money paid at settlement to forestall negative amortization can be deducted.

In addition to conventional GPM mortgages, such financing is also available under FHA Sec. 245 for owner-occupied, single-family homes and condos. This program features assumable financing with low down payments—usually less than 5 percent plus the value of deferred interest (negative amortization) and has five repayment plans:

Plan I. Monthly payments increase 2.5 percent each year during the first 5 years of the loan.

Plan II. Monthly payments increase 5 percent each year during the first 5 years of the loan.

Plan III. Monthly payments increase 7.5 percent each year during the first 5 years of the loan.

Plan IV. Monthly payments increase 2 percent each year during the first 10 years of the loan.

Plan V. Monthly payments increase 3 percent each year during the first 10 years of the loan.

Certain buyers may also be interested in a somewhat different FHA program known as Sec. 245(b). This is a graduated mortgage program intended for first-time home buyers or for those who have not owned a home in the past three years and who do not otherwise qualify for other FHA programs. It can be used to purchase new or "substantially rehabilitated" housing. The attraction of this program is that it requires somewhat less money down than the Sec. 245(a) program and offers an additional repayment schedule: monthly payments increase 4.9 percent each year over a period of ten years.

The GPM concept can be combined with an adjustable rate to produce a GPARM, or graduated payment adjustable rate mortgage. With a GPARM, there would be set—but rising— monthly payments in the first few years of the loan. Since payments are set but the interest rate is not it is possible that negative interest will occur in the first years of the loan. After the initial period when monthly payments are set, a GPARM would behave just like a regular ARM with payments and interest rates that could vary throughout the life of the loan.

A GPARM is probably a better financing choice than an ARM, especially for young property buyers. Individuals first entering the work force are the people least able to cope with rapidly rising housing costs because they have relatively little disposable income. By fixing initial costs, a GPARM gives buyers the below-market interest levels that ARMs often feature at first plus some time in which incomes can rise.

GPM loans in general represent one of the best forms of first-time financing, because they are fixed-rate mortgages attuned to the needs of entry-level purchasers. Be aware, however, that because they feature negative amortization in their first few years, buyers who intend to move in less than five years may find that they owe more with GPM financing at settlement than they borrowed.

Questions to ask:

What is the GPM interest rate?

How many points, if any, are being charged for conventional financing and for GPM loans?

When points are considered, what is the true annual percent rate (APR) for a GPM loan?

What GPM formats are available from local lenders?

How much money down would you need for a conventional GPM? How much for an FHA-backed GPM?

How is negative amortization handled? By an enlarged down payment? By higher monthly payments through most of the life of the loan? By a balloon payment? By extending the term of the loan?

If you are selling a home with a GPM where you have paid additional money up front to account for negative amortization, have you received any credit from the purchaser?

If you are assuming a GPM loan, is a balloon payment scheduled?

GROWING EQUITY MORTGAGES (GEM)

For 50 years the fixed-rate conventional loan has been the standard against which "creative" financing has been measured. But in the early 1980s a new loan, the "growing equity mortgage" or "GEM" loan, was developed. Radically different from conventional mortgages, the GEM loan has a unique payment concept that can readily cut interest costs by $100,000 or more for most loans.

With GEM financing monthly payments for the mortgage are figured on a 25- or 30-year amortization schedule, depending on the plan. However, the mortgage term is nowhere near 25 or 30 years because GEM loans have a rapid repayment feature.

Instead of paying a set amount each month, GEM loans have graduated payment increases that can be calculated two ways:

First, the monthly payments can be increased 2, 3, 4 or 5 percent annually during the first years of the loan. Thereafter monthly loan payments are flat.

Second, one could tie monthly payment increases to an index. For example, if the Commerce Department cost-of-living index rose 4 percent, monthly mortgage payments in the coming year would rise by some portion of that figure, say 60 percent of the increase, or 2.4 percent. The idea of indexing GEM loans to an inflation barometer was imported from nations where triple-digit inflation rates are common. Without indexing, loans of any type in such countries would be impossible.

So far it sounds as though a GEM loan is nothing more than a graduated payment mortgage but there is one significant difference: As monthly GEM payments rise, additional dollars paid by the borrower are only used to reduce the principal balance of the mortgage. The result is that GEM loans with fixed monthly increases can often be repaid in less than 15 years.

Rapid repayments create substantial advantages for borrowers. Even though GEM monthly payments are increased annually, the sum total of those payments is nowhere near the aggregate cost of 360 monthly payments. Look how interest costs between a 30-year, $85,000 conventional mortgage at 10 percent interest would compare with two $85,000 GEM loans.

The 30-year conventional loan would have 360 monthly payments of $745.94. The total value of all payments would be $268,538. Subtracting the original principal of $85,000 would leave a potential interest cost of $183,538.

An $85,000 GEM loan would start with payments of $745.94. If monthly payments rose by 5 percent each year the entire loan would be repaid in 174 months—a little over 14 years— and the total interest cost would be $73,625. If monthly payments were raised by 2 percent annually, the loan would have

220 payments (18.33 years) and a total interest cost of $85,000.

It doesn't take an electronic calculator or a strong familiarity with the new math to see that GEM loans substantially cut interest costs. With the first GEM format, potential interest expenses drop by $109,911.90, while the second format creates interest savings of $98,536.90—more money in either case than the original value of the loan!

Short repayment schedules are extremely attractive to lenders, since they represent less risk than long-term financing. Less risk means lower interest rates and that is another important GEM feature.

TABLE 22
Conventional Versus GEM Financing (Monthly Payments for $85,000 Loans)

Year	Conventional ($)	2 percent GEM* ($)	5 percent GEM** ($)
1	745.94	745.94	745.94
2	745.94	760.86	783.24
3	745.94	776.08	822.40
4	745.94	791.60	863.52
5	745.94	807.43	906.69
6	745.94	823.58	952.03
7	745.94	840.05	999.63
8	745.94	856.85	1,049.61
9	745.94	873.99	1,102.49
10	745.94	891.47	1,157.20
11	745.94	909.30	1,215.06
12	745.94	927.48	1,275.81
13	745.94	946.03	1,339.60
14	745.94	964.95	1,406.58
15	745.94	984.25	.00
16	745.94	1,003.94	.00
17	745.94	1,024.02	.00
18	745.94	1,044.50	.00
19	745.94	1,065.39	.00
20–30	745.94	.00	.00

*Three payments of $1,065.39 in the final year and one payment of $919.76.
**Five payments of $1,406.58 in the final year and one payment of $1,225.50.

Lower interest rates allow buyers who could not qualify for financing at market rates to get GEM mortgages, or—seen another way—to get larger mortgages at any income level. Lower rates also speed the amortization process, since less interest is required to pay back the loan.

One could refine the GEM concept even further for buyers with limited incomes. Suppose, for example, our purchasers can afford initial monthly payments of just $650.00 a month rather than $745.94 as in the examples above. Could we formulate a loan that would accommodate such purchasers, one that would allow them to qualify for a mortgage? Sure. Assuming that the buyers will have rising incomes, we could have a loan that's a 5 percent GEM in its first seven years and then a level-payment mortgage thereafter. Table 23 illustrates how the monthly payments would look.

TABLE 23
Bonus GEM Mortgage

Year	Payment ($)	Loan Balance ($)
1	650.00	85,732.99
2	682.50	86,134.36
3	716.63	86,148.95
4	752.46	85,714.83
5	790.08	84,762.50
6–30	770.24	—

The attractions of this loan format are that initial monthly payments are far below current market rates, and overall payments never reach the steep upper limits found with traditional GEM financing. Indeed, this loan even offers a "bonus" of sorts: monthly payments *drop* in the final 25 years.

The problem with this mortgage, however, is that while monthly payments are low, interest costs are high. Interest fees over the life of a 30-year "bonus" GEM total $231,359 in this example—almost $48,000 more than one would pay with a 30-year conventional loan. Also, because the loan has negative amortization in its first four years, a buyer who sold during that time would owe more money to the lender than was originally borrowed.

Are there cases when a "bonus" GEM would be attractive? Such loans could be useful with investment property when low monthly costs are important. But for home owners generally, a "bonus" GEM is not a bargain.

From the borrower's viewpoint there are three negative aspects of a GEM loan:

First, there is the monthly payment, which rises each year. Not everyone will be able to afford such payments but for those who can it is comforting to know that since the entire amount of the increase is going toward amortization rather than interest, such increases represent nothing more than a form of forced savings.

Second, because less interest is being paid, the value of the mortgage interest tax deduction is greatly reduced. While it is true that GEMs offer less tax shelter, it is also true that they require far fewer payment dollars. With less to spend on the mortgage a borrower has more dollars to place elsewhere, including, perhaps, alternative investments that produce significant tax advantages. (If a home interest tax shelter is important, a borrower could always refinance in the last years of the loan.)

Third, a GEM is not a good financing vehicle for those who anticipate declining incomes. GEMs require an increasing proportion of available income at a time when there are fewer dollars to spend. For this reason, GEMs should be avoided by those who expect to retire within the next ten to fifteen years.

In addition to conventional GEM mortgages there is also an FHA-backed GEM program. Yearly payment increases from 1 to 5 percent are allowed, but the maximum size of such loans is limited according to the same terms as the FHA 203(b) program. As predicted in the first edition of this guide, FHA GEMs are freely assumable, offer the low down payments normally associated with FHA financing and may be prepaid in whole or in part without penalty. This is an attractive GEM program because its assumption and prepayment features are a benchmark against which other GEM formats can be compared. It offers flexibility in the event plans change, the property is sold or a borrower elects to make a prepayment.

Because of their inherent advantages—below-market interest rates, predictable payment increases and rapid amortization —GEMs should be regarded as one of the best of the new mortgage formats. Because they neatly balance the needs of both lenders and borrowers and because they offer the potential to substantially reduce homeownership costs, GEM financing is well within the definition of a common-sense mortgage. Simply stated, GEM financing is a mortgage concept that should not be overlooked.

Questions to ask:

What is the initial GEM interest rate? How does that rate compare with conventional financing costs?

How much money down is required?

How much will the monthly payments increase each year? How many years will the increases continue?

Does the rate of interest change during the term of the loan?

How long will it take to pay off the loan?

Is the loan assumable?

Can GEM financing be prepaid in whole or in part without penalty?

Are FHA-guaranteed GEMs available? If so, under what terms?

HOME EQUITY MORTGAGES

Real estate has traditionally been considered a non-liquid asset, property that could be converted to cash only by selling or refinancing—two very expensive and time-consuming ways to raise capital. But the old image of real estate is now changing. Today property can be converted to cash immediately through the use of a home equity loan secured by real estate.

Credit is the great wonder of American society. You can be born on credit, live on credit and probably die on credit. Like gravity, credit is silent, invisible and with us every moment.

While credit is all around us all forms of credit are not identical. Consumer credit differs from traditional real estate financing, another form of credit, in three ways:

First, the credit represented by hundreds of millions of flat plastic cards is unsecured debt. When you make a credit purchase the card company advances money to a gas station or department store on the theory that you will repay. Real estate debt, in contrast, is secured by the value of your property. If you don't pay the property will be sold to pay off what you owe.

Second, real estate debt is normally advanced at one time. Consumer debt is usually a revolving line of credit. You may have the right to borrow $5,000 from a single credit card company but you don't have to. If you borrow only $150 you pay interest only on the outstanding debt. Moreover, once you pay back the $150 you can again borrow up to $5,000. With most real estate loans, it's understood that once you pay back any portion of the principal the lender is not obligated to loan to you again.

Third, there are few if any charges to get consumer credit. Companies will gladly send you credit cards with the fervent hope you really do buy now and pay later. Real estate lenders will not only charge a fee to apply for financing but they also have a variety of closing costs which the borrower must pay.

Home equity mortgages are hybrid loan products that take features both from traditional mortgages and consumer credit practices. A real estate loan with a line of credit could work like this:

The Taylor house is worth $125,000 in today's market and has a $40,000 mortgage balance. The Taylors feel they may need some ready cash in the next two years to start a small business and to send Junior to college, and so their lender suggests a credit line arrangement.

The lender says the Taylors can borrow up to 70 percent of the equity in their home and values their equity like this: 70 percent of $125,000 equals $87,500 less the remaining mortgage balance, $40,000, equals $47,500.

The lender tells the Taylors that the minimum home equity loan is $5,000 and the minimum loan advance is $1,000. Since they have equity worth $47,500, the Taylors elect to get a $25,000 line of credit.

To get this loan the Taylors pay for a credit report, title search and other closing expenses. Their application costs are figured on the basis of a $25,000 loan but they do not, however, pay any points. While interest rates for second trusts at the time of their application average 8 percent, the Taylors pay 1.5 percent over the prime rate charged by a major bank, or 9.5 percent in this case. The lender has the right to change the rate of interest every three months. In contrast, it should be noted that the cost of consumer credit ranges from 16 to 24 percent.

The lender explains that the Taylors may select any loan term they choose, from 1 to 30 years. They select 15 years and make their first draw, $12,000, eighteen months after their application is approved. This means they have a maximum of 13.5 years to repay the $12,000 debt. The Taylors can repay the loan in advance, however, without penalty.

How do the Taylors withdraw their money? The lender offers four choices: a check mailed to their home or business; a deposit in a savings or checking account maintained with the lender or at another financial institution; a telephone transfer or, most interestingly, a book of blank drafts which the Taylors can use up to their credit limit.

After 6 years the Taylors have paid down their debt to $7,000. Because of the revolving nature of the credit line system, the Taylors can still borrow $40,500. In effect, by making their monthly payments they have raised their available credit line from a low of $35,500 ($47,500 less $12,000) at the time they made their first draw.

Home equity loans are attractive to lenders because they can collect processing fees up front even though actual monies may not be advanced for months or years—or at all. Also, such loans are commonly adjustable rate mortgages, which means that lenders are largely protected against inflation.

Borrowers like credit lines because they have the ability to instantly convert bricks and pipes to cash with relatively little cost up front and far lower interest than they would normally pay for unsecured consumer credit. The access to such credit may prove extremely valuable. For instance, when they wish to buy a new home the Taylors in the example above need not wait to sell their house before placing a down payment on a new property. Instead they can just advance the money from their credit line as long as they are able to make the proper payments. As soon as the property is sold the debt would be paid in full from the proceeds of the sale.

Home equity loans also have several features that should concern potential borrowers.

Since a home equity loan is a second trust a borrower who defaults could be foreclosed. The difficult issue here is this: Suppose a homeowner has a $10,000 credit line, becomes unemployed and for some reason borrows $500 on a credit line mortgage which is not repaid. Could a lender foreclose if only $500 was outstanding? Absolutely. Would a lender necessarily foreclose? The answer depends on the facts and circumstances in each case and the policies of the lender. As a matter of good public relations it seems likely that most lenders would try to work out some arrangement before seeking foreclosure.

Another potential problem may seem somewhat contradictory. Home equity loans may be too accessible for certain borrowers. Many otherwise responsible people overextend themselves with unsecured credit card loans and it is probable that some homeowners will do the same with credit lines secured by real estate.

As this is written, for example, several lenders permit the withdrawal of relatively small sums, say $300, $400 or $500. To prevent frivolous expenditures that could result in foreclosure, lenders may set higher minimum draws, say $1,000, as they gain more experience with this type of financing.

Questions to ask:

What is the interest rate for conventional financing?
What is the interest rate for unsecured consumer credit?
What is the market value of your home?

What portion of your equity can be used to calculate a maximum credit line? Various lenders are likely to have different standards, so speak to several loan officers in your community.

Is the home equity loan structured as an adjustable rate mortgage? If so, how often is the rate adjusted? Which index is used? How frequently can payments be adjusted? Is there an interest cap? Is there a payment cap? Can there be negative amortization?

What is the lender's policy on late or missed payments?

What is the minimum and maximum credit line?

What is the minimum and maximum draw?

How long is the loan term?

What is the full, up-front cost of establishing a home equity mortgage?

Do you have the right to repay in whole or in part without penalty?

MUNICIPAL, OR BOND-BACKED, MORTGAGES

There is no limit to the artful ways in which tax policies can be written. At this time we have a system that provides subsidies for some industries but not for others, a tax break for those over 65 but not over 61 and a deduction for the blind but not the lame.

In this maze of exemptions, deductions, exceptions, interpretations, rulings, codes and court cases are benefits which greatly favor property ownership. Without tax exemptions for mortgage interest and real estate taxes the number of residential property owners would be greatly reduced—as would the number of construction workers, real estate brokers, mortgage loan officers, appliance manufacturers, lumberjacks, etc.

One tax exemption of some interest is the right of governmental bodies such as cities, counties and states to issue tax-exempt bonds which can be used to build dams, roads, industrial parks or whatever.

Issuers like tax-exempt bonds because it means public projects that produce local employment and other benefits can be funded cheaply. Investors like such bonds because they often produce a higher after-tax income than alternative investments.

Suppose a tax-exempt bond pays 8 percent interest. A bond buyer in the 28-percent tax bracket would have to earn 10.24

percent from a taxable investment to have the same net return after taxes. Since not all investments pay 10.24 percent, and since private securities are not backed by the taxing authority of a governmental entity as are many bonds, tax-exempt bonds are attractive to investors looking for good yields with little risk.

If tax-exempt bonds can be used to build factories and roads, why can't bonds be used to underwrite home mortgages? After all, cheap mortgages mean more real estate sales and more sales mean more local employment. The answer is that tax-exempt bonds worth billions of dollars are issued each year to underwrite local home mortgages. Here's an illustration:

South County sells bonds worth $75 million and paying 6 percent interest to investors. The money from the bonds is then used to underwrite 8 percent mortgages for local home buyers at a time when conventional rates are 10 percent. The principal and interest home buyers pay is used to pay off the bond holders, and so South County will not raise taxes to repay the debt—a politician's dream. In some cases, as in this example, the issuing jurisdiction actually profits by charging homeowners more interest than bond holders receive.

Although tax-exempt bonds can bring millions of mortgage dollars into an area, that money is not available to everyone. Instead, only individuals with a certain income, family size, and length of residency within the jurisdiction can apply for financing in most cases. Also, many programs will not issue mortgages to otherwise-qualified individuals who have owned property within the past three years.

Tax-exempt mortgage revenue bonds have stirred considerable controversy. Critics argue that tax-exempt bonds unnecessarily shift billions of dollars from the federal treasury tc well-heeled investors. Worse, they say, bonds are not an efficient way to stimulate home ownership.

Supporters believe that bonds are necessary and that without such funds home ownership would not be possible for most participating borrowers. Also, bond backers believe that comparing the benefits of bonds with other housing programs, such as Sec. 8 subsidized housing, is not realistic because of what they see as the inherently different nature of each program.

The politics and economics of tax-exempt mortgage revenue bonds are simply irrelevant if you are the one looking for mortgage money. If you qualify, such financing may represent the cheapest money source in town and that fact by itself may make bond-backed financing the common-sense mortgage for many first-time and moderate-income buyers.

Because bond-backed mortgages are a good deal, there is considerable demand for these loans when they become available. Waiting lists, lotteries and all-night vigils outside banks have been known to occur. In a sense, part of the qualification process for these loans may include luck and physical stamina as well as how many dollars you earned last year.

When considering bond-backed mortgages potential borrowers should be aware that such financing often contains specialized restrictions. For example, bond-backed mortgages are usually not available to investors; there may be renting limitations; individuals may be required to live in the property for a certain number of years; and loans may be assumable only by individuals who are qualified to participate in the program.

Information about mortgages backed from tax-exempt bonds is available from real estate brokers, local lenders (who often service such loans), home builders, community groups and governmental officials. Because this type of financing is often snapped up the day it becomes available, borrowers should obtain program information as much in advance as possible. With advance information plus prepared applications and supporting documents in hand you'll have the best shot at bond-backed mortgages when they are announced.

Bond-Backed Mortgages at a Glance

Q. Who buys bonds?

A. Investors, pension funds, etc.

Q. Why are bond returns so low?

A. Interest on bonds issued by governmental agencies is generally exempt from federal taxation.

Q. Are bond-backed mortgage rates lower than conventional financing?

A. Yes, in virtually all cases.

Q. Are bond-backed mortgages always available?

A. No. Occasionally Congress has made an effort to stop or curtail bond-backed mortgages nationwide. In addition, bond-backed mortgages are not available in every jurisdiction at every moment, in part because funding is usually limited. If you're interested in bond-backed financing, be certain to keep up with the latest developments in your community.

Q. Who qualifies for financing with bond-backed mortgages?

A. Standards vary but low-to-moderate-income individuals buying a first home generally qualify.

Q. Are bond-backed mortgages available to investors?

A. Usually not for single-unit purchases such as an individual home or condo.

Q. Are bond-backed mortgages ever awarded on the basis of employment or union membership?

A. Yes. When a pension fund makes a large-scale bond purchase—sometimes the entire issue—it is often stipulated that a portion of the money raised will be available to organization members first.

Q. If I qualify for a bond-backed mortgage are there any restrictions?

A. In some programs there may be restrictions on renting property and assuming loans.

Questions to ask:

What is the current rate of interest for conventional financing?

Are bond-backed mortgages available in the jurisdiction where the property is located?

What is the current interest rate of bond-backed mortgages?

What are the income, family size and residency requirements, if any, associated with bond-backed mortgages?

How much cash down is required?

When will bond-backed mortgages next be available? Is there a waiting list? If so, how do you get on it?

Can you get a bond-backed mortgage from a local lender? If so, what are the proper application procedures?

Are you part of a group that has a pension fund that is buying a large quantity of bond-backed mortgages? If so, you may be able to get preferential treatment.

Are you required to live in the property for a certain period, say 5 years?

Are you allowed to rent all or part of the property once you have obtained bond-backed financing?

Is the mortgage assumable? If it is assumable must the buyer be qualified to participate in the program?

Can the loan be prepaid in whole or in part without penalty?

PLEDGED AND RESERVE ACCOUNT MORTGAGES

The idea of "no money down" financing should mean that no cash is required to purchase a property. Yet it is possible to have a sale with "no money down" that is offset by cash elsewhere in the deal. Such loans are called pledged account mortgages (PAM) and reserve account mortgages (RAM).

For example, with a PAM loan, Mrs. Tilton, the borrower, gets 100 percent financing under the best available rates and terms. Rather than making a down payment, money is instead deposited by Tilton or a seller with a lender in a pledged, interest-bearing account.

The lender then takes a certain sum from the account, say $150 or so a month, to offset Tilton's regular mortgage payments until the account is drawn down. If Tilton defaults, the lender can claim the entire account immediately and foreclose on the property. In effect, the pledged account money offsets the lender's risk, since it is a substitute for the security of a down payment.

As an illustration, if Mrs. Tilton buys property for $100,000 a seller could set up a $10,000 pledged account with a lender. Tilton would get a $100,000 mortgage but her monthly payment would be reduced by $150. The $150 comes from the interest-bearing pledged account. Once the money in the pledged account, including interest, is used up, Tilton would then have to make the entire monthly payment.

In most instances PAM accounts are established by sellers as a form of buy-down financing to aid purchasers with limited incomes and little capital. Since they are not getting their money out of the property in cash, however, it follows that sellers will want higher prices when they sell. If higher prices are not possible because of depressed market conditions, PAMs may represent a genuine discount.

Pledged accounts are not necessarily buy-downs, however. When a pledged account is established by a friend or relative, that individual can withdraw a specified sum from the account each month. The money taken out coincides with the reduced mortgage balance and growing equity in the property.

The attraction of this arrangement is that it enables individuals to help buyers without making a direct cash contribution toward the property's purchase price or acting as a co-signer or co-owner. If the buyer defaults, however, the money remaining in the pledged account would go immediately to the lender.

A RAM is a specialized type of loan that can offer 100 percent financing at conventional rates to buyers with limited capital but good incomes. (See Table 24.)

TABLE 24
PAM versus RAM

	PAM	RAM	Conventional
Down payment	None	None	20 percent
Account size	5 percent minimum	5 percent minimum	None
Monthly withdrawal	Regular sum, say $100 or $150	None	None
Term held	Until paid out	Until sufficient equity is established in property	None
Account money returned	None	Deposit plus accrued interest	None
Can account be taken in foreclosure?	Yes	Yes	Not appropriate

Suppose RAM financing was used by Robertson to buy a home valued at $85,000. Robertson would get an $85,000 loan at conventional rates and no money down except closing costs. The lender would also get something: security worth at least 5 percent of the property's value in the form of a pledged asset such as a certificate of deposit or funds in a passbook savings account. Interest on the security deposit would be paid to whoever puts up the deposit.

The question is: Who did put up the deposit? One choice would be the borrower. Rather than using money for a down payment Robertson could deposit money with a lender under a RAM arrangement.

The idea from Robertson's viewpoint is to get interest income from money that would otherwise be used for a down payment. The problem is this: If mortgage money costs, say, 10 percent, and reserve accounts pay 8 percent interest, it is better to have a larger down payment. The interest earned in the reserve account in this case is offset by higher mortgage costs.

Another possibility, and one that is far more sensible, is that a friend or relative of Robertson places money in a reserve account. Essentially this would be an assisted loan in a situation where someone wanted to help a Robertson, again without becoming either a co-signer, co-owner or actually contributing cash to the purchase.

A third deposit source could be a seller. To get the most money out of a deal, a seller (possibly a builder or developer) might offer to deposit cash in a reserve account to assure the purchase of his property. The problem here is one of economics: sellers are looking for maximum profits and one way to justify a reserve account is to charge premium prices when possible.

The purpose of the reserve account is to protect the lender in the event of a loan default. This means a lender will want access to the reserve account until a certain point, say until the value of the loan is less than 90 or 95 percent of the overall property value. This sounds fine until one realizes that no down payment has been made. If property values remain stagnant or decline the lender may not be obligated to release reserved funds for many years.

If you haven't got the capital or the income, PAMs and RAMs are better than rental stubs. However, these programs raise four issues:

First, with both loans 100 percent financing means bigger mortgages and larger interest payments.

Second, with PAMs set up by sellers one has to ask if the borrower would simply be better off with a discounted price. (See section on buy-down financing.)

Third, if you are the party putting up money for an account with a lender, where is your security, if any? Is your account considered a second trust secured by the property or is it merely a personal loan? In the event of foreclosure how do you get your money back?

Fourth, if the return of reserve account money is dependent on a certain loan-to-value ratio there is no specific time when this ratio will be achieved and therefore there is no absolute time when the money will be returned. This can be a problem if the donor needs funds by a certain date.

While alert buyers can benefit from PAM and RAM financing, particularly when friends and relatives are involved in the purchase, such loans are often outside the definition of a common-sense mortgage when it is a seller, developer or builder who underwrites such accounts. If you've got the cash you're probably better off bargaining for a lower sales price and a loan format that requires little or nothing down, such as mortgages backed by the VA, FHA or private mortgage insurance.

Questions to ask:

What is the prevailing interest rate for conventional financing?

How much money is required to set up either a PAM or RAM account?

How much is withdrawn monthly from a PAM account?

If you set up a reserve account for a friend or relative who defaults on the mortgage, do you have any recourse to get your money back? In other words, if a reserve account is not intended to be a gift is it a lien against the property?

With either PAM or RAM financing, does the donor have a choice of accounts in which the money can be deposited, such as certificates of deposit, money market accounts, etc.?

With either PAM or RAM financing, does the donor have

any liability beyond the money originally placed in an account with the lender?

In the case of a PAM loan set up by a seller, would the buyer be better off with a direct price reduction instead?

REVERSE MORTGAGES

All the gold in Fort Knox represents nowhere near the value found in America's non-mortgaged housing stock. At the end of 1983, there were approximately 43 million owner-occupied homes, each on less than ten acres of land. Of these, according to the Census Bureau, over 15.75 million were owned free and clear of any mortgage debt. With a median value of $48,800 these 15.75 million homes had a total net worth over $769 billion.

In many cases the owners of mortgage-free properties are age 60 and above and find that while they have property with a substantial economic value, they cannot transform that value into cash without selling the property or having it refinanced. Selling is not a good choice because it merely substitutes the problem of a house and no cash for cash and no house. Refinancing is not a good choice either, because it means making monthly payments at a time when income may be limited.

Reverse mortgages, in contrast, are designed for people with real estate equity but limited cash flow. They allow individuals to retain home ownership while providing needed cash.

Mr. and Mrs. Nelson are each 65 years old and about to retire. Their house, which is worth $125,000, is mortgage free. They would like more cash once they retire and so they speak to a lender who suggests reverse financing.

A reverse mortgage, says the lender, works like this: Each month we give you so many dollars. That money earns 10 percent interest for us. The Nelsons are told that with their projected income they could get an $85,000 reverse mortgage.

Unlike other mortgage formats where the sum of $85,000 would only represent principal, with a reverse mortgage $85,-000 is equal to the combined total of all principal and interest.

The final term of this loan is 10 years and 3 months, and at the end the borrower actually owes $85,213.59. Of this total, $49,200 represents principal and the balance of $36,013.59 is interest. (See Table 25.)

TABLE 25
Reverse Mortgage at a Glance
[An $85,000 Loan at 10 Percent Interest]

Month Number	Deferred Cost ($)	Principal ($)	Balance ($)
1	400.00	400.00	400.00
2	403.33	400.00	803.33
3	406.69	400.00	1,210.03
4	410.08	400.00	1,620.11
5	413.50	400.00	2,033.61
123	1,100.94	400.00	85,213.59

To control interest costs it's best to have a reverse mortgage with set monthly payments rather than payments designed to last a given number of years. For example, if the loan was structured so that the total obligation was simply $85,000 paid out over 15 years, a borrower would receive only $205 per month. The total principal payoff would be $36,900, while interest would total $48,066.42.

A second way to control interest costs is to have larger payments. If the $85,000 loan illustrated here was arranged so that the borrowers received $250 a month, the loan would run 13 years and six months. However, interest payments would total $44,500, while principal would amount to $44,577.

The loan above will end if the Nelsons sell, lease, or refinance the property, if they fail to maintain the property, or if they do not pay property taxes. In addition, the loan will terminate when both die. If the Nelsons die before the entire $85,000 is paid out, their estate would simply owe less money to the lender. If it should happen that the Nelsons outlive the loan term the lender, in this case, will refinance the property at then-current rates.

As an alternative to a reverse mortgage the Nelsons consider several other strategies. They could get a regular $85,000 mortgage and invest that money. However, it may not be possible to get a return above the loan's rate of interest. They could also finance the house and purchase an annuity. Annuity income, however, may be taxable.

Another alternative would be to get an $85,000 mortgage and then invest the money in a tax-free annuity. The problem here is that the mortgage interest may not be deductible, since the purpose of the mortgage loan is to generate tax-exempt income.

Since money received under a reverse mortgage is principal rather than income, such advances are not taxable. The issue of interest deductions is more complex, however.

The Nelsons owe interest but they have not actually made payments to a lender. According to IRS spokesman Roy Young, if the borrowers use a cash-based system of accounting they are not entitled to a deduction until payments have been made. If they have an accrual-based system, a form of accounting often used by businesses, then deductions may be possible. When the loan is paid off, by the Nelsons or their estate, it is then that payments have actually been made and a deduction may be in order. For specific advice speak to a tax attorney or CPA.

The reverse mortgage concept can be attractive for some of those with debt-free homes but it may not be so appealing to lenders.

First, interest from the loan accumulates until the entire value of the mortgage is due. This means lenders are getting a credit for income not actually received but which may be subject to taxation. Lenders may charge more points or higher interest to offset this problem.

Second, security for the loan—the house—could be tied up in probate court for years as relatives argue over who is entitled to the property.

Third, because the loan can be terminated by death or other reasons, reverse loans do not produce an assured income over time and are thus not attractive to pension funds and others who buy mortgages. This means most local lenders will have difficulty selling a reverse loan to bring new funds into the community.

Fourth, if a reverse mortgage sours, a lender could have an unseemly public relations problem. One can just picture the headline, "Local Lender Forecloses on 94-Year-Old Widow of Town Minister."

Questions to ask:

Are local lenders making reverse loans? Groups such as the American Association of Retired Persons (AARP) may be able to suggest lenders who offer reverse mortgages.

What is the value of your property? A lender will want an appraisal.

What reverse mortgage terms are best for you? Have a lender provide you with amortization statements to show which alternative monthly payments and terms would work best.

How will a reverse mortgage affect your income tax obligations? Speak to a tax consultant.

How will a reverse mortgage affect your pension and Social Security benefits? Speak to appropriate professionals and administrators.

Does the loan include a written guarantee to refinance the

property at then-current rates in the event you reach the reverse loan limit?

Is a will required as part of a reverse mortgage? Even if it isn't, do you have an adequate will? Speak to an attorney for more information.

Would a life insurance policy equal to the value of the reverse mortgage be a good purchase? In the event of death the proceeds of the policy could be used to retire the reverse mortgage debt. Would your heirs want to pay for such a policy on your behalf? If so, what are your obligations to them, if any?

FHA TITLE I: IS THIS THE BEST SMALL LOAN IN TOWN?

There are many people who simply don't like the idea of refinancing their homes. When they need extra dollars they use checking account overdraft credit, credit cards, and signature loans—anything but the equity in their homes. For these people, and for many others, the FHA has devised a unique form of financing that straddles both real estate and personal finance.

If you need $17,500 or less for home improvement purposes, it may pay to look at the FHA Title I program. If the amount sought is less than $2,500, the loan is regarded as a personal debt and not recorded as a lien against property. From $2,500 to $17,500 the loan is recorded as a lien but one that is subordinate to other loans. That means you can get Title I financing even with other loans on your property. Since 90 percent of the loan is guaranteed by FHA, the risk to your lender is minimal and there should be little resistance to giving a loan that could be regarded as a personal loan or as a first, second or even third trust, depending on such other loans as may be in place on the property and the size of the debt.

The FHA loan program provides for a maximum term of 15

years and an interest rate that is usually not much higher than conventional loans and lower than credit card financing.

Not all lenders handle FHA Title I home improvement financing, so you may have to call your local FHA office (it's part of the U.S. Department of Housing and Urban Development) to get the name of area lenders who are active in the program.

Questions to ask:

What is the Title I interest rate?
What is the maximum Title I loan?
How much Title I money can you borrow as a personal loan?

WRAPAROUND LOANS

One of the most innovative forms of creative financing is the wraparound mortgage, a type of loan which in the best of circumstances provides below-market financing for purchasers and above-market yields for lenders. While high yields and low rates sound like the definition of the ideal loan there are potential complications that make wraparound financing difficult, if not unacceptable, to large numbers of borrowers and lenders.

A wraparound loan consists of two parts: First, there is the original financing on the property. This loan remains in place at its original rate and terms. Second, there is the wraparound loan, financing which is in addition to the original loan.

Imagine that a home is sold for $150,000. There is a freely assumable loan on the property with a remaining balance of $50,000. The assumable loan has an 8 percent interest rate and 20 years left on a 30-year term. This loan requires a monthly payment of $418.22.

To buy this property a purchaser, Mr. Morton, knows that with $100,000 in cash he could merely assume the original loan. Few people, however, have $100,000 in ready cash, so Morton looks into assuming the original loan and having a lender or the seller take back a second trust. As good as it sounds, this approach has problems too. Second trusts tend to have short terms, high rates and balloon payments. Add up the first and second trust payments and the monthly mortgage bill is far more than Morton can afford.

As an alternative, Morton could put $30,000 down and qualify for conventional financing at the market interest rate, perhaps 12 percent in this case. The problem here is that 12 percent interest would leave Morton with few dollars for anything other than mortgage payments.

To get a better rate—and to reduce monthly payments—Morton suggests a wraparound deal under which the seller will take back a $120,000 mortgage at 10 percent interest from the purchaser. The term of the loan will be the remaining length of the assumable loan, 20 years in this case. The seller, however, remains responsible for the original $50,000 first trust.

The effect of this deal is to provide Morton with 10 percent financing in a 12 percent market. Not only does Morton get a good rate, but he saves extra interest payments worth $166,-434.41. In addition, if it is the seller who takes back the loan many settlement expenses can be avoided. (See Table 26.)

For the seller or wraparound lender the deal looks like this: the loan appears to generate 10 percent interest. However, the original 8 percent loan must be repaid and thus the seller receives 10 percent interest on $70,000 ($120,000 less $50,000) and 2 percent on $50,000 (10 percent interest from the buyer less 2 percent which must be paid on the assumable loan).

If yield is defined as the return on money actually loaned, the seller is taking in far more than 10 percent interest. Since the

TABLE 26
Wraparound Loan versus Conventional Financing

	Conventional Loan	Wraparound Loan
Cash down	$30,000	$30,000
Assumable financing	None	$50,000
Interest rate	12 percent	10 percent
New financing	$120,000	$70,000
Term	30 years	20 years
Monthly payment	$1,234.34	$1,158.03 (on total debt of $120,000 [$50,000 old loan + $70,000 new financing])
Potential interest cost	$324,360.64	$157,926.23
Extra potential interest	$166,434.41	None
First trust liability of wraparound lender	None	$50,000
Net buyer liability	$120,000	$120,000
Recorded debt	$120,000	$170,000
Recorded price	$150,000	$150,000

seller is not actually lending the first $50,000, the yield in this illustration is 11.36 percent.

The Wraparound Note Holder

1. Gets a monthly income of $1,158.03.
2. Makes a monthly first trust payment of $418.22.
3. Has a net monthly return on $70,000 of $739.81.
4. Earns an annual return of 11.36 percent on $70,000.

The interest earned by a wraparound note will be taxed as regular income, while the principal payments are likely to be treated as a capital gain if the lender is a seller. For borrowers, the interest paid is deductible in the same sense as any mortgage interest payment.

As good as this deal looks, and in practice properly structured wraparounds can work well, it does raise a number of concerns which need to be carefully reviewed. Here are some of the issues that both borrowers and seller/lenders should discuss with a knowledgeable attorney before making a wraparound commitment.

- Is wraparound financing a first trust or a second trust? It is sometimes argued that a wraparound has the effect of a first trust, while others maintain that it is nothing more than a glorified second trust. The difference can be important for two reasons:

   First, many states have different usury limits for first mortgages and second trusts. How a wraparound mortgage is defined could determine whether or not usury statutes are being violated.

   Second, what is the order of repayment in the event of default? In the example above, there are liens on the property for both the original first trust and the wraparound financing, a total of $170,000. What if the buyer gets still another loan secured by the property? Is it a second claim? A third claim?
- What happens if the buyer wants to prepay the first trust?
- What happens if the buyer wants to get additional financing above the value of the wraparound loan? How does this affect the security of the wraparound lender?
- What if a payment is missed? If the wraparound lender fails to make a payment on the first trust it is possible that the original lender could foreclose, in which case the borrower could lose his home and the wraparound lender could lose his equity.

   One way to resolve the missed payment problem is to have

the buyer issue separate checks each month, one to the first trust holder and a second to the wraparound lender for the balance due. Another approach is to deposit payments with a local lender who then pays the original lender and the holder of the wraparound note. This approach assures that a precise record of all payments will be made and avoids the potential problem of payments lost or delayed in the mail.

- What about property taxes? Both the original financing and the wraparound note will be recorded liens against the property for $170,000 in the illustration above even though the actual sales value of the property was only $150,000. An unsympathetic assessor could read those numbers and assign a higher value to the property for tax purposes than might otherwise be warranted. Check with local assessors to find out how such matters are handled.

- Is a wraparound a good deal? To analyze this question one must consider alternative monthly costs and potential interest expenses.

Also, if a buyer intends to occupy a property for only a few years and a seller is willing to hold either a wraparound or a second trust, then consideration must be given to the fact that up-front, one-time financing charges are being avoided—a significant cost reduction in the short run.

For sellers, holding a wraparound becomes attractive if such financing provides an equal or better rate of return than alternative investments of similar risk. Also, wraparounds may be extremely attractive in those situations where market interest levels are high and few buyers qualify for financing. In such circumstances, no financing means few sales and so a seller who can hold financing has a decided marketing advantage. The fact that interest rates are high generally also insures a good rate of return on a wraparound.

Questions to ask:

What is the current interest rate for conventional financing?

What is the remaining loan balance on the property?

Is the current loan freely assumable?

How many years remain on the original loan?

Will the seller hold wraparound financing?

How much cash down is required if a wraparound is to be used to buy property?

Do commercial lenders in the jurisdiction where the property is located make wraparounds?

What are the precise terms of the proposed wraparound? How much are the monthly payments, what is the interest rate, how long will the loan last?

How does a wraparound deal compare with assuming the first trust and getting a second mortgage for the balance of the financing?

For purposes of defining usury limits, is a wraparound regarded in your jurisdiction as a first trust or as a second trust?

ZERO-INTEREST (ZIP) MORTGAGES

By definition, the idea of a no-interest mortgage seems to be a contradiction in terms. Is a loan without interest a gift? How can a lender profit if there is no interest? Who would make an interest-free loan?

With an $85,000 zero-interest (ZIP) loan the payments for a $127,500 house would look like this: one-third of the price down ($42,500) plus 60 monthly installments of $1,417. That's it.

In comparison, with 20 percent down ($25,500), a 30-year, $85,000 conventional mortgage at 10 percent interest would have 360 payments of $745.94 and a total interest cost over 30 years of $183,536.40 (360 × $745.94 equals $268,538.40 less $85,000 equals $183,538.40). (See Table 27.)

TABLE 27
ZIP versus Conventional Purchases

	ZIP	Conventional
Sales price	$127,500	$106,250
Down payment	$42,500	$25,500
Loan size	$85,000	$85,000
Interest rate	10 percent	10 percent
Monthly payment	$1,416.67	$745.94
Income required	$60,714	$31,968
Number of payments	60	360
Total payments	$85,000	$268,538.40
Total interest	None	$183,536.40

Why no interest? The answer lies elsewhere. Buried in the deal is a higher price for the property, a bigger down payment and the world of discounted loans.

Suppose a property is marketed for $106,250. With 20 percent down there would be an $85,000 mortgage. The builder, paying some closing fees, would net in the area of $100,000.

If the same property were sold with a ZIP loan, the price would be higher, say $127,500. Here the buyer would put down $42,500 and get an $85,000 zero-interest mortgage for the balance.

In many cases, it is the builder who first holds the zero-rate mortgage. Since the builder wants cash from the loan, he'll sell the note to an investor. The investor would see that the note has a term of five years, a $1,416.67 monthly payment and an $85,-000 face value. If the investor wanted a 12 percent return he would buy the $85,000 mortgage at discount and pay $63,-686.45 in cash to the builder. (Alternatively, a lender could make a zero-rate loan if a builder pays points up front. This arrangement would have the same effect as an investor buying the loan at discount.)

The builder has now collected $42,500 from the buyer and $63,686.45 from the investor, or a total of $106,186.45 for his property.

The note holder—whether builder, lender or investor—will view zero-rate mortgages as low-risk loans. They have short terms, usually five to seven years, and represent only a reasonable fraction of the market value of the property, 80 percent or less.

Because ZIP loans have limited risk, qualification standards for such mortgages are generally far more liberal than the guidelines used for conventional financing. With a ZIP loan perhaps one-third of an individual's gross income can be applied to principal and interest payments, up from 25 to 28 percent with conventional mortgages.

It should be said that even with easier qualification standards a ZIP borrower will not get a larger loan than a conventional borrower. For example, a person earning $35,000 a year could afford monthly mortgage payments of $972.22 per month for a ZIP loan with a total value of $58,333 (60 × $972.22). At 28 percent the maximum allowable monthly mortgage payment for principal and interest would drop to $816.67. This smaller monthly figure, however, will support a 30-year, $93,060.22 conventional mortgage at 10 percent interest.

ZIP loans, as good as they seem, raise four issues for borrowers.

First, is it worth paying a premium purchase price to obtain zero-rate financing? In this example, the buyer has paid $42,500 up front to save as much as $183,536.90 in future interest payments. If you've got the cash there are few investments of equal risk (none) or economic potential (savings are not income and are therefore not taxed). However, it should be noted that the borrower does pay a premium up front and loses potential income that the premium payment may have earned.

Second, some borrowers will be bothered by the apparent lack of interest payments. No interest payment could mean no tax deduction. However, the IRS may allow an "imputed" rate of interest as a tax deduction. To find the latest IRS rulings with regard to zero-interest loans and to determine the size of any possible imputed interest claim, check with a CPA or tax attorney before buying property with a zero-interest mortgage format.

Third, resale profits over a short period of time may be hindered by ZIP financing. Prices for properties of equal size, location and quality will have to rise before the market value of your property exceeds its purchase price.

Fourth, because ZIP financing is generally associated with premium prices borrowers might pay higher taxes when local assessors check selling prices.

While zero-interest loans are generally available only through new home builders, a seller could conceivably take back a zero-interest loan directly from a purchaser. This can be an attractive sales tool, particularly if combined with a premium price and down payment. However, be aware that there may be income tax to pay on the imputed interest that is credited to the seller but not actually received. Again, see a tax specialist for current advice in this area before making commitments.

Although premium prices are associated with ZIP financing there is no rule which requires owners to raise asking values. In a "buyer's market" or where property is not selling well, it may be possible to get both ZIP financing and a normal price—a deal that effectively offers a steep discount. In any case buyers would be well advised to negotiate.

ZIP loans are clearly designed for people who can afford to put a significant sum of money down and pay large monthly costs for a few years thereafter. Even with premium property

prices ZIP loans deserve careful consideration by qualified borrowers, particularly if an imputed tax benefit is available. If you
are a buyer without sufficient dollars to afford ZIP financing on
your own, a shared-equity arrangement could help get the cash
you need.

Questions to ask:

What is the interest rate for conventional financing?

What is the price of comparable properties financed con-
ventionally?

How much cash down is required for a ZIP loan?

What are the monthly payments?

Can you claim a tax deduction for imputed interest? If so,
at what rate?

If you hold ZIP financing, will you pay a tax on interest not
actually received? If so, what portion of the loan is regarded
as taxable income?

12
Loans to Avoid

There is a vast array of loan choices available to the public at any time and yet borrowers are often lured into transactions that are implausible if not unworkable. Often these arrangements are described in glowing terms as "too good to be true," a phrase which is literally correct in too many instances.

Different arrangements work for different borrowers, so with the exception of fraudulent transactions there are few strategies that are not right for someone. The problem is that a given strategy that is "right" for one person may be "wrong" for virtually everyone else. Three such mortgages are land contracts, roll-over loans and 40-year mortgages.

LAND CONTRACTS

If one were to concoct the worst possible consumer mortgage it would be difficult to construct a concept less appealing than the land contract, an arrangement in which borrowers have debt without title.

With a land contract a borrower makes payments on a loan but *title* (ownership) is not conveyed until a certain number of payments, or all payments, have been made. Since ownership has not officially changed hands a buyer has only an "equitable" interest in the property. In the event a single payment is missed the borrower can lose the property, including the value of the down payment, monthly principal reductions and all accumulated equity because title is in the name of the lender.

This arrangement, which is also called an *installment contract, contract for deed* or a *conditional sales agreement,* is commonly used in recreational land sales and timesharing purchases because the developer has many, many small units to sell and the cost of foreclosing on tiny loans is prohibitive. By using land contracts the developer is assured of either getting paid or being able to re-sell the property quickly, since he has not given up title.

Since recreational land sales and timeshare purchases tend to be relatively small real estate deals, buyers should consider personal loans as an alternative to land contracts. With homes, where far more money and much deeper personal concerns are at stake, land contracts should be avoided. Indeed, the suggestion of land contract financing for a private home should cause buyers to look at the entire deal with caution.

Although title does not change hands immediately when land contracts are employed, borrowers should ask if the deal will at least be filed in public records, a requirement in a growing number of jurisdictions. Recordation alerts the public to the claims of the title holder and the existence of any rights a borrower may have with a land contract.

In most instances land contracts involve either newly developed properties or sales with freely assumable financing. However, when interest rates are high it sometimes happens that a home is sold with a loan that cannot be assumed. To get around the assumption ban, buyer and seller may try to use a land contract which is not recorded in public records.

The seller in such cases continues to make monthly mortgage payments to the original lender, while the buyer, in turn, pays the seller on a monthly basis. The buyer gets to record title when interest rates drop and the property can be refinanced or when the debt to the seller is paid off.

This is an area of great controversy, since some attorneys argue that a land contract does not violate assumption bans, so-called due-on-sale clauses. Other lawyers strenuously disagree because, they contend, the seller has no intention of regaining occupancy and has therefore effectively given up possession.

In those situations where the loan is assumable, it makes far more sense for the buyer to assume the loan, get a second trust or wraparound note from the seller and record the entire transaction to assure that all legal and equitable rights have been fully protected. If the original loan is not assumable, then one has to ask if the purpose of an unrecorded transaction, where the original mortgage is not paid off, is to deny the rights of a lender. If there is a question about whether or not the loan is assumable, then one should consult with a knowledgeable real estate attorney before making a commitment.

In discussing land contracts there has, as yet, been no mention of interest rates or terms. The reason is that any loan format can be the basis of a land-contract arrangement as long as title does not pass to the borrower at the beginning of the loan.

Note that a *land contract* is entirely different from a *land lease* or a *ground lease*. A land lease is an arrangement in which ground and improvements are owned separately. For instance, Mr. Hubbard could erect an apartment building on ground owned by Mrs. Thornton. Thornton would rent the use of the land for a given period, say 75 years, at which point Hubbard's rights as a renter would end and Thornton or, more likely, Mrs. Thornton's heirs, would then own the building.

From the questions that follow, it should be clear that land contracts raise a variety of basic issues not found in other financing arrangements. If, for some reason, a land contract seems enticing at least have a knowledgeable real estate attorney review the deal before getting involved.

Questions to ask:

If a payment is late is there a grace period?

What are the rights of the borrower if a payment is missed entirely?

Who pays the property taxes?

What are the rights and credits, if any, of the borrower if a single payment is missed?

Since he or she is not an owner of record, what right does the borrower have to modify the property? Must the title holder give permission before the property is painted or the hot-water heater is updated?

What right, if any, does the buyer have to raise capital by getting a second trust? What lender would make such loans to someone without actual title?

Is the installment contract assumable? Can it be prepaid?

What right does the borrower have to sell the property?

In those jurisdictions that have rent control, is the borrower a tenant under such regulations? If so, what rights and obligations are created?

What are the rights of the buyer if the seller fails to pay the original lender?

Who pays for fire, theft and liability insurance, the borrower or the seller? (Lenders often find out about unrecorded land contracts when they receive annual renewal notices from insurers. When the names of the owner of record and the insured don't match, lenders will ask why.)

If the property burns down, who gets the insurance money? The owner of record (the seller)? The borrower? Neither? Both? If both, who gets what portion?

Who pays property taxes? If you are not an owner can you get a tax deduction? Speak to a CPA or tax attorney for advice.

ROLL-OVER LOANS

Outside of a land contract there is no loan with less innate appeal than a roll-over mortgage. Roll-overs feature interest at or near conventional rates, conventional down payments, short terms and mammoth balloon payments—a foul recipe for virtually all borrowers. (See Table 28.)

TABLE 28
Roll-Over versus Conventional Financing

	Roll-Over	Conventional
Interest rate	At or marginally below market	Market
Down payment	20 percent	20 percent
Initial term	Usually 5 years	30 years
Balloon payment	Yes	No

When self-amortizing, long-term conventional loans were first popularized in the 1930s they largely replaced the "term" mortgage. A term mortgage was a short loan, say 5 years, which usually required only payments for interest. At the end of the term the borrower repaid the entire principal.

Since borrowers did not normally have the entire value of the mortgage in cash at any one time, at the end of each term they would merely go out and get new financing. This process meant that loan balances were forever outstanding and that new fees and interest rates could be charged every few years.

Today the term loan with minor modifications is back, only now it is called a *roll-over* or *Canadian roll-over* mortgage. (Roll-overs are used more widely in Canada than in the United States.) With a roll-over loan, a borrower gets a mortgage for a stipulated amount and with payments figured on a 25- or 30-year term. The loan, however, lasts only 5 years.

At the end of 5 years there's a gargantuan balloon payment to consider. Because of the way that 25- and 30-year loans are amortized, the size of the balloon payment will not be very much smaller than the original principal balance. For example, at the end of five years, a fixed-rate $85,000 loan at 10 percent interest will have a remaining balance of $82,088.17.

What does a buyer do now? In many cases, roll-over loans have a provision through which the lender "guarantees" to provide another 5-year note. However, unless there is a cap the interest rate in the second term may be any number selected by the lender.

The lender at the end of the first 5-year term is in a marvelous position to get a premium rate, since the borrower's alternative, other than selling or being foreclosed, is to refinance with someone else. Refinancing is likely to involve costly loan origination fees, points, and settlement charges—new title searches, appraisals, etc. A premium interest rate in such circumstances may be the best of several poor choices.

TABLE 29
Roll-Over Amortization

Loan size	$85,000
Interest rate	10 percent
Monthly payment	$745.94
Loan balance at the end of	
Year 1	$84,527.50
Year 2	$84,005.53
Year 3	$83,428.90
Year 4	$82,791.89
Year 5	$82,088.17
Balloon payment	$82,088.17

Even if a second 5-year term is guaranteed, a third term usually is not. At this point a borrower must find new financing if the property is to be retained.

The lack of a long-term loan commitment raises all the problems associated with balloon financing generally: There is no guarantee that funds will be available to refinance the roll-over note and there is no promise that if such funds are available the borrower will qualify for financing. Even if money is available, interest rates may be so high that new financing is ludicrously expensive anyway. Finally, a roll-over loan is nothing more than a short-term balloon note—a terrible arrangement from the borrower's standpoint.

It is difficult to imagine a situation in which roll-over financing is advantageous to borrowers. If interest rates are abnormally high, the time when roll-over loans are more likely to be in style, one would be better off with ARM financing. The ARM interest rate is likely to be at or below current market levels. Moreover, an ARM is a long-term commitment by a lender. While borrowers may worry about rising monthly payments with an ARM, at least they are not faced with the certainty of a giant balloon payment in a few years.

If interest rates are low the need for a roll-over loan approaches zero. Why get a loan that is essentially term financing when plenty of money is available in more attractive formats?

Questions to ask:

What is the interest rate for conventional financing?

What is the interest rate for a roll-over loan?

How much cash is required for a down payment?

What is the term of the roll-over loan?

Does the lender guarantee to continue the loan for an additional term?

Must you be "financially qualified" to continue roll-over financing for a second term?

Will the lender continue the loan for a third term? A fourth?

Will the lender allow you to convert to conventional financing if interest rates decline to a certain point? What point?

If the lender does guarantee to renew the loan, how much notice will you receive regarding any new interest rate?

Is there a cap on the interest level for a second term?

Is the roll-over loan assumable?

Can the roll-over loan be prepaid in whole or in part without penalty at any time?

THE 40-YEAR MORTGAGE

Whenever money is tight some bright person comes up with this thought: Monthly mortgage payments would be lower if loan terms were stretched from 30 to 40 years. If monthly payments were lower more people could qualify for financing. Therefore, why not have more 40-year loans? Here's why:

Suppose you want to borrow $85,000 at 10 percent. A 30-year note for this sum will require monthly payments of $745.94, while a 40-year loan will have monthly installments of $721.77. However, for the monthly saving of $24.16, a figure which is positively minute in the context of this loan, the 40-year note will require 120 additional monthly payments. (See Table 30.)

TABLE 30
Conventional Loan Comparison by Term

Loan size	$85,000	$85,000	$85,000
Loan term	15 years	30 years	40 years
Interest rate	10 percent	10 percent	10 percent
Number of payments	180	360	480
Monthly payment	$913.41	$745.94	$721.77
Monthly cost differential	+167.47	None	−24.17
Balloon payment	None	None	None
Total potential interest	$79,413.80	$183,536.90	$261,449.60

If paid out over their respective terms, the ultimate difference between the two loans will be $77,911.10 ($745.94 × 360 payments vs. $721.77 × 480 payments). Thus by making 360 additional monthly payments of $24.17—or $8,701.20 over 30 years—a borrower could potentially save over $77,900, or almost the entire value of the original loan.

Huge potential interest costs plus marginal monthly savings suggest that longer loans are simply unfavorable to most buyers. If in the context of an $85,000 mortgage it's important to save $24.17 per month, both buyer and lender would be better off if the purchaser bought a smaller, more affordable property.

Questions to ask:

What is the monthly cost of a 30-year mortgage?

What is the monthly cost of a 40-year loan?

How much cash is required for a down payment with 40-year financing?

What is the possible interest cost for a 30-year loan? (To find the total potential interest cost of a 30-year mortgage, multiply 360 times the value of the monthly payment and subtract the original face value of the mortgage.)

What is the potential interest cost of a 40-year mortgage? (Multiply 480 times the monthly payment and subtract the original face value of the mortgage.)

13

Loan Restructuring:

Four Profit Strategies
Produce Big Mortgage Interest Cuts

Many people believe that once a mortgage has been made its terms are set in stone. Year after year they make regular payments without a thought to restructuring their loans and as a result they fail to quickly and easily cut interest costs by thousands of dollars.

As attractive as refinancing may be, it has become a more complex process under tax reform. Prior to tax reform, if you refinanced a house the interest on your new loan was fully deductible. Under tax reform, however, interest costs may be deductible, not deductible or possibly deductible only in part.

In basic terms, if you refinance a primary residence or a second home today the interest cost is deductible up to the original purchase price of the property plus all capital improvements. "Capital improvements" might include an addition to the property or a new furnace.

Suppose you bought a home in 1970 for $35,000. Today it's worth $190,000. If you refinance now for $100,000, interest on the first $35,000 is fully deductible while charges on the $65,000 balance are not.

Interest on the $65,000 remainder is partially deductible in 1987 (65 percent), 1988 (40 percent), 1989 (20 percent) and a meager 10 percent in 1990. After 1990, forget it.

Naturally, a 900-page reform act devoted to simplicity and

fairness would be incomplete without a few exceptions. You can deduct interest for loans above the property's original purchase price plus improvements if the money is used for education or medical expenses. Also, if a home is used to secure commercial debt, it seems likely that all interest is deductible in that case because the loan is for an active business purpose.

Points are another tax issue to consider when refinancing. Points have traditionally been deductible in the year in which they were charged, the theory being they're a form of interest. In 1986, however, new rules stipulated that although points used to acquire real estate were deductible at the time of purchase, points charged for *refinancing* were not. Instead, deductions for points must be allocated over the loan's term.

Interest deductions and points are two major issues which should concern property owners who refinance. Before you restructure a loan, be certain to *first* check with a CPA or tax attorney for the latest rules, regulations and interpretations. In particular, the concept of allocating deductions for points over the life of a loan is being debated in Washington and it's possible by the time you read this book that Congress may have changed the system back to the old rule.

A REFINANCING QUARTET

Restructuring a loan means nothing more than changing the terms of repayment on an existing mortgage with few if any fees to the lender. For example, Mr. Conrad has a 30-year, $85,000 mortgage at 10 percent interest. After 5 years the principal balance is down to $82,088.17.

Rather than make 300 more payments (25 years) of $745.94, Conrad decides to pay off the loan in 20 years. He does this by merely increasing his monthly payments $46.23 a month to $792.17. The result is that over 20 years he makes additional payments of $11,095.20 (240 months $\times$ $46.23). He saves $44,-

756 (60 months × $745.94). His net benefit is $33,660.80 ($44,-756 less $11,095.20). (See Table 31.)

TABLE 31
Mr. Conrad's Restructured Loan

	Original Terms	New Terms
Loan amount	$82,088.17	$82,088.17
Remaining term	25 years	20 years
Monthly payment	$745.94	$792.17
Extra monthly cost	None	$46.23
Total extra cost	None	$11,095.20
Total payment	$223,782	$190,120.80
Cash saved	None	$33,660.80

Before mortgages can be revised a borrower must first find out about prepayment rules and penalties.

Prepayment penalties are fees and charges designed to stop or discourage borrowers from making early repayments. Lenders, however, cannot always charge prepayment fees, since they are regulated in many jurisdictions and with certain types of loans.

For example, there is no prepayment penalty with FHA loans, provided the prepayment is not less than the monthly installment. In some jurisdictions there is no prepayment penalty if a loan is over three years old or if the prepayment is above a certain size, say $10,000 in the first year. Moreover, it should be said that in many cases lenders will wave penalties to rid their books of an unwanted (read "low yield") mortgage.

Conceivably, if a loan is silent on the matter of prepayments or permits the borrower to repay the note at any time in whole or in part without penalty, a borrower has the right to restructure a loan at will as long as monthly payments do not drop.

To restructure a loan one must first examine the lowly amortization statement, a table showing monthly mortgage payments, payment allocations for interest and principal and the mortgage balance.

Except for adjustable rate loans, where future monthly payments, interest rates and principal balances cannot be guaranteed, amortization schedules demonstrate how various mortgage formats compare. They also illustrate how rapid repayment strategies can produce tremendous mortgage savings.

With a 30-year, $85,000 conventional mortgage at 10 percent interest the monthly payments will be $745.94 per month for 360 months. Yet while the payments are equal, the pace of amortization is not.

- In the first month only $37.60 of the $745.94 payment goes to reduce the principal balance. In fact, in the first year the total principal reduction is just $472.50, while interest payments amount to $8,951.23.
- At the end of the tenth year, payment #120, the mortgage balance is $77,297.32—despite total payments of $89,512.80 (120 × $745.94).
- At the end of the fifteenth year, payment #180, the mortgage balance drops to $69,414.88—after total payments of $134,269.20 (180 × $745.94).
- In the twenty-ninth year, the principal reduction is $8,484.-65, while interest amounts to only $466.58. (The last month's payment is $745.95, or $0.01 more than the previous 359 installments.)

The nature of mortgage amortization means that prepayments at the beginning of the mortgage term have greater financial impact than those at the end. With this principle in view, here are four rapid repayment programs for a 30-year, $85,000 mortgage at 10 percent interest.

Program 1: The Steady Payment Approach. Prior to settlement you see that your $85,000 mortgage requires monthly payments of $745.94. However, if the same loan were repaid over a 15-year period, the payments would move up to $913.41—a difference of $167.47 per month. Since you anticipate a rising income, you elect to spend a week of vacation at home in the coming year to raise the additional $2,009.69 needed for the first 12 monthly payments. Future pay raises will cover the additional cost in the following years.

You tell the lender of your plan and the lender agrees, in writing, to waive any prepayment penalties. Why? Because most loans are outstanding less than 15 years anyway and by making regular monthly payments at a set rate the lender has few bookkeeping problems.

Potential Savings: You pay an additional $167.47 for 180 months, or $30,144.60 over 15 years. You save $104,076.00 (180 payments × $745.94 equals $134,269.20 less $30,193.20).

TABLE 32
Amortization Schedule

	30-Year Loan	15-Year Loan
Loan amount	$85,000	$85,000
Interest rate	10 percent	10 percent
Number of payments	360	180
Payment size	$745.94	$913.41
Extra monthly payment	None	$167.47
Potential interest cost	$183,538.40	$79,413.80
Potential saving	None	$104,076.00

Program #2: The Double-up Plan. You check the amortization schedule and see that in the first month the payment is $745.94, but only $37.60 goes to reduce principal. In the second month you see that the same payment is made but the principal balance drops by the munificent sum of only $37.92. You decide to go from payment #1 to payment #3. When it comes time

to make your first payment you write out a check for $783.86
($745.94 plus $37.92). The principal balance has now been reduced by both $37.60 and $37.92.

	Interest	Principal	Balance
Month 1	$708.33	$37.60	$84,962.40
Month 2	$708.02	$37.92	$84,924.48
Month 3	$707.70	$38.23	$84,886.25

Potential Savings: You effectively move down the amortization schedule from month 1 to month 3 and therefore do not
pay $708.02 in interest for month 2. However, you do make
your regular payment in the second month and in all following
months. If you hold the loan to maturity there will be one less
payment to make.

Note that by paying ahead your interest deduction for the
year has hardly dropped at all. Instead of paying interest on
months 1 through 12, a total of $8,478.73, you pay interest on
month 1 ($708.33) and months 3 through 13 ($7,766.78), a total
of $8,474.80. For tax purposes, then, the amount of interest you
could deduct for the year is reduced $3.93.

Program #3: The Lump-Sum Rapid Reduction. Lenders
are not normally too pleased about an advance payment of
$37.92, and your lender requires prepayments of at least a full
month's usual payment, or $745.94 in this case. At the end of
the first year you have made 12 payments and the mortgage
balance is reduced to $84,527.50. By making an additional pay-
ment of $745.94 you reduce the loan balance to $83,781.56.
Had you followed the usual amortization program you would
not have reached this level until payment 37, when the principal balance was scheduled to total $83,378.20.

Potential Savings: You have skipped ahead 25 payments
worth $18,648.50. To achieve this advantage you spent $745.94

	Interest	Principal	Balance
Payment 12	$704.74	$41.20	$84,527.50
Payment 37	$695.24	$50.70	$83,378.20

Your maximum potential net benefit is $17,902.56 ($18,648.50 less $745.94).

Program #4: Large Lump-Sum Rapid Repayment. You see from the amortization statement that the principal balance of the loan will be $69,414.88 after 15 years of payments—a drop of only $15,585.12. The first year you get the mortgage you decide to postpone the purchase of a new car and instead get a $16,000 personal loan from a local lender at 13 percent interest. The loan must be repaid over 4 years with monthly payments of $429.24, or a total cost of $20,603.52. (Alternatively, you receive a gift of $16,000 from a relative, sell stock or whatever.) You take the $16,000 and eliminate 182 mortgage payments.

Potential Savings: You spent $20,603.52 but save $136,104.21 (182.46 × $745.94). The maximum net benefit is $115,500.69 ($136,104.21 less $20,603.52). At the beginning of the loan, you have effectively created a self-amortizing loan with an initial principal of $69,414.88 that can be paid off with 180 equal monthly installments of $745.94. (See Table 33.)

The benefits of the above strategies can be measured within two boundaries. If you hold a mortgage through its full term you will get the total benefit cited in each example. If, however, you sell a property before the mortgage is paid off your minimum benefit will be interest not paid, taxes not assessed on interest "savings" and a smaller loan balance to pay off when you sell.

In addition to saving money, each of these mortgage-reduction strategies offers a series of important advantages:

First, each program is at the option of the borrower. You

TABLE 33
Large Lump-Sum Repayment Plan

Car loan principal	$16,000
Monthly payments	$429.24
Number of payments	48
Total cost	$20,603.52
House loan principal	$85,000
Monthly payments	$745.94
Number of payments	360
House loan less money from car loan	69,000
Monthly payments	$745.94
Number of payments	177.54
Payments saved	182.46
Dollars saved	$136,104.21
Less car loan cost	$20,603.52
Net benefit	$115,500.69

don't have to develop an interest-reduction program but it is good to know that you can.

Second, in each case 100 percent of the principal is being repaid. This means that the loan has not been discounted and since there is no discount there is no income to tax.

Third, all property owners should periodically review the mortgage market to see if an interest-reduction program is appropriate. Deals which may not have been possible at the time property was acquired may arise in later years.

Fourth, many people view a home mortgage as a discomforting burden which should be repaid even if rapid repayments are not the best financial choice. Interest-reduction programs are especially valuable for such individuals.

Questions to ask:

Can you repay present financing in whole or in part at any time without penalty?

If there is a penalty what is it?

Will the lender waive the penalty if you agree to higher but steady payments?

What is the current interest rate on your mortgage?

What is the prevailing, post-tax return on alternative investments such as money market funds, savings accounts or government securities?

What are the tax consequences if you rapidly repay your mortgage? Speak to a CPA or tax authority for more information.

Should you refinance or restructure or is your money better invested elsewhere? What about reducing credit card balances or paying off car loans?

What are the tax consequences of your prospective new financing?

FULL CURTAILMENTS: HOW TO PAY OFF LOANS AT DISCOUNT

If that stock market hunch finally paid off or Uncle Jasper left you with a large chunk of cash, you may want to examine the idea of repaying your current mortgage with a single lump sum, a process known as a full or total *curtailment*.

A full curtailment differs from a restructuring program in two ways.

First, the loan is being paid off at one time.

Second, a full curtailment often involves a principal discount. Part of the loan debt is usually forgiven in exchange for the prepayment, particularly when the lender wants to close an unprofitable loan.

Suppose you can get 9 percent interest from a simple savings account. Suppose also that you have a 6 percent mortgage with a remaining balance of $25,000 and 15 years left on it.

At 6 percent, $25,000 will earn $1,500 a year in simple interest. If you can get 9 percent, a savings account with $16,666.67

will yield the same $1,500. If you had $25,000 in the account you would earn $2,250.

	Interest Rate	Yield
$25,000	6 percent	$1,500
$25,000	9 percent	$2,250
$16,666	9 percent	$1,500

Clearly you would do better to leave your money in the savings account rather than pay off the remaining loan balance. But what would happen if the lender said, "Look, give us the $16,666 and we'll consider the loan fully paid." Would you take an $8,334 cash discount—a one-third savings in this case?

While the lender would obviously prefer to get the entire $25,000, a curtailment could be a better deal than another 15 years of low-interest payments. For the lender, getting back almost $17,000 means getting rid of your old loan and putting more cash in the vault, money that can be re-loaned as new, higher-rate financing with up-front points and fees.

Loan curtailments are possible at any time but discounts are unlikely when your home is on the market. If the lender is aware that you are selling property, he is also aware that your loan is likely to be repaid in full at settlement—particularly if the loan value is a small portion of the total sales price. For this reason borrowers looking for a curtailment should approach lenders well before placing their homes for sale.

However, if you have a buyer who can finance the property with or without the loan, you again will be in a position to seek a discount.

One word of caution: As this is being written the value of a mortgage discount, that is, the difference between the remaining principal balance and the cash used to repay the loan, is regarded as regular income for tax purposes. Thus a discount may raise your taxable income, so when calculating the value of a discount, attention must be paid to the possible tax costs involved, taxes which will reduce the benefit of any discount you obtain.

Note that a discount on a principal balance is treated differently than a loan which is structured to pay less interest. If you pay less interest that is merely a "saving" and therefore not taxable.

For current information about curtailment tax angles speak to a tax attorney or CPA.

Questions to ask:

What is the interest rate on your current financing?

What is the rate of return on alternative conservative investments such as savings accounts or money market funds?

How much cash do you have available for a curtailment?

What deal can you make with a lender?

If you pay off an FHA mortgage where the insurance premium was pre-paid, how much of the premium will be refunded? When can you expect a refund? Speak to your lender or whoever services the mortgage for details.

What are the tax consequences of a curtailment?

DON'T FORGET HIDDEN REFINANCING COSTS

When considering either a partial or complete refinancing borrowers should be concerned with more than interest rates.

Because of the many add-on charges involved, the full cost of refinancing is often concealed in a maze of charges, fees, and accounting concepts that can easily distort the advantages of lower rates.

Suppose Mr. Grayson has a 30-year, $85,000 mortgage at 13

percent interest. The monthly payments for principal and interest are $940.27. With 10 percent money, the monthly cost drops to $745.94, a difference of more than $2,330 per year.

Although the new rate is certainly attractive, one must consider the one-time, up-front expenses requried to get the better financing. If you expect to sell your property within a few years, these costs may wipe out the benefits of lower interest rates. Here are some of the charges to anticipate, items that alone may seem small but when added together seriously affect the true cost of borrowing.

- Points (loan discount fees): A point is equal to 1 percent of the value of a mortgage. Unlike a sales situation where buyer and seller may split the cost of financing, with a refinancing situation there is no one with whom the fee can be divided. Cost: 1 percent or more of the mortgage. For Mrs. Grayson at least $850.
- Loan Origination Fee: Essentially a charge by the lender to grant the loan. Cost: 1 percent of the loan.
- Appraisal: An appraisal will be required by the lender to establish the property's value. Cost: $200 and up.
- Credit Report: A lender will examine your finances and charge a credit report fee. Cost: $25 to $50.
- Application Fee: A payment to the lender for processing the loan. Cost: varies and may be waived when refinancing with the lender who holds the current mortgage.
- Prepayment Penalty: A charge established in the original mortgage to discourage early repayment. Such charges are limited in many jurisdictions and in some cases may be waived by lenders. Cost: from zero to a fixed percentage of the remaining mortgage balance or the value of interest for a certain period, perhaps six months.
- Survey: In some cases, a lender may require a survey, particularly for detached property. Cost: varies considerably.

- Termite Inspection: May be required by lenders. Cost: $35 to $75.
- Taxes: Local jurisdictions charge recording fees to place documents in public files, others actually tax new financing. Cost: varies considerably.
- Title Insurance: Lenders will commonly require title insurance up to the value of their loan. In the event the title is faulty, "lenders" title insurance assures that the party making the mortgage will be repaid. Cost: varies by jurisdiction and according to the size of the new mortgage. Suggestion: see if you qualify for a "re-issue" rate. In cases where there has been a title search in the past five to ten years, many insurers offer a discounted rate and you may save 10 to 20 percent.
- Legal: New financing requires a new title search, document preparation, and other legal and paralegal services. Cost: expect to pay for specific services according to local regulations and the requirements of the lender.

Borrowers often ask if it is better to refinance in whole or in part. While there is no absolute answer that is correct in all cases, it should be said that partial refinancing is frequently advantageous for two reasons. First, with partial refinancing such as second trusts and wraparound loans, original mortgages with low interest rates can often be retained. Second, non-interest costs are generally cheaper with partial refinancing because the overall loan size is smaller.

Time is also important when refinancing. If you expect to hold property for a relatively short period it may actually pay to keep current, high interest loans. The reason: the benefit of low interest financing may be offset by high non-interest expenses. To make the best decision, check with local lenders to see whether interest and non-interest costs make refinancing worthwhile in your situation.

14
Saving Money with Short-Term Strategies

Despite all the attention and emphasis adjustable-rate loans have received since the early 1980s, there has always been an interest in fixed-rate financing, loans without gimmicks, indexes or the possibility of rising monthly payments. But if conventional 30-year loans have proved so costly in today's high-interest world, what is the alternative?

An increasing number of borrowers, particularly those who are refinancing or purchasing homes for the second time, are turning to 15-year mortgages. Such loans offer all the advantages of conventional financing but without enormous interest costs.

In addition, bi-weekly loans have been introduced around the country as an alternative to adjustable-rate financing. While such loans have received extensive publicity, they as yet represent a wrinkle in the marketplace rather than a trend.

THE 15-YEAR MORTGAGE

If there is a single word to describe the mortgage world of the 1980s, it is "complexity." We have GPARMs, GEMs and RAMs, loans with variable interest rates and mortgages with which you can wind up owing more than you borrow. But instead of all this confusion, what about something simple? Why not a self-amortizing loan with level monthly payments, one interest rate (preferably something low) and sensible overall interest costs?

At first it might seem that cutting a loan term in half will double monthly payments, but this is not the case. For an $85,-000 mortgage paid out over 30 years at 10 percent interest, the monthly cost will be $745.94. If the loan term is only 15 years, the monthly payment will rise to $913.41, a difference of $167.47 per month.

The very fact that a loan has a term of 15 years rather than 30 years means monthly payments must be higher because there are fewer of them. However, because the loan term is shorter, less principal is outstanding over time and so interest costs are greatly reduced. The potential interest bill for the 30-year loan above is $183,537, while the greatest possible cost for the 15-year mortgage is only $79,413.80—a savings of $104,-113.20.

So now we have an example where the loan term is cut in half, monthly payments rise by $167.47, and we can save as much as $104,113. Sounds okay, but there is one slight problem: this example is wholly unrealistic.

The reason this illustration does not work goes back to the concept of risk. The longer the loan term, the greater the risk to the lender. Conversely, the shorter the loan term, the smaller the risk. Less risk, in turn, means lenders can accept lower interest rates.

In the example above we compared two loans with identical interest rates. Although some lenders will gladly charge equal rates, smart borrowers should be able to do better. How much better depends on local market conditions, but interest savings of one-quarter to one-half percent should be readily available.

If we cut the interest rate on the 15-year loan above to 9.5 percent, we will have monthly payments of just $887.59, an increase of $141.65 per month. Total potential interest costs will drop to $74,766.38, and so we could save as much as $108,-

770.52 when compared to our model 30-year mortgage at 10 percent interest.

TABLE 34
15-Year versus 30-Year Financing

Loan amount	$85,000	$85,000	$85,000
Loan term	30 years	15 years	15 years
Interest rate	10 percent	10 percent	9.5 percent
Monthly payment	$745.94	$913.41	$887.59
Additional monthly cost	None	$167.47	$141.65
Potential interest	$183,536.90	$79,413.80	$74,766.20
Potential savings	None	$104,123.10	$108,770.70

The use of 15-year financing clearly results in significant interest savings. It is also clear that such mortgages are becoming increasingly common. But is a 15-year mortgage appropriate for everyone? Should it be the new "conventional" mortgage, the loan by which other mortgage formats are measured?

Even though 15-year loans have obvious economic benefits, the reality of the marketplace is that many people will not be able to select such financing. In the context of the loan above, an additional $141.65 may not be feasible for first-time home buyers, purchasers with limited means or those buying on the brink of affordability. Fifteen-year mortgages can be extremely attractive, however, and they seem to make sense for three groups of borrowers:

- Second-time buyers who have accumulated cash from the sale of house number one. Such individuals typically can make larger down payments than first-time buyers and have larger incomes to support monthly payments.
- Those seeking an enforced savings program—people with additional money to spend each month but who will otherwise fritter the money away if not obligated to spend it for mortgage payments.

- Borrowers who look at potential interest costs and recognize that huge savings are possible with minimal additional payments.

Another growing use for 15-year mortgages is in the area of refinancing. Suppose Mr. Castle bought property in 1984 and obtained a 30-year conventional mortgage for $85,000 at 13 percent interest. His monthly payments are now $940.27. By mid-1987, Mr. Castle could refinance his property with a 15-year loan at 9.5 percent. His new monthly payment will be $887.59—a monthly saving of $52.68

TABLE 35
A Look at Mr. Castle's Refinancing

	Old Loan	New Loan
Loan amount	$85,000	$85,000
Loan term	30 years	15 years
Interest rate	13 percent	9.5 percent
Monthly payment	$940.27	$887.59
Additional monthly cost	$52.68	None
Potential interest	$253,497.20	$74,766.20
Potential savings	None	$178,731.00

Not only will monthly costs decline, but Mr. Castle will also cut his overall interest bill. With the 30-year mortgage he faced a potential interest cost of $253,497. With his new mortgage his interest bill is limited to $74,766. Total potential savings: $178,-731.

Mr. Castle, however, must ask a question: How much will it cost to refinance the property? If his cost is $3,000, then he must remain on the property for 57 months ($3,000 divided by $52.-68) if he is to recover his refinancing costs from monthly savings alone. In addition, of course, he is paying off his debt faster and accumulating equity more quickly than with a 30-year mortgage.

Still another use of the 15-year mortgage is to raise additional capital in a refinancing situation. If Mr. Lawrence, like Mr. Castle, has a 30-year mortgage at 13 percent, he too is paying $940.27 a month. But what if he needs additional money? If he refinanced for 15 years at 9.5 percent and elected to still pay $940.27 per month, he could get a $90,045 loan. His potential interest cost will equal $84,248.60. Thus Mr. Lawrence can maintain his monthly payments, refinance, pull in an additional $5,045 in cash and still cut his potential interest bill by $168,-893.45. Although some of his new-found money will undoubtedly go for up-front refinancing expenses, Mr. Lawrence is still ahead.

TABLE 36
How Mr. Lawrence Raised Additional Capital

	Old Loan	New Loan
Loan amount	$85,000	$90,045
Loan term	30 years	15 years
Interest rate	13 percent	9.5 percent
Monthly payment	$940.27	$940.27
Additional monthly cost	None	None
Additional cash	None	$5,045
Potential interest	$253,497.05	$84,603.60
Potential savings	None	$168,893.45

Whatever the economics of 15-year mortgages, these loans at least have the advantage of being understandable to consumers. With a 15-year mortgage no one worries about obscure indexes or negative amortization—the loan and its terms are clear. Lenders also like the 15-year concept because it offers less risk and fewer administrative problems than long-term mortgages or loans with changing payments and interest levels.

As for the interest "lost" by lenders under a 15-year repayment schedule, don't worry. The faster a loan is paid off, the faster lenders can turn around and issue new loans that generate not only interest but also additional fees, charges and points. All together, not a bad deal for everyone.

Questions to ask:

What is the interest rate for conventional financing?

What is the best local interest rate for a 15-year mortgage?

What is the cost per month for conventional financing?

What is the cost per month for a 15-year loan?

What is the additional monthly cost for 15-year financing?

What is the total potential interest cost for a 30-year mortgage?

What is the total potential interest cost for a 15-year mortgage?

What are the potential savings from the use of a 15-year mortgage?

What is the difference in terms of interest and monthly payments between your current mortgage and a 15-year loan?

How much will it cost to refinance your property?

If you refinance your property, based on monthly savings alone, how long should you remain in the house to recapture refinancing costs?

If you continued to make your present monthly payments but switched to 15-year financing, how much additional capital could you raise?

THE BI-WEEKLY MORTGAGE

In the eternal search for better mortgages, lenders and borrowers have tried every possible financial concoction. Today we have a tremendous number of loan alternatives, including what may be the most publicized and least-used home financing idea in recent history, the bi-weekly mortgage.

The bi-weekly mortgage is distinguished by the fact that instead of 12 mortgage payments per year, borrowers make 26 payments to lenders. Each payment, however, is only half the size of a regular monthly payment, and so the results are lower costs per payment, higher costs per year, faster loan amortization, shorter loan terms and reduced interest costs.

If we borrow $85,000 on a conventional 30-year basis at 10 percent interest, we will have monthly payments of $745.94. The interest bill over 30 years will total $183,536.90.

Here's what happens if we borrow $85,000 at the same interest rate but on a bi-weekly basis:

First, we just about divide the conventional payment in half, paying out in this case $391.94 every two weeks.

Second, we make 26 bi-weekly payments per year.

Third, the loan is paid off in 18 years.

Fourth, the interest bill totals just $98,425, a savings of $85,-111.90 over the conventional loan.

So we have a loan that does indeed result in a huge interest saving. But although the bi-weekly loan produces significant interest economies, it does so in a needlessly complex manner.

The basic question about the bi-weekly loan is this: why bother? There are other ways to accomplish the same goal with far less hassle. For instance, why not just make monthly payments of $849.87? The loan will be repaid in the same 18 years and the potential interest bill will total $98,571.31—again a huge savings when compared with conventional financing. Just as important, the annual cost of mortgage payments will remain essentially equal, going from $10,190.44 ($391.94 × 26) to $10,-198.41 ($849.87 × 12). (See Table 37.)

From the lender's point of view, the bi-weekly mortgage poses new administrative headaches. There are 26 payments to record each year and 26 chances to enter the wrong information on a computer. At a time when lenders have their hands

TABLE 37
The Bi-weekly Mortgage Compared

Amount borrowed	$85,000	$85,000	$85,000
Interest rate	10 percent	10 percent	10 percent
Loan term	30 years	18 years	18 years
Number of payments per year	12	26	12
Payment size	$745.94	$391.94	$849.87
Annual cash cost	$8,951.28	$10,177.44	$10,198.44
Additional cost per year	None	$1,226.16	$1,247.16
Potential interest cost	$183,536.90	$98,427.92	$98,571.92
Potential savings	None	$85,108.98	$84,964.98

full trying to account for ARM variables, why would any lender joyously suggest a loan that is difficult and costly to administer?

One answer is probably related to lender competition rather than the economics of the bi-weekly loan. Lenders vigorously compete for business, and lenders who can get an extra bit of notice are likely to attract more borrowers than those lenders who are virtually anonymous. The bi-weekly mortgage is something to talk about, it draws publicity. Whether it makes sense as a practical mortgage option for either lenders or consumers can be debated.

Another possible attraction of bi-weekly financing is that payments can be tied to automatic deposit plans, which means borrowers must maintain accounts with the lender. Rather than sending in a check every two weeks, payments are deducted directly from an account with the lender. The lender benefits by opening additional accounts (which he hopes will allow him to generate extra loans and interest) and by the possibility of offering additional services to the borrower, such as auto loans and checking accounts.

Although one would expect lower interest rates as loan terms become shorter, this is not necessarily true with bi-weekly mortgages. Even though there is a shorter pay-back period, which should mean less risk and therefore lower interest rates, the high administrative costs associated with bi-weekly financing may limit or disallow interest discounts. Until lenders can accurately assess administrative costs for such loans over several years—and until default patterns become clear—bi-weekly loans are not likely sources of discount financing.

Are bi-weekly mortgages a plausible financial option? They certainly save money when compared with 30-year loans, but one has to compare such programs with simple 15-year or 18-year financing as well as other mortgage options to make a valid decision.

Questions to ask:

What is the interest rate for conventional financing?

What is the interest rate for bi-weekly financing?

What is the monthly payment for a conventional loan?

What is the payment cost for each bi-weekly installment?

What is the total annual cost of a bi-weekly mortgage?

Can you repay the loan whole or in part without penalty?

If you obtain a 15-year or 18-year loan with monthly payments, how much will you pay per month? How much will you pay per year?

If you have a bi-weekly mortgage, must you open a savings or checking account with the lender? If so, what interest will your funds earn?

15
Your Questions Answered

The idea of cutting real estate mortgage costs is not revolutionary, unique or implausible. It can be done and it is being done by borrowers across the country. Travel to any city, speak with consumers and lenders, and you hear example after example of people who have cut mortgage interest bills by tens of thousands of dollars and often far more.

Since *The Common-Sense Mortgage* was first introduced early in 1985, I have met with journalists, participated in seminars and appeared on radio and television programs nationwide. Hundreds and hundreds of questions have been raised, and although most were originally addressed in the first edition of this guide, there are certain issues that were not specifically discussed or that should be reviewed in greater detail than was possible in the original text. Here are the most representative questions I've gathered from around the country.

Q. Loan qualification standards are getting tougher. What does this mean to me?

A.   If you buy property with at least 10 percent down, probably very little. But if you're looking for a deal with little or no money down, you may have a hard time getting a loan. For the past few years borrowers have been able to put down 5 percent of the purchase price and get loans based on the use of 28

percent of their gross yearly income for basic mortgage costs—
that is, principal, interest, taxes and insurance. If you had a
household income of $30,000, then $8,400 ($700 per month)
could be used for basic mortgage costs.

Today standards have been tightened. Most lenders will now
qualify applicants who put down less than 10 percent only on
the basis of a 25 percent income allocation for housing. For our
$30,000-income earner, this means only $7,500 ($625 per
month) can be used for basic mortgage costs.

Here's the difference. If you allow $25 per month for prop-
erty insurance and $75 per month for property taxes, under the
old standard $600 would be available for principal and interest.
If the interest rate is 10 percent, you could borrow $68,370.49
with a 30-year conventional loan. Under the new guidelines
only $525 will be available for principal and interest and you
will only be allowed to borrow $59,824.18.

Another change concerns ARMs. In the past, lenders have
often qualified ARM borrowers on the basis of initial rates. Since
ARM interest rates are typically 2 to 3 percentage points less
than conventional fixed-rate mortgages—at least at first—borrowers could get far larger loans by using ARMs. Now most
lenders will qualify ARM borrowers only if they can afford
enough fixed-rate financing to buy the property.

Under the old standard, our $30,000 wage earner might con-
sider either a 10 percent fixed-rate loan or perhaps an 8 percent
ARM. He could get $79,765.57 with the fixed-rate loan or $95,-
398.45 with an ARM. Under the new standard, he could only
qualify for a $79,765.57 loan in either case.

Another way to look at the new standards is to consider
affordability in terms of income. Suppose a home is selling for
$90,000. If you put down five percent ($4,500) you'll need a
mortgage for $85,500. If interest rates are 10 percent, if you can
only qualify for financing on the basis of 28 percent of your
income and if taxes and insurance total $100 per month, you

could get by with an income of $31,173 with the old formula. Under the new 25 percent standard, you will need an income of $34,914.

Since lenders are wholly independent, many will not adhere to the new "standards." If getting a home with little or no money down is important, then shop around for lenders who make nonstandard or "nonconforming" loans or sellers willing to take back financing. Otherwise, be prepared to scrape up more money for a down payment or to borrow less.

Q. Why are lenders asking for tougher standards?
A. Because, basically, many loans should never have been made in the past few years.

In a speech to the American Bankers Association, David O. Maxwell, chairman and chief executive officer of the Federal National Mortgage Association (Fannie Mae), said, "In all candor, in our efforts to survive as an industry, we probably qualified many people who should have remained out of the home-buying market in 1981 and 1982. In addition, we also created some new mortgage products that were ill advised—particularly those causing almost immediate negative amortization for the borrower."

If you look at the mortgage industry in the past few years, you can see that many loans were made with the expectation that housing prices would rise and so if a borrower defaulted on a loan, lenders could just foreclose and recapture their money. In essence it was felt there was little risk, particularly since prices had skyrocketed between 1970 and 1980.

Unfortunately prices don't always rise or rise as much as people expect. Worse yet, those nice, low foreclosure figures from the 1970s began to rise. Farmers failed, businesses in the Rust Bowl closed and creative financing deals in California and elsewhere backfired. The result: tougher loan standards to protect lenders.

Q.   You make a point of steering borrowers away from ARMs with negative amortization. Hasn't negative amortization been abandoned by lenders?

A.   Lenders have not abandoned negative amortization, clauses which allow increases in mortgage principal when monthly payments are insufficient to pay down the loan. Depending on whom you ask, negative amortization can be found in 10 to 15 percent of all ARMs.

Q.   What are the most common ARM caps?

A.   ARMs typically offer three types of caps. First, virtually all ARMs have a lifetime interest cap. In the past this cap has usually been set 5 percent above the initial interest rate, so if you started out with 8 percent financing your interest rate will never rise above 13 percent. Now, however, about one ARM in four has a cap pegged just 4 percent above the initial interest rate—good news for consumers!

A second type of cap is designed to limit periodic interest increases. About 75 percent of all ARMs limit interest increases to 2 percent a year or less.

The third type of cap is a limitation on annual payments. Usually cap is set at 7.5 percent; so if you are paying $500 per month this year, your maximum payment will be $537.50 next year.

The curious aspect of payment caps is that they are becoming less common. A study by the U.S. League of Savings Institutions shows payment caps were found in 59.1 percent of all ARMs in 1984 but in only 39.9 percent in 1985.

What these caps mean is that some lenders are making ARMs more attractive by limiting potential interest rates. At the same time, lenders are also expecting borrowers to pay increases in full as indexes rise. In effect there has been a trade-off of interests in the marketplace. You won't have negative amortization because all monthly payment increases will be paid in full.

Conversely, if you don't have the dollars to make larger monthly payments, you could face foreclosure.

Q.   What are "basis points"?

A.   When you or I talk about mortgage interest costs we might speak about a 12 percent mortgage or a 14 percent loan. The difference to us is 2 percent, but to a lender it is "200 basis points." Therefore, 100 basis points equal 1 percent, 50 basis points equal 0.5 percent and 25 basis points equal 0.25 percent of interest.

Q.   What's a reasonable interest spread between an ARM and 30-year fixed-rate financing?

A.   Assuming an equal number of points for both loans, an ARM should be discounted by at least 2 percent. If you can get fixed-rate financing at 10 percent then an ARM should be avoided unless the initial rate—which should be in effect for at least a year—is no greater than 8 percent.

Q.   What is the best ARM index?

A.   The best ARM index should cover the longest possible span of events. Unfortunately, there has been a turn in the opposite direction. Figures from the U.S. League of Savings Institutions show that nearly 62 percent of all ARMs made in May 1985 used rates based on one-year Treasury securities, up from 26.3 percent in June 1984.

The use of one-year Treasuries is attractive when rates are declining, as they did in 1985, because one-year Treasuries respond rapidly to changes in the marketplace. But what happens if interest rates rise? Treasuries can also go up rapidly. As an alternative, borrowers should consider the use of a cost-of-funds index, which is less prone to sudden movement.

Q. It seems so much easier to get an ARM rather than a fixed-rate mortgage. Why is this?

A. ARMs appear to be popular for three reasons. First, they have evolved in the past few years so that many of the conditions which once made ARMs unacceptable to borrowers have now been modified or removed. The result is a refined loan concept which can be attractive for selected borrowers and in specific situations.

Second, ARMs are heavily promoted. You don't see too many ads for FHA financing, VA mortgages or conventional loans. ARMs have also gotten extensive press coverage, in part because they are new, different and forever subject to change.

Third, ARMs have simply become more acceptable to the general public. The one-sided terms of the first ARMs have been replaced, millions of such loans are now outstanding, and so there is a body of public experience and low up-front rates which make them a loan format that cannot be ignored.

Q. We track our ARM payments closely and it seems as though our figures and the lender's have differed for the past few months. Could the lender have made a mistake?

A. Lenders—like the rest of us—make mistakes, and with lenders often tracking many loans and indexes it is entirely possible to have an error. Why not call your loan officer, describe the situation and get it straightened out?

Q. We bought a house for $100,000 two years ago. The seller took back a 30-year first trust for $80,000 at 13 percent interest and a seven-year second trust for $18,000, also at 13 percent interest, on which we pay $250 per month. We put up $2,000 in cash and will have to make a balloon payment on the second trust in five years. Interest rates have now fallen to 10 percent and we want to refinance but no lender will help us. What's the problem?

A.   The problem is that you have almost no equity in the property plus a balloon note due in just a few years. The manner in which you've financed your home makes the whole package a risky deal for lenders. Until you've got more at stake, no lender will want to take a chance on your deal.

In this situation you might try to get an extension on the second trust—something the seller may favor, considering the interest rate. Another strategy would be to open an account with a lender in which you put the monthly savings that result from refinancing. Through refinancing your monthly payments will fall from $1,134.96 to $772.26—a difference of $362.70. If you set aside your monthly savings in an account with the lender you'll accumulate $21,761.82 over five years. Add interest to your monthly savings and you should be able to pay off the $10,525.78 balloon payment with little trouble. Be aware, however, that refinancing will require certain costs up front which will either have to be paid in cash or financed. Also, the lower interest payments will reduce the size of your tax deduction.

Q.   We bought a home with a 10 percent down payment and the lender required us to take out private mortgage insurance (PMI). When can we cancel such coverage?

A.   You cannot cancel coverage without the lender's approval. Lenders typically require PMI coverage when property is bought with less than 20 percent down. While the borrower pays the premium, the lender is the beneficiary of the policy and thus has little incentive to see it canceled.

Still, you may be able to have your PMI premiums canceled if 20 percent of the original principal balance has been paid off or if the value of the property has risen to a point where the remaining principal balance is less than 80 percent of the total value of the property. Note that in either situation, dropping PMI coverage is entirely at the lender's *option*. If you have made timely and regular payments, however, and the value of the property could easily cover the balance of the loan in the event of foreclosure, many lenders will allow borrowers to cancel PMI coverage.

For those borrowers whose loans are held by the Federal Loan Mortgage Corporation (Freddie Mac) but serviced by local lenders or mortgage bankers, new rules *require* them to drop title insurance coverage after seven years if the borrower has a good payment record, the outstanding loan balance is less than 80 percent of the market value of the property and the borrower requests dropping such insurance coverage.

In general it's a good idea to ask lenders about title insurance coverage, when—if ever—policies are typically canceled and if your loan has been sold to Freddie Mac.

Q. The economics of a 15-year loan look good, but couldn't I do just as well by getting a 30-year mortgage and then making regular prepayments? That way if I had a cash crunch I wouldn't be obligated to make the larger payments associated with 15-year financing.

A.   Yes. Getting 30-year financing and voluntarily making prepayments can be a sound strategy *provided* that the lender allows prepayments without penalty.

If you are getting a new mortgage, ask the loan officer about the lender's policies. If prepayments without penalty are allowed, make certain this information is written into the loan agreement in clear, understandable language. If you already have financing, ask the lender about his policies. If prepayments without penalty are allowed, get a letter from the loan officer confirming this information. If you want to set up a prepayment program on a regular basis, tell the lender of your plans so he can more easily track your payments.

One potential problem with voluntary prepayments is the matter of bookkeeping. Make certain all payments are properly recorded by the lender. To avoid confusion, you may want to send in two checks each month, one for the amount actually owed and a second check for the extra payment.

Q. My parents want to help us buy a home with an equity-sharing agreement. Since we're on great terms with them, do we need a formal written agreement?

A.   Absolutely. Here's why. Suppose you have a fight and they no longer make monthly mortgage payments, then what?

Not only do you need a formal agreement, but each party needs an appropriate will. What happens if your parents intend to give you their interest in the property as an inheritance but they have no will? A relative might claim your house is part of the estate and that your parent's interest belongs to the entire family. Alternatively, suppose you are in a car crash and die without a will? Who gets your interest in the property? As gory and unpleasant as these questions seem, they are not unrealistic.

Before these problems and others arise, make certain you have a formal agreement with your parents and appropriate wills, documents that should be prepared by a knowledgeable attorney.

Q. My friend and I have a nifty home-buying plan. We each will buy property and then rent it to the other; that way we can get all the tax breaks that come from investing. Will lenders help us finance such deals?

A.   If you have a legitimate rental arrangement, lenders are likely to treat your application as they will any other appeal for investment financing. The question is: Do you have a legitimate rental situation?

When asked about such cross-rental/cross-ownership deals, IRS spokesman Wilson Fadely said in certain cases, depending on the facts and circumstances involved, "it doesn't appear there is anything we can do to attack it or that the statute would prohibit it." However, Fadely said deductions could be disallowed if such an arrangement were merely a sham.

A sham, he continued, might involve a situation where the owners did not take the risks normally found in property ownership or where economic validity—an effort to obtain the greatest market return for the use of the property—was missing.

In considering whether the arrangement was a sham, Fadely said the IRS might look at a variety of factors. Is there a valid written lease? Is each tenant paying a fair market rental? Who carries the insurance for the property and who is the beneficiary? Will a party be compensated if one property rises in value but not the other? Are there special provisions not normally found in a rental arrangement?

Cross-rental/cross-ownership deals raise issues outside the usual scope of real estate finance. For specific information and advice, be sure to contact a knowledgeable tax attorney before establishing such an arrangement.

Q.   I want to buy my first house. How can I find out if I qualify for a low-interest municipal or bond-backed mortgage?

A.   Ask local real estate brokers. Brokers keep abreast of such financing, particularly those who deal in low-priced properties. Also, you can contact the government office in charge of such mortgage programs. They usually have brochures and applications and are happy to answer questions.

Q.   Where can I get information about veterans' mortgage programs?

A.   Try local brokers or look in the Yellow Pages for "Veterans' Administration" under "U.S. Government."

Q.   Interest costs are paid out over many years in dollars that become less valuable over time because of inflation. Doesn't it make sense to invest your money in something other than a mortgage?

A. Maybe. The real issue here is the question of alternatives. Suppose you have a 10 percent mortgage. Can you get a 10 percent return after taxes with as little risk elsewhere? Can you get returns greater than 10 percent?

Some real estate entrepreneurs argue that realty investors should get returns of at least 15 percent on their money and that repaying a mortgage quickly is a waste of money. But when you ask for specifics, when you ask about alternatives, the suggestions you hear are often unappealing. For example, one choice might be to invest in second trusts created by home sellers.

Such second trusts are bought at discount and often produce high returns. But such loans also represent a substantial level of risk that many people will prefer to avoid, particularly those who do not hold large portfolios of second trusts. There is a big difference between the investment pro who has 100 second trusts and the small guy with just one loan in his "portfolio." The pro can survive if one note is in default, but the situation is far tougher for the novice.

When deciding whether to pre-pay a mortgage, borrowers must look at each case individually based on such factors as interest rates, risk, tax consequences, personal income and investment preferences. There is no answer that is always right, but it is fair to say that in many situations, the opportunity to reduce mortgage debt can be an attractive, conservative, low-risk investment that appeals to a broad range of people.

Q. Don't borrowers, particularly those in the upper income brackets, always benefit from large mortgages because Uncle Sam effectively pays much of the interest?

A. For the well-to-do of the world, those in the 28 percent tax bracket in 1988, the issue of reducing mortgage costs is somewhat complicated. True, it is beneficial to reduce unnecessary interest costs. But it's also true that the money used to reduce mortgage expenses can often produce better after-tax earnings when spent elsewhere.

As an example, given a choice, someone in the 28 percent bracket will probably do better investing $1,000 in a tax-exempt bond that pays 9 percent interest rather than paying down a 10 percent mortgage. Why? Because such bonds offer an effective rate of return equal to 11.52 percent before taxes.

Even for the rich, however, it's tough if not impossible to justify excess interest costs. Borrowing $500,000 at 10 percent is a better deal than borrowing the same amount of money with the same type of mortgage at 12 percent interest. The fact that federal tax rates are now lower than in the past gives even less incentive to pay high interest costs—as though any further incentive were necessary.

For those not in the 28 percent bracket—the overwhelming majority of all home owners—the interest tax deduction makes housing more affordable by transferring payments to lenders that will otherwise go to the government. In effect, if we spend money in ways approved by the tax codes we get more control over our dollars.

Q.   If I'm only going to live in a house for five years, how will cutting my mortgage make a difference?

A.   Few mortgages are held to maturity. What usually happens is that we buy our first house, sell it and invest any profit in the purchase of a second house. We then sell house number two to get our third home and so on.

In this process of moving and selling we are also financing. If we get a 30-year, $85,000 mortgage at 10 percent for our first home and sell after five years, here's what happens.

First, we have made 60 monthly payments of $745.94.

Second, these 60 payments total $44,756.40.

Third, of the $44,756.40 paid out, only $2,911.83 is used to reduce principal. The rest is interest.

Fourth, when the house is sold we still owe the lender $82,-088.17.

However, it doesn't have to be this way. If, in the simplest case, we had a 15-year mortgage at 10 percent interest, the monthly payments will be $913.41 per month—an increase of $167.47 per month. Over 60 months we will pay out a total of $54,804.60, of which $15,880.80 is principal and $38,923.80 is interest. When the house is sold we'll owe the lender $69,119.20 —or $12,968.97 less then someone with a 30-year loan.

But we are not likely to find both 30-year and 15-year loans at the same interest rates. The 15-year mortgage should be available at a lower interest rate, and thus monthly payments will be reduced and the advantages of short-term financing will be even greater.

Q.   Don't lenders always oppose efforts to cut interest costs?
A.   Lenders are often elated to see loans with shorter terms and faster pay-offs.

Mortgage lenders traditionally lend money on a long-term basis but finance such mortgages with short-term borrowing. The difference between the interest charged and the interest paid is their margin, a portion of which is profit. In addition, mortgage lenders have two other profit centers. First, money can be made from up-front charges such as "points" and loan origination fees. Second, money can be earned by "servicing" loans for investors (such as insurance companies) by making monthly collections and, if necessary, foreclosing in the event of default.

In the late 1970s, short-term interest rates began to greatly exceed long-term interest rates. Home owners often had 5 percent, 6 percent and 7 percent mortgages, while lenders were borrowing on a short-term basis at 9, 10 and 11 percent. The result was obvious: massive lender losses that only got worse in the early 1980s, when short-term rates went still higher.

In response to these conditions, lenders began seeking alternatives. One alternative was the adjustable-rate mortgage (ARM), where interest rates can rise or fall during the life of the loan. Another choice is the trend to short-term mortgages. Why? Because loans with short terms mean lenders can recycle funds more quickly, make more loans and thus collect more fees and charges up front. It is these fees and charges that now represent a significant portion of lender profits. The interest not paid by one borrower will be paid by the next when the money is recycled as a new loan.

Q.   Isn't it true that 30-year mortgages have lower interest rates than short-term financing?

A.   No. Loans with shorter terms represent less risk to lenders than 30-year financing. If rates for 30-year loans range between 10 and 11 percent, you can expect 15-year rates of 7.5 to 8.5 percent, with an equal number of points for either type of financing.

Q.   Won't most lenders charge a penalty if you want to make prepayments?

A.   While some loans prohibit or limit prepayment options, many mortgages do not. Adjustable-rate mortgages (ARMs) typically allow prepayments without penalty. FHA and VA loans usually permit prepayments provided the lender receives at least 30 days' notice and the prepayment is not less than one month's usual installment. Older loans, those made before 1978, often allow prepayment without penalty. Also, prepayment penalties are barred in some states. In all cases read the loan agreement to see what is permitted—but remember, even when prepayment penalties are allowed, they may be waived at the lender's option.

Q. We got a good buy on a home, but to move quickly we took a 30-year mortgage. We figured the lender would welcome prepayments but we were wrong. The lender will assess a huge prepayment penalty if we're ahead more than a dime during the first 10 years of the loan term. Now what?

A.   No problem. Suppose you have a $100,000 mortgage at 10 percent which you want to pay off in 17 years. With the 30-year loan you're paying $877.57 per month. To pay off the loan in 17 years you'll have to raise your payment to $1,021.21, a difference of $143.64 per month. Instead of giving the additional money to the lender, place it in a money market account, a savings account, or in a place where the principal is not at risk and you can earn interest.

Because you are making monthly contributions to your own private prepayment fund that equal what you need to pay off the loan in 17 years, you will have sufficient money available to curtail the loan on time. There are two other benefits as well. First, if finances are tight you don't have to add to your private account. Second, your account will earn interest, which will allow you to pay off the loan well before 17 years if you want. Third, interest savings from the shorter loan can potentially total $107,598.83 in this example. Note, however, that the interest on a balancing account will be taxed and so the real level of possible savings is somewhat diminished.

Q.   My loan has a "due-on-sale" clause, which means the mortgage cannot be assumed when I sell the house. My loan also has a stiff prepayment penalty built in. Will I have to pay a prepayment penalty if I sell the property and thus am forced to retire the note?

A.   Some lenders have created loans that pose a no-win situation for borrowers. The loans can't be assumed and yet the lender charges a prepayment penalty if the property is sold. What to do?

First, always choose loans, if possible, where prepayment penalties, in whole or in part, are prohibited. If a total ban on prepayment penalties is not feasible, ask for a written (not oral) waiver so that no penalty will be charged in the event of a sale. Second, many lenders will not assess a prepayment in a sale situation. Third, you may be able to get a prepayment waiver if you borrow from the lender on your next house or if your buyer gets a loan to purchase your property through the original lender.

Q. Isn't cutting the length of the mortgage term the only way to cut mortgage costs?
A. No. There are an unlimited number of strategies that can result in substantial mortgage savings when compared with traditional 30-year loans. Such options include the use of second trust and wraparound mortgages, blend loans, buy-downs, bond-backed mortgages and even a loan format without any interest, so-called zero interest (ZIP) mortgages.

Q. My lender is supposed to pay my real estate taxes but I recently got a bill from the local government showing they are unpaid. What should I do?
A. Contact your lender to see if payment has been made since you received the notice. If payment was made, make sure the local government corrects its records, since property taxes are a lien against your home and if they are unpaid you could be foreclosed.

If the taxes have not been paid, then you have to ask why. A lender who collects money from you and holds that money in trust for the specific purpose of paying property taxes has an obligation to make timely, correct payments. If the lender has made a mistake, make sure the taxes are paid by the lender and that the lender agrees to be responsible for any additional interest and penalties. If the lender refuses to pay the taxes, contact an attorney immediately.

Q.　I have a large property that can be subdivided into two lots. Can I subdivide without the lender's approval?

A.　Your property—all your property—is security for the lender's note. Clearly if you sell a portion of the property you reduce the lender's security and thus change the terms of the mortgage contract. Ask your lender if you can sell the lot, perhaps pledging a portion of the net proceeds from settlement as a mortgage reduction. If your interest rate is reasonably current, many lenders will agree.

The world of real estate finance changes almost daily and the information presented here is designed to illustrate general principles and concepts. For specific information concerning individual mortgage options, check first with such professionals as realty brokers, local lenders, attorneys, financial planners and/or tax advisors before taking any action.

Appendix A:
Amortization Statement

The following amortization table shows the monthly interest cost, principal reduction and loan balance for a 30-year, $85,000 mortgage at 10 percent interest. Monthly payments are $745.94 throughout the term of the loan.

The figures presented in this chart are for illustrative purposes only and may vary somewhat from tables developed by individual lenders. For information regarding specific loan arrangements be certain to get amortization charts directly from the lender with whom you will be working.

Loan amortization	$85,000.00
Interest	10.00 percent
Number of years	30
Monthly payment	$745.94
Total interest cost	$183,536.90

Payment	Interest payment ($)	Principal payment ($)	Balance due ($)
1	708.33	37.60	84,962.40
2	708.02	37.92	84,924.48
3	707.70	38.23	84,886.25
4	707.39	38.55	84,847.70
5	707.06	38.87	84,808.83
6	706.74	39.20	84,769.63
7	706.41	39.52	84,730.11
8	706.08	39.85	84,690.26

Payment	Interest payment ($)	Principal payment ($)	Balance due ($)
9	705.75	40.18	84,650.07
10	705.42	40.52	84,609.56
11	705.08	40.86	84,568.70
12	704.74	41.20	84,527.50
Year 1	8,478.73	472.50	84,527.50
13	704.40	41.54	84,485.96
14	704.05	41.89	84,444.08
15	703.70	42.24	84,401.84
16	703.35	42.59	84,359.25
17	702.99	42.94	84,316.31
18	702.64	43.30	84,273.01
19	702.28	43.66	84,229.35
20	701.91	44.02	84,185.33
21	701.54	44.39	84,140.94
22	701.17	44.76	84,096.17
23	700.80	45.13	84,051.04
24	700.43	45.51	84,005.53
Year 2	8,429.26	521.97	84,005.53
25	700.05	45.89	83,959.64
26	699.66	46.27	83,913.37
27	699.28	46.66	83,866.71
28	698.89	47.05	83,819.66
29	698.50	47.44	83,772.22
30	698.10	47.83	83,724.39
31	697.70	48.23	83,676.16
32	697.30	48.63	83,627.52
33	696.90	49.04	83,578.48
34	696.49	49.45	83,529.04
35	696.08	49.86	83,479.17
36	695.66	50.28	83,428.90
Year 3	8,374.60	576.63	83,428.90
37	695.24	50.70	83,378.20
38	694.82	51.12	83,327.09
39	694.39	51.54	83,275.54
40	693.96	51.97	83,223.57
41	693.53	52.41	83,171.16

Payment	Interest payment ($)	Principal payment ($)	Balance due ($)
42	693.09	52.84	83,118.32
43	692.65	53.28	83,065.04
44	692.21	53.73	83,011.31
45	691.76	54.17	82,957.14
46	691.31	54.63	82,902.51
47	690.85	55.08	82,847.43
48	690.40	55.54	82,791.89
Year 4	**8,314.22**	**637.01**	**82,791.89**
49	689.93	56.00	82,735.88
50	689.47	56.47	82,679.41
51	689.00	56.94	82,622.47
52	688.52	57.42	82,565.06
53	688.04	57.89	82,507.16
54	687.56	58.38	82,448.79
55	687.07	58.86	82,389.93
56	686.58	59.35	82,330.57
57	686.09	59.85	82,270.72
58	685.59	60.35	82,210.38
59	685.09	60.85	82,149.53
60	684.58	61.36	82,088.17
Year 5	**8,247.51**	**703.72**	**82,088.17**
61	684.07	61.87	82,026.30
62	683.55	62.38	81,963.92
63	683.03	62.90	81,901.02
64	682.51	63.43	81,837.59
65	681.98	63.96	81,773.63
66	681.45	64.49	81,709.15
67	680.91	65.03	81,644.12
68	680.37	65.57	81,578.55
69	679.82	66.11	81,512.44
70	679.27	66.67	81,445.77
71	678.71	67.22	81,378.55
72	678.15	67.78	81,310.77
Year 6	**8,173.83**	**777.40**	**81,310.77**
73	677.59	68.35	81,242.42
74	677.02	68.92	81,173.51

Payment	Interest payment ($)	Principal payment ($)	Balance due ($)
75	676.45	69.49	81,104.02
76	675.87	70.07	81,033.95
77	675.28	70.65	80,963.30
78	674.69	71.24	80,892.05
79	674.10	71.84	80,820.22
80	673.50	72.43	80,747.78
81	672.90	73.04	80,674.75
82	672.29	73.65	80,601.10
83	671.68	74.26	80,526.84
84	671.06	74.88	80,451.96
Year 7	**8,092.42**	**858.81**	**80,451.96**
85	670.43	75.50	80,376.46
86	669.80	76.13	80,300.33
87	669.17	76.77	80,223.56
88	668.53	77.41	80,146.15
89	667.88	78.05	80,068.10
90	667.23	78.70	79,989.40
91	666.58	79.36	79,910.04
92	665.92	80.02	79,830.02
93	665.25	80.69	79,749.34
94	664.58	81.36	79,667.98
95	663.90	82.04	79,585.94
96	663.22	82.72	79,503.23
Year 8	**8,002.49**	**948.74**	**79,503.23**
97	662.53	83.41	79,419.82
98	661.83	84.10	79,335.71
99	661.13	84.80	79,250.91
100	660.42	85.51	79,165.40
101	659.71	86.22	79,079.17
102	658.99	86.94	78,992.23
103	658.27	87.67	78,904.56
104	657.54	88.40	78,816.16
105	656.80	89.13	78,727.03
106	656.06	89.88	78,637.15
107	655.31	90.63	78,546.53
108	654.55	91.38	78,455.14

Payment	Interest payment ($)	Principal payment ($)	Balance due ($)
Year 9	7,903.15	1,048.08	78,455.14
109	653.79	92.14	78,363.00
110	653.03	92.91	78,270.09
111	652.25	93.69	78,176.41
112	651.47	94.47	78,081.94
113	650.68	95.25	77,986.69
114	649.89	96.05	77,890.64
115	649.09	96.85	77,793.79
116	648.28	97.65	77,696.14
117	647.47	98.47	77,597.67
118	646.65	99.29	77,498.38
119	645.82	100.12	77,398.27
120	644.99	100.95	77,297.32
Year 10	7,793.40	1,157.83	77,297.32
121	644.14	101.79	77,195.52
122	643.30	102.64	77,092.88
123	642.44	103.50	76,989.39
124	641.58	104.36	76,885.03
125	640.71	105.23	76,779.80
126	639.83	106.10	76,673.70
127	638.95	106.99	76,566.71
128	638.06	107.88	76,458.83
129	637.16	108.78	76,350.05
130	636.25	109.69	76,240.37
131	635.34	110.60	76,129.77
132	634.41	111.52	76,018.25
Year 11	7,672.16	1,279.07	76,018.25
133	633.49	112.45	75,905.80
134	632.55	113.39	75,792.41
135	631.60	114.33	75,678.08
136	630.65	115.29	75,562.79
137	629.69	116.25	75,446.55
138	628.72	117.21	75,329.33
139	627.74	118.19	75,211.14
140	626.76	119.18	75,091.96
141	625.77	120.17	74,971.79

Payment	Interest payment ($)	Principal payment ($)	Balance due ($)
142	624.76	121.17	74,850.62
143	623.76	122.18	74,728.44
144	622.74	123.20	74,605.24
Year 12	7,538.23	1,413.00	74,605.24
145	621.71	124.23	74,481.02
146	620.68	125.26	74,355.76
147	619.63	126.30	74,229.45
148	618.58	127.36	74,102.10
149	617.52	128.42	73,973.68
150	616.45	129.49	73,844.19
151	615.37	130.57	73,713.62
152	614.28	131.66	73,581.96
153	613.18	132.75	73,449.21
154	612.08	133.86	73,315.35
155	610.96	134.97	73,180.38
156	609.84	136.10	73,044.28
Year 13	7,390.27	1,560.96	73,044.28
157	608.70	137.23	72,907.05
158	607.56	138.38	72,768.67
159	606.41	139.53	72,629.14
160	605.24	140.69	72,488.45
161	604.07	141.87	72,346.58
162	602.89	143.05	72,203.53
163	601.70	144.24	72,059.29
164	600.49	145.44	71,913.85
165	599.28	146.65	71,767.20
166	598.06	147.88	71,619.32
167	596.83	149.11	71,470.21
168	595.59	150.35	71,319.86
Year 14	7,226.81	1,724.42	71,319.86
169	594.33	151.60	71,168.26
170	593.07	152.87	71,015.39
171	591.79	154.14	70,861.25
172	590.51	155.43	70,705.83
173	589.22	156.72	70,549.10
174	587.91	158.03	70,391.08

Payment	Interest payment ($)	Principal payment ($)	Balance due ($)
175	586.59	159.34	70,231.73
176	585.26	160.67	70,071.06
177	583.93	162.01	69,909.05
178	582.58	163.36	69,745.69
179	581.21	164.72	69,580.97
180	579.84	166.09	69,414.88
Year 15	**7,046.24**	**1,904.99**	**69,414.88**
181	578.46	167.48	69,247.40
182	577.06	168.87	69,078.53
183	575.65	170.28	68,908.25
184	574.24	171.70	68,736.55
185	572.80	173.13	68,563.41
186	571.36	174.57	68,388.84
187	569.91	176.03	68,212.81
188	568.44	177.50	68,035.32
189	566.96	178.97	67,856.34
190	565.47	180.47	67,675.87
191	563.97	181.97	67,493.90
192	562.45	183.49	67,310.42
Year 16	**6,846.77**	**2,104.46**	**67,310.42**
193	560.92	185.02	67,125.40
194	559.38	186.56	66,938.84
195	557.82	188.11	66,750.73
196	556.26	189.68	66,561.05
197	554.68	191.26	66,369.79
198	553.08	192.85	66,176.94
199	551.47	194.46	65,982.48
200	549.85	196.08	65,786.39
201	548.22	197.72	65,588.68
202	546.57	199.36	65,389.32
203	544.91	201.02	65,188.29
204	543.24	202.70	64,985.59
Year 17	**6,626.40**	**2,324.83**	**64,985.59**
205	541.55	204.39	64,781.20
206	539.84	206.09	64,575.11
207	538.13	207.81	64,367.30

Payment	Interest payment ($)	Principal payment ($)	Balance due ($)
208	536.39	209.54	64,157.76
209	534.65	211.29	63,946.47
210	532.89	213.05	63,733.42
211	531.11	214.82	63,518.60
212	529.32	216.61	63,301.98
213	527.52	218.42	63,083.56
214	525.70	220.24	62,863.32
215	523.86	222.07	62,641.25
216	522.01	223.93	62,417.32
Year 18	**6,382.96**	**2,568.27**	**62,417.32**
217	520.14	225.79	62,191.53
218	518.26	227.67	61,963.86
219	516.37	229.57	61,734.29
220	514.45	231.48	61,502.80
221	512.52	233.41	61,269.39
222	510.58	235.36	61,034.03
223	508.62	237.32	60,796.72
224	506.64	239.30	60,557.42
225	504.65	241.29	60,316.13
226	502.63	243.30	60,072.83
227	500.61	245.33	59,827.50
228	498.56	247.37	59,580.12
Year 19	**6,114.03**	**2,837.20**	**59,580.12**
229	496.50	249.43	59,330.69
230	494.42	251.51	59,079.18
231	492.33	253.61	58,825.57
232	490.21	255.72	58,569.84
233	488.08	257.85	58,311.99
234	485.93	260.00	58,051.99
235	483.77	262.17	57,789.82
236	481.58	264.35	57,525.46
237	479.38	266.56	57,258.91
238	477.16	268.78	56,990.13
239	474.92	271.02	56,719.11
240	472.66	273.28	56,445.83

Payment	Interest payment ($)	Principal payment ($)	Balance due ($)
Year 20	5,816.94	3,134.29	56,445.83
241	470.38	275.55	56,170.28
242	468.09	277.85	55,892.43
243	465.77	280.17	55,612.27
244	463.44	282.50	55,329.76
245	461.08	284.85	55,044.91
246	458.71	287.23	54,757.68
247	456.31	289.62	54,468.06
248	453.90	292.04	54,176.02
249	451.47	294.47	53,881.56
250	449.01	296.92	53,584.63
251	446.54	299.40	53,285.24
252	444.04	301.89	52,983.34
Year 21	5,488.74	3,462.49	52,983.34
253	441.53	304.41	52,678.94
254	438.99	306.94	52,371.99
255	436.43	309.50	52,062.49
256	433.85	312.08	51,750.41
257	431.25	314.68	51,435.72
258	428.63	317.30	51,118.42
259	425.99	319.95	50,798.47
260	423.32	322.62	50,475.86
261	420.63	325.30	50,150.55
262	417.92	328.01	49,822.54
263	415.19	330.75	49,491.79
264	412.43	333.50	49,158.28
Year 22	5,126.17	3,825.06	49,158.28
265	409.65	336.28	48,822.00
266	406.85	339.09	48,482.92
267	404.02	341.91	48,141.00
268	401.18	344.76	47,796.24
269	398.30	347.63	47,448.61
270	395.41	350.53	47,098.08
271	392.48	353.45	46,744.63
272	389.54	356.40	46,388.23
273	386.57	359.37	46,028.86

Payment	Interest payment ($)	Principal payment ($)	Balance due ($)
274	383.57	362.36	45,666.50
275	380.55	365.38	45,301.12
276	377.51	368.43	44,932.69
Year 23	**4,725.64**	**4,225.59**	**44,932.69**
277	374.44	371.50	44,561.19
278	371.34	374.59	44,186.60
279	368.22	377.71	43,808.89
280	365.07	380.86	43,428.03
281	361.90	384.04	43,043.99
282	358.70	387.24	42,656.75
283	355.47	390.46	42,266.29
284	352.22	393.72	41,872.58
285	348.94	397.00	41,475.58
286	345.63	400.31	41,075.27
287	342.29	403.64	40,671.63
288	338.93	407.01	40,264.62
Year 24	**4,283.16**	**4,668.07**	**40,264.62**
289	335.54	410.40	39,854.23
290	332.12	413.82	39,440.41
291	328.67	417.27	39,023.14
292	325.19	420.74	38,602.40
293	321.69	424.25	38,178.15
294	318.15	427.78	37,750.37
295	314.59	431.35	37,319.02
296	310.99	434.94	36,884.07
297	307.37	438.57	36,445.51
298	303.71	442.22	36,003.28
299	300.03	445.91	35,557.37
300	296.31	449.62	35,107.75
Year 25	**3,794.35**	**5,156.88**	**35,107.75**
301	292.56	453.37	34,654.38
302	288.79	457.15	34,197.23
303	284.98	460.96	33,736.27
304	281.14	464.80	33,271.47
305	277.26	468.67	32,802.80
306	273.36	472.58	32,330.22

Payment	Interest payment ($)	Principal payment ($)	Balance due ($)
307	269.42	476.52	31,853.70
308	265.45	480.49	31,373.21
309	261.44	484.49	30,888.72
310	257.41	488.53	30,400.19
311	253.33	492.60	29,907.59
312	249.23	496.71	29,410.88
Year 26	**3,254.36**	**5,696.87**	**29,410.88**
313	245.09	500.85	28,910.04
314	240.92	505.02	28,405.02
315	236.71	509.23	27,895.79
316	232.46	513.47	27,382.32
317	228.19	517.75	26,864.57
318	223.87	522.06	26,342.50
319	219.52	526.41	25,816.09
320	215.13	530.80	25,285.29
321	210.71	535.23	24,750.06
322	206.25	539.69	24,210.38
323	201.75	544.18	23,666.19
324	197.22	548.72	23,117.48
Year 27	**2,657.83**	**6,293.40**	**23,117.48**
325	192.65	553.29	22,564.19
326	188.03	557.90	22,006.29
327	183.39	562.55	21,443.74
328	178.70	567.24	20,876.50
329	173.97	571.97	20,304.53
330	169.20	576.73	19,727.80
331	164.40	581.54	19,146.26
332	159.55	586.38	18,559.88
333	154.67	591.27	17,968.61
334	149.74	596.20	17,372.41
335	144.77	601.17	16,771.25
336	139.76	606.18	16,165.07
Year 28	**1,998.82**	**6,952.41**	**16,165.07**
337	134.71	611.23	15,553.84
338	129.62	616.32	14,937.52
339	124.48	621.46	14,316.07

Payment	Interest payment ($)	Principal payment ($)	Balance due ($)
340	119.30	626.64	13,689.43
341	114.08	631.86	13,057.58
342	108.81	637.12	12,420.45
343	103.50	642.43	11,778.02
344	98.15	647.79	11,130.23
345	92.75	653.18	10,477.05
346	87.31	658.63	9,818.42
347	81.82	664.12	9,154.31
348	76.29	669.65	8,484.66
Year 29	**1,270.82**	**7,680.41**	**8,484.66**
349	70.71	675.23	7,809.43
350	65.08	680.86	7,128.57
351	59.40	686.53	6,442.04
352	53.68	692.25	5,749.79
353	47.91	698.02	5,051.77
354	42.10	703.84	4,347.93
355	36.23	709.70	3,638.23
356	30.32	715.62	2,922.61
357	24.36	721.58	2,201.03
358	18.34	727.59	1,473.43
359	12.28	733.66	739.78
360	6.16	739.77	0.01
Year 30	**466.58**	**8,484.65**	**0.01**

Appendix B:
Loan Release Tips

Borrowers with financing who wish to get a release of liability will need the approval of both the lender who issued the loan and the organization which provided the guarantee, if any.

Veteran borrowers can be released from all VA liability, according to that agency "by having the purchaser assume all of the veteran's liabilities in connection with the loan and having VA approve the assumption agreement and specifically release the veteran from all further liabilities to VA."

Being released from liability is a process distinct from the possible restoration of a VA entitlement. Again quoting VA materials, borrowers may have their entitlements restored when: A, "the loan has been paid in full, or the VA otherwise has been relieved of the obligation under the guaranty and the home has been disposed of"; or B, a VA-qualified buyer has "agreed to assume the outstanding balance of the loan, has consented to substitute his or her entitlement for that of the original veteran-borrower" and meets all other current VA requirements. For more information, contact the nearest VA office and ask for Pamphlet 26-4 and the "ROL/SOE Package."

The release procedure through the FHA varies somewhat from the VA format. With FHA loans, lenders submit an application for release (FHA Form 22-10) and a credit report (Form 2900) on the new borrower. If the FHA is satisfied with the credit-worthiness of the new borrower it will inform the lender.

Note that there is no requirement for the lender to release original borrowers even if they are released by the FHA. Also, FHA procedures, unlike those of the VA, envision communication between a lender and the agency rather than the agency and an individual borrower.

In the case of loans generally, as well as those backed by private mortgage insurers, be certain to contact your lender for complete release and assumption information. Ask for a list of all charges, if any.

For loans held or backed by the VA, FHA, Freddie Mac, Fannie Mae, private mortgage insurers or Ginnie Mae there may be restrictions on the extent to which lenders can charge release or assumption fees. Write or call these organizations for more information if you have questions not answered to your satisfaction by a lender.

Appendix C: Specialized FHA Loan Programs

While a variety of FHA-backed loan plans are described in detail throughout the book, there are additional FHA programs which may be of interest to limited numbers of single-family home buyers.

Sec. 203(h). This FHA program is directed toward individuals who live in major disaster areas. It provides up to the full value of Sec. 203(b) financing for home replacement or reconstruction.

Sec. 203(i). If you have an interest in acquiring a farm home with at least 2.5 acres this program will provide mortgage insurance. The maximum loans available under this section, however, are limited to 75 percent of the maximums permitted under 203(b). If the 203(b) maximum for a single-family home in a given area is, say, $90,000, then the maximum 203(i) loan would be $67,500.

Sec. 213. One of the most interesting FHA programs, this section is designed to guarantee co-op housing loans. Under this section, the FHA can guarantee loans for entire projects as well as individual units. As of January, 1987, however, no individual co-op unit has been refinanced under this program. The reason: Sec. 213 could only be used for the purchase of individual units in projects with overall FHA financing and the co-op board could not block a purchase under the program. In 1984, however, this section was revised. First, new legislation now allows Sec. 213 to back the acquisition of single units in projects which do not have overall FHA funding. Speak to your lender for current information.

Sec. 221(d)(2). A program designed for individuals and families displaced by governmental action such as urban renewal or the construction of a new highway, Sec. 221(d)(2) provides mortgage insurance for up to $36,000 to individuals who need single-family, owner-occupied housing, more money for families of five or more or those who acquire two to four units.

Sec. 203(k). This FHA program is designed to insure financing for the purchase and/or rehabilitation of housing. Initially such loans are viewed as construction financing and then, upon completion of the work, the loan is converted into permanent financing. This is an excellent program for both investors and those who do their own repairs and thus earn "sweat equity."

Sec. 223(e). Not all properties meet FHA underwriting guidelines for 203(b) loans and in those cases where homes are unqualified because they are located in "declining" areas, financing may be available under Sec. 223(e). Down payment and maximum mortgage amounts available under Sec. 223(e) vary but such financing may represent a last-ditch financing choice since regular FHA lending standards are waived.

VA-Qualified Buyers, National Guard Personnel and Reservists. Individuals who are VA qualified or who have served in the National Guard or a branch of the military reserve should be aware that FHA Sec. 203(b) contains a small, but significant, advantage for those looking for single-family, owner/occupied housing. Sec. 203(b) provides that a portion of the down payment normally required for FHA financing will be waived for qualified individuals. The FHA includes guardsmen and reservists with at least 90 days of continuous active duty service— including training periods—among those who qualify for this benefit.

Index